THE ESSENTIAL GUIDE TO
Dual Sport Motorcycling

EVERYTHING YOU NEED TO BUY, RIDE, AND ENJOY THE WORLD'S MOST VERSATILE MOTORCYCLES

CARL ADAMS

WITH A FOREWORD BY MALCOLM SMITH

Whitehorse Press
Center Conway, New Hampshire

All illustrations are provided by the author unless otherwise noted: Suzanne Adams 6, 108, 148, 149, 150; John Austin 37, 42, 50, 62, 82, 90, 189; Baja Designs 72; Baja Off-Road Tours 190; Jim Bradbury 94, 95, 115, 119, 122, 123, 124, 125, 130; Dean Chaney 13, 25, 26, 42, 43, 76, 89, 110, 111, 118, 123, 127, 129, 134, 138, 141, 148, 156, 163, 164, 169, 174, 178, 179, 182, 190; Mick Collins 157; Cycle Pump 188; DeLorme 172, 173, 175, 178, 182; FMF Racing 78; Garmin 176; Helmet House 56, 59, 83; Harry Keast 168; Mikuni 77; NHTSA 48; Precision Concepts 105; Progressive Suspension 98; Race Tech 98, 105; Dave Schulte 22, 26, 36, 107, 127, 138, 139, 155; Seal Line 83; Don Simone 27, 31, 89, 184; Snell Memorial Foundation 52; Tucker Rocky 53; Mike Wallace 137; Whitehorse Press 35, 55, 62, 68, 96, 97, 99, 100, 101, 112, 121, 162, 185

Whitehorse Press books are also available at discounts in bulk quantity for sales and promotional use. For details about special sales or for a catalog of Whitehorse Press motorcycling books, write to the publisher:

Whitehorse Press
107 East Conway Road
Center Conway, New Hampshire 03813
Phone: 603-356-6556 or 800-531-1133
E-mail: CustomerService@WhitehorsePress.com
Internet: www.WhitehorsePress.com

ISBN-13: 978-1-884313-71-4

5 4 3 2

Printed in China

CONTENTS

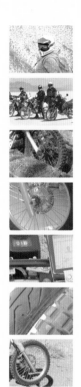

FOREWORD

Motorcycles have been my passion for more than 50 years, and at age 67 I'm still riding lots and putting on the annual "No Wimps" Dual Sport Ride. Fortunately, my life in this engaging sport has been filled with wonderful, rewarding experiences including winning races, starting Malcolm Smith Racing (MSR), and operating a successful dealership. Over the years though, more relaxed off-road adventuring has replaced racing as my primary off-road activity, and I find that I particularly enjoy sharing my enthusiasm for this newer interest with others.

Much of the motorcycle press focuses on racing, but most riders do not race—especially as they mature and develop family and business obligations. They still crave adventure and excitement, but can't afford to get injured or spend excessive time practicing and training. For these riders dual sport motorcycling can be the perfect outlet.

Dual sport motorcycles range from agile lightweight machines that are completely at home on trails and rough terrain, to powerful heavyweights that are more suitable for graded roads and pavement. They are all legal for use on public roads and highways, greatly expanding riding opportunities at a time when our public lands are increasingly closed to motorized recreation. Whatever their size, dual sports can be your ticket to exciting adventures in new places.

Despite the growing appeal of dual sport, I have seen no books that deal comprehensively with the topic. Most new riders learn by watching their buddies, who may only have rudimentary skills themselves. For newer riders, there is a lot to absorb and even old hands can always learn new tricks. There are numerous books about motocross, but dual sport enthusiasts have been largely ignored, until now.

I was interested when first asked to contribute a foreword to this book, but also a bit skeptical. A proper treatment of dual sport motorcycling demands knowledgeable coverage of a wide range of topics. I had never met the author and wondered whether he could write a substantial book about this complex subject, one that could convey the fun of the sport without trivializing the need to learn to do it properly.

Happily, I found that *The Essential Guide to Dual Sport Motorcycling* is packed with useful information, presented skillfully, and illustrated abundantly. The author's love of dual sporting and the knowledge he has gained through long experience shine through the chapters, providing a helpful introduction to dual sporting for newcomers and a comprehensive resource for riders having more experience. I hope to see many of you, armed with this new book, out on the trails enjoying our wonderful sport.

Malcolm Smith

Malcolm Smith was a winner of the Baja 1000, eight gold medals at the International Six Day Trials, a featured rider in the movie On Any Sunday, *and is owner of Malcolm Smith Motorsports, and founder of the Malcolm Smith Motorsports Foundation.*

ACKNOWLEDGEMENTS

It would have been impossible to complete this book without key contributions from a number of people whom I would like to thank.

Malcolm Smith has been a hero and role model ever since I read of his gold medals in the International Six Day Trials during the 1960s and I subsequently saw him ride in the movie On Any Sunday. His willingness to furnish a foreword to this book is a high point of my effort to write it.

ISDE legend Drew Smith of Works Enduro Rider reviewed the chapters on riding technique. Scott Hodgson, Director of Application Engineering at Progressive Suspension reviewed the material on suspension setup and tuning. Dual sport event organizers Jerry Counts and Larry Langly read early versions and made valuable suggestions.

My very experienced riding buddies Don Simone and Dean Chaney offered encouragement and valuable suggestions, plus many pictures. Jim Bradbury took the photos of riding techniques. Mick Collins, Jerry Mather, John Austin, and Dave Schulte provided many excellent photos. The Dust Devils Motorcycle Club of Reno gave permission to use materials from their events. Harry Keast, Jay Tullis, and Pat Cody helped move the project forward at key points. Jon King and Darrol Taylor rode with me on many days when conditions were too hot, too cold, or too wet for anyone else.

My editor Dan Kennedy of Whitehorse deserves special mention. He encouraged me to make the book better in many ways and is entirely responsible for the professional layout that would have been far beyond my abilities. He is also a joy to work with.

Finally, I would like to thank my wife Suzanne who helped with the editing and patiently listened to me talk about "the book" for a very long time.

This volume is more a labor of love than a commercial endeavor. In an effort to return something for my many years of dual sport enjoyment, the author's royalties have been assigned to the Pediatric Brain Tumor Foundation.

INTRODUCTION

At the most basic level, dual sport motorcycles that are both competent in the dirt and licensed for use on the street. Depending on the model, a dual sport may be designed for use primarily in the dirt with short trips on pavement, for use equally in both environments, or for use primarily on pavement with short trips in the dirt. Although this description is accurate, it fails to convey the real potential and excitement of dual sporting.

Dual sports are the world's most versatile motorcycles. They can be ridden to work all week and then used to explore dirt roads and trails on Sunday. They can carry you and a partner to dinner in the city on Friday and you to a remote fishing spot on Saturday. They can be taken on long trips in remote areas and run errands in the neighborhood. They are a tremendously useful alternative to specialized offerings such as motocross, cruiser, touring, and sport bikes.

This book is addressed both to new riders and to current enthusiasts who want to improve specific techniques. There are many good books about street riding and touring, so this book emphasizes the dirt side of dual sport. It is organized into four sections covering motorcycle selection, setup, riding technique, and dual sport activities. Several chapters include exercises to help you improve riding and learn new skills. The book also contains many references and sources which can increase your knowledge and enjoyment.

New riders, and those coming to dual sport from a street riding background, will find chapters covering every dual sport topic, from types of dual sports to multi-day tours. I explain all terms and describe riding techniques in detail. The book also covers topics of interest to more experienced riders, many of whom come to dual sport with prior dirt riding experience. These riders often expect dual sports to be "racing bikes

Carl Adams

with license plates" and miss the rich possibilities of dual sport. The chapters about equipment selection, mental attitude, and various dual sport activities are designed to broaden this perspective, foster safe riding, and increase your enjoyment.

Very few riders take formal instruction in riding technique. Most watch their friends and develop comfortable methods. However, they may be repeating the same small mistakes year after year, compensating for them with quick reactions. The riding exercises I suggest in this book are a good way for experienced riders to polish their skills.

Section 1 is about selecting a dual sport. It covers the uses of dual sport motorcycles, the types that are available, and selection of a model that is right for you. Section 2 covers motorcycle preparation and riding gear. It includes basic setup, popular accessories, tires, riding gear, and suspension tuning. Section 3 covers basic riding. It includes safety, basic and advanced riding techniques, and trailside repair. Section 4 is about dual sport activities. It describes organized activities, off-highway navigation, and touring.

This book began as a half-day training session for new members of the Dust Devils Motorcycle Club of Reno, Nevada. Some of the students were novices, some were returning to dual sport after raising a family or retiring, and others were experienced riders who wanted to improve specific techniques. I created a course outline, improved it over several years, and added another class on dual sport navigation.

In conversations with club members, the same questions arose year after year. What is the best dual sport? How do you set it up for local conditions? How can you ride without getting hurt? How do you find good places to ride? Wanting to improve the classes, I began looking for a book

A license plate, dirt-oriented tires and long-travel suspension allow this dual sport rider to enjoy a wide variety of pavement and off-road adventures.

about dual sport which I could recommend to the students. A search of *Books in Print* listed over 80 books about motocross and off-road racing, but nothing written specifically for dual sport.

Eventually, I decided to use my course outlines to write a short book covering the most important topics. Whitehorse Press expressed interest in publishing it, but encouraged me to make it more comprehensive, expanding the original concept. As the project progressed, several long-time riding partners and experts contributed generously of their ideas, photos, and comments. The result is based on their collective wisdom, derived from thousands of hours of dual sport riding experience.

I have been a dual sport enthusiast since buying a BSA 500cc single in 1961, with a detour into enduro racing in the 1970s. Hopefully, my love of dual sport will shine through the pages of this book and encourage you to get involved, or to ride more.

Section 1

CHOOSING A DUAL SPORT

Dual sport riding can be an elegant, intensely satisfying ballet of man and machine. Choosing the right dancing partner is extremely important.

Some types of motorcycling are narrowly defined. For example, motocross bikes, motocross riding techniques, and motocross tracks have evolved under the pressure of competition into a narrow and highly specialized niche. Selecting a motocrosser is relatively simple. Decide whether you want a 250 or 450, read the shootouts in dirt bike magazines, note what the stars are riding, and go for it.

Dual sport is completely different. There are no races, no shootouts, and no stars. There are few organized events and very little promotion. Some dual sports are optimized for rough singletrack trails, others are at home in a wide variety of conditions, and yet others are more comfortable on pavement and graded roads. You are completely free to choose where and how you will ride—smooth forest service roads, rough singletracks, or long trips.

Manufacturers continually introduce new models and promote them against back-drops of famous races or exotic locations which have little to do with the machine's best potential or the needs of specific riders. In this environment even experienced riders can make mistakes in selecting a motorcycle.

The first step is to appreciate the wide range of dual sport riding possibilities. Then you need to grasp the relative advantages and disadvantages of different dual sport motorcycle offerings—how things like weight, power, suspension, comfort, cruising range, and durability affect the riding experience.

The next step is honestly assessing your own needs. Are you a casual rider or are you an expert? Do you crave speed, or do you enjoy mellow outings? Where will you ride and who will be your riding buddies? A good list of your needs is essential to making a good choice. Finally, you must match your requirements with a specific motorcycle, choosing from the many models that are available.

The chapters in Section 1 will guide you through every step of the selection process.

This club ride has attracted 30 dual sports ranging from 250cc lightweights to 650cc middleweights. Each machine has been carefully chosen to match the type of riding its owner most enjoys.

1

The Dual Sport Experience

This chapter tells four very short stories about typical dual sport rides. They illustrate different kinds of riding and are intended to help you start the process of defining, or possibly rethinking, your own dual sport experience.

Most motorcycles are designed for specific purposes and everyone, even non-riders, can easily picture riding a motorcycle. We see cruisers and sport bikes each day on the highway, and racing bikes on television. It is easy to imagine being in the saddle and doing the things we see.

It is usually possible to convey the intended use of a motorcycle in a single iconic image. The cover of a book on adventure touring shows a motorcycle with lots of luggage, parked in front of a monastery with Buddhist prayer flags, high in the Himalayas. The cover of a book about motocross technique depicts a well-known champion launching over a jump. These images, alone, are sufficient to create a shared understanding of how the motorcycles are used.

Dual sport is different. Remote trails and dirt roads are their preferred venues but most people never see them in action. Furthermore, they are designed to be competent in a wide variety of uses. For every possible iconic image, there are numerous alternatives with equal meaning—riding a shady trail, traveling to the bottom of Copper Canyon, pounding across the desert, exploring a sand wash, winding along a country road, discovering what lies beyond the pavement—all of these images depict the essence of dual sport with equal validity.

Even experienced dual sport owners may fall into ruts, using their machines over and over for the same types of rides, and missing much of the variety. They may even buy additional motorcycles to do different things that can all be done very enjoyably on a dual sport.

Manufacturers love to create new market niches so they can sell more motorcycles. We have adventure motorcycles, hooligan bikes, supermoto, and naked bikes, to name a few. Presumably, the well-equipped motorcyclist will buy one of each. A dual sport is a refreshing alternative to niche bikes—one capable motorcycle, at home in a multitude of settings.

However, merely saying that dual sports are versatile doesn't begin to convey their possibilities, and it is pointless to begin this book without a common understanding of their potential. As you read the following stories of typical dual sport rides, imagine yourself in the saddle—experiencing the many possibilities of dual sport.

These riders think they're in paradise, but the desert is only one of many settings for dual sport enjoyment.

AN AFTERNOON DIVERSION

This first story is very ordinary. There are no exotic destinations, no feats of daring and skill, and no memorable adventures. A story like this will never grace the pages of a magazine. Yet, it may be the most relevant dual sport story of all—a short, enjoyable outing near home, riding an unpretentious motorcycle, on a pleasant afternoon.

It's nearly 1 p.m. on Saturday and his morning's chores are done, or more accurately, as done as they will get. It's been a busy week. The commute, job, and family have taken virtually every waking hour and it's time for a break. He's not whining; life is good, but everyone needs a few hours off.

He thumbs the starter of the Honda and the motor settles into a quiet, steady idle. Twenty minutes later he turns from the highway onto his favorite road. It used to be the main route to the next town, but a new highway leaves it virtually unused.

The old road is neglected now with potholes, stretches of broken pavement, and occasional stretches of dirt and gravel. Old trees cast their shadows on the surface and reveal glimpses of the river below.

He putts lazily along, feeling the warm wind through his sweatshirt and jeans, hearing the sound of the motor, and enjoying the sensations of leaning into the curves. This road could be ridden much faster, but that's not the goal.

As miles roll by, cares of the week fall behind. Concentrating on accelerating, braking, and leaning frees his mind from thoughts of the boss, the job, the commute, the bills, the things he should have done, and the things he has to do.

His ride is a moving meditation on scenery and sensation.

A break in the trees beckons toward the river. He stops, locks his helmet to the frame and walks down to sit on a rock, listen to birds, and watch the lazy current. Life is good.

A couple of hours later, he reaches the town

Short trips close to home can be a welcome break in the weekly routine.

and cuts back to the highway. Neighbors are coming to dinner and it's time to head for home.

The Honda is just as happy on the highway at 65 mph as it was by the river at 40, and he is content to flow along with traffic. Three cruisers thunder by in the opposite direction making enough noise to reenact the Normandy invasion. He waves, but they pointedly ignore him, secure in the superiority of their black leather uniforms and chrome encrusted show-quality motorcycles.

He couldn't care less. Jeans and a sweatshirt match the day, the Honda matches his budget and the afternoon is perfect.

Afternoons like this won't make the news, but they can make your week. In some ways these rides are the very essence of dual sport—short, low-key rides on simple, uncomplicated motorcycles.

This book goes into detail about equipment selection, accessories, dirt riding techniques, and organized activities because they are all relevant to the dual sport experience. But remember that these are opportunities, not obligations; the choices are yours. The objective is to have fun; it can be as simple or involved as you want it to be.

The pavement ends, and excitement begins.

A VARIED DAY IN THE SADDLE

The next story shows another aspect of dual sporting: riding a wide variety of roads and trails in changing conditions. No other motorcycles offer as many riding options.

It is early June in Reno, but still snowy in the mountains—in my opinion, the best time of the year for dual sport adventures. I roll the Suzuki out and begin the mandatory pre-ride checks of gas, oil, and tire pressure, with a quick scan to make sure everything looks tight and right.

With some choke and a couple of kicks the old motor settles into a quiet idle. Turning out onto the street, we head for Boomtown and a splash of gas. The Suzuki and I need to be at Little Truckee Summit by 8 a.m. to meet Jon, my riding partner, and start the real adventure. There is no gas there, or where we are going, so a full tank is mandatory.

I could load the motorcycle into a truck and drive to the Summit, but why would anyone want to start a motorcycle ride by driving? Most other dirt bike riders have no license plate and no choice. They will be driving to some trailhead while I am already enjoying the ride.

The quickest way to Boomtown is on the freeway and soon the Suzuki is keeping up with traffic at 70, going about as fast as it can, making a mixture of dirt-tire-on-pavement, and slightly stressed engine noises. It is only about 12 miles before we are topped off, over the state line into California, and onto dirt at the Dog Valley Road.

As the wheels leave pavement, my riding style changes. Holding the lane, maintaining distance, and daydreaming won't cut it here. Heavy winter rains have resurfaced this usually well-graded road. Now it's all exposed rocks, loose stones, rain ruts, and washouts. It's time to focus, stand on the pegs, flex my knees, move my head over the steering stem, and scan ahead for problems.

The bike is tuned for local conditions. It doesn't have neck-wrenching power, but it's smooth, quiet and supple, soaking up hits from the biggest rocks and hooking up when I give it the gas. We are throwing a big plume of dust as I alternate between standing for the straights and sitting to break into corners, then power sliding with the throttle.

My senses are fully engaged and I am excited and happy. This is what I live for—cool morning air, squirrel critters scampering out of the way, and the sound of the motor.

At the saddle overlooking Stampede Reservoir I am greeted by a 180 degree view of the Sierras. The snow has been receding since April, but the peaks are still deeply covered. It looks like a good day for the Meadow Lake loop.

The familiar roads flow like rivers beneath the wheels and the dust plume is my wake. A movie of rushing trees and bushes fills my peripheral vision. The air is perfumed with vanilla pine and the flinty odor of mountain earth. I see no person and think no thoughts, totally absorbed in the physical act of riding—moving meditation on flowing, sliding speed.

At 7:45, I turn from Highway 89 into the parking lot at Little Truckee Summit. I have been riding dirt roads for 30 minutes, but the time has passed unnoticed. Jon is waiting for me in the lot, sitting astride his KTM.

He makes a big deal of looking at his watch as if I am late, but it's just a tease. We are both early, and both ready to go. If we had tails and could bark we would be straining at our leashes like

You deserve days such as these—riding through pines toward distant snow-capped peaks.

hounds at a hunt. There is nothing we love more than riding in the mountains and we are always eager for more.

A left turn brings us up the crumbling pavement of an old logging road and then back onto dirt. At 6500 feet, the ground is still moist from recently melted snow and the traction is superb. Small streams bisect the trail as I dodge fallen trees using throttle, brakes, and body position to steer. All my senses are engaged and tingling. It doesn't get any better for a woods rider.

Overgrown roads lead us up and down ridges, past Lake of the Woods, and onto the Yuba Pass Road as another hour flies by. Then Jon notices an old logging road leading in the general direction of Meadow Lake and we decide to try it. Within a few hundred yards it is obvious that no one has used it for a long time and it is not likely to go anywhere. Perfect! We love these roads.

Thick grass covers the two-track, hiding big rocks and logs. Our speed drops to a crawl as we zigzag though. Spring is just reaching this elevation and gaps in the trees show Coppins Meadow, all covered with lush grass and sprinkled with bright flowers.

Fallen logs become more numerous; we dodge some and cross others. The Suzuki hangs on a log and I lift it over. Going up the bank to avoid a big log I am surprised by a ditch hidden in brush. I hesitate, the front wheel hits a rock, forward motion stops, the bike starts to fall, and I throw myself uphill. It's an easy fall with no damage and I am soon right side up and going again.

The road turns into skid trails and then the skid trails end. It is time to turn around. We have been on this road to nowhere for another forty minutes, but it is time well spent, and one of the highlights of the day.

Another hour passes and we descend a sunny west-facing road to Meadow Lake where, at higher elevation, it is still winter. There are deep puddles on the road and big snow drifts in the shadows. We weave our way through mounds of old snow, repeatedly melted and refrozen. They support our weight and allow us to charge

Dual sports can easily chug through short stretches of hard spring snow.

through for short distances. We turn north away from the lake, but the snow deepens, forcing us to turn around and head for an alternate way down.

Deep drifts greet us again at the top of Weber Lake Road. It seems prudent to retreat the way we came in, but Jon starts down the road before I can stop him. I wait, thinking he will come to his senses, but soon he is too far down to get back up the slope. There is nothing to do but follow.

The snow is hard enough, but this is a popular snowmobile route in winter. The sleds, like motorcycles in a sand wash, have beaten four foot whoops into the snow. I am using all my skill to gain speed on the down sides of the whoops and use momentum to climb the up sides. The front wheel is sliding and I shuffle and slog with my feet to keep from falling. This is hard, clumsy work, but I am moving and the fear of getting stuck motivates steady progress.

I pass Jon with his back wheel down to the axle. It serves him right for starting down here and I keep on slogging. After a mile, drifts yield to a patch of clear road, but deep snow returns at the next bend. Time, which passed so quickly before, now drags, as I sweat and worry. The snow gets softer and I start pushing harder with my feet. Fortunately, I am still on top of the drifts and moving. I put it in second and chug slowly, but steadily forward. After several miles the road opens up for as far as I can see and it's time to wait for Jon.

More roads and challenges lead us back to pavement near 2 p.m. Being hungry and low on gas, we decide to ride Highway 49 to Sierraville for lunch and fuel. Then, it's goodbye to Jon and back on graded roads to Reno. I arrive home about 4 p.m. with 170 miles on the odometer and a grin that keeps recurring for the rest of the week as I remember sections of the ride.

Dual sports are at home on freeways, highways, and byways. They are a blast to ride on dirt roads and trails whether it's dry, muddy, or snowy. They thrive on sand, rocks, ravines, logs, ledges, washes, and ridges. Big four-wheel-drive trucks are better at crossing deep water, modified Jeeps are better at climbing huge boulders, and road racing motorcycles are faster, but none of these machines can do so many things so well as a dual sport.

Riding all of the various conditions and surfaces takes skill. It's not something that you can do without preparation and practice, but it is the ultimate expression of dual sport and just about the most fun you can have on a motorcycle.

AN INTENSE TRAIL RIDE

The next story reveals another aspect of dual sport: the ability to travel at speed across long expanses of rugged country, and then ride into town for gas and food. Not limited to riding short loops around some gas cans in a truck, you can go anywhere you want, for as long as you want, as fast as you want.

Darrol turns his KTM high on the damp side of a narrow, twisted sand wash in the Nightingale Mountains. Eight feet above the rutted bottom, he feels the 525EXC carve the apex and start down as he looks intently toward the entrance of the next blind corner. The outside of this one is bordered by a vertical, rocky face so he drops to the bottom, brakes, and leans sharply into the turn.

As ruts in the deep sand grab his wheels, he weights the outside peg, twists the throttle hard, and rockets forward on a short straight. Then it's up on the wall again for the next turn. The wash twists by in an ecstasy of turning, climbing, plunging speed.

Climbing ever higher into the mountains, the wash gets narrower and rocks begin to appear in the bottom. He pivots around the bigger stones and hits the smaller ones as squarely as possible. The KTM was made for this. Its powerful motor and long travel suspension come straight from a long line of successful off-road racers.

The wash ends in a single-track leading higher into the mountains and the dance of man and machine continues up through sage and rabbit bush toward the snow-dusted spine of the range. Here the rhythm of the ride changes again. This trail is barely wider than his wheels with short sections of straight connecting sharp turns around bushes. He accelerates hard for a few dozen feet, brakes hard, pivots around the next bush with rear brake and throttle, and then squirts forward again.

His many years of racing experience serve him well and he opens an ever widening gap on his

A brisk ride leading to a spectacular view is as good as it gets for this trail rider.

friends riding behind. He is starting a new business and no longer has time to race every weekend, but he loves riding like this—going as fast and as hard as he can in tight terrain. The dual sport gets him out of the office a couple of times every month when things are slow.

The trail twists up into the mountains and onto a ridge. Overlooking Winnemucca Lake, he pauses to let his buddies catch up. Small rugged ranges rise abruptly above a dry flat extending 50 miles north. Light snow blankets the peaks and flanks of ridges under a moody winter sky. He's raced these trails before but didn't have time then to stop and enjoy the truly spectacular scenery.

His buddies arrive and they decide to follow the ridge north, then ride the highway to Empire for fuel and a sandwich.

Riding at race speed takes practice, experience, and skill. There are no course markings or danger warnings and you are totally responsible for choosing routes and anticipating hazards. For some people, these challenges are the most meaningful and enjoyable experiences in life. Everything else is just waiting until the next ride.

DUAL SPORT TOURING

Touring motorcycles are usually large machines optimized for comfort and luggage-carrying capacity. Dual sports are a terrific alternative for long trips on dirt roads and two-tracks. They excel in rough country and harsh conditions.

Jan and Will are camped by a small stream flowing into the Yukon River near Eagle, Alaska. Jan squeezes the last air from her Thermarest sleeping pad, slides it into a waterproof bag, and straps it to her mud spattered, Kawasaki KLR650. It's near 8 a.m. and the sun at this far northern latitude has been up since 4, but they are in no hurry to go. Getting somewhere is the last thing on their minds. They came to savor the country, not blast through it.

These friends have been on the road with their KLRs for more than a week, traveling from Seattle to Port Hardy on the highway and then via ferry to Prince Rupert. They turned the bikes north onto Highway 37, taking side trips to Stewart and Telegraph Creek, going on past Dease Lake, and onto the Alcan Highway near Whitehorse. They have been traveling in easy stages, setting up camp early in the afternoon, and fishing nearby rivers and lakes below spectacular ranges.

The past two days have been rainy and cool, but Jan and Will are seasoned backpackers and dual sporters from the Pacific Northwest. It takes more than a bit of rain to spoil their fun. Even so, this morning's warm sun is a welcome change.

Riding is enjoyable, but they derive equal pleasure from trip planning and practicing back country skills. For them, the dual sports are simply the best way to travel long distances in rough country.

Their neat camp and carefully chosen equipment reflect long experience with wilderness camping. The month they chose to travel was a studied compromise between good weather and minimum mosquitoes. It's bear country and their campsite is immaculately clean, with all scented and edible items packed in vapor proof containers and hung in a tree, well away from the

For some riders scenery is more important than equipment. Dual sports are just the best way to get there.

sleeping area. The tents, sleeping bags, and rain gear are of good quality and field tested.

They both ride KLR650s so that the same spare tubes, hand levers and cables can be used on either bike. Their camp stove runs on the same unleaded gas the motorcycles use. Both bikes are equipped with sturdy luggage racks and small, watertight, aluminum panniers.

The riders in this story are polar opposites of the intense trail riders who see the dual sports as the ticket to thrills. These campers see dual sports as enjoyable, practical transportation into remote areas. For them, the bikes are supporting actors while mountains, rivers, lakes, and seacoasts play the starring roles.

FURTHER THOUGHTS

One of the great attractions of dual sporting is sharing it with friends. Whether it's joining a club or meeting some riders at a shop or trail head, you will find people who love dual sporting and want to ride with you.

Dual sporting is a good opportunity for new experiences. Most people have busy lives with many interests, but want to try something different. A dual sport can be your ticket to different scenery and exciting memories. You don't need to make a total commitment; a few rides each summer may be exactly what you need.

Dual sports make terrific city bikes. The smaller models are light, agile, and cheap to buy, operate, and insure. They are easy to park, superb at weaving through traffic jams, and rugged enough to withstand the assaults of clumsy motorists who back into them. You can use them for errands, short commutes to work, and taking your spouse or adventurous date to dinner. They can add a whole new dimension of mobility in urban areas and still be ready for a weekend outing in the dirt.

They are great companions to motor homes and campers. With them, you can arrive early, get a good space by the lake, and leave to explore the surrounding area. Dual sports are equally at home on the main streets of small towns, forest service roads, or designated trails. They are happy fetching beer and ice from the country store or following winding logging roads over nearby peaks.

These riders are sharing a peak moment—reaching the summit of Mt. Patterson at 11,500 feet.

It's great fun to tinker with dual sports if you are mechanically inclined. Working on cars and trucks can be hard, messy work. Automotive components are often computerized, covered in oily dirt and buried beneath air conditioning assemblies and body panels. Single-cylinder dual sport engines are simple, accessible designs with relatively few parts. You can clean everything with a power washer before starting and reach nuts and bolts without contortions.

Some dual sports are gorgeous machines. They come in exciting colors—red, orange, yellow, and blue—and are the true embodiment of "form follows function" design with all of their lovely mechanical parts on display. They are accented with stainless steel, polished aluminum, and racy decals. You can customize them with a huge selection of relatively inexpensive bodywork and accessories. They can be rare and exotic contrasts to endless hordes of cruisers. A set of street oriented tires transforms them into terrific canyon bikes—light, quick, and responsive.

Dual sports can also carry passengers. Spending an afternoon on a relaxed ride in pleasant surroundings with child, spouse, or date is a terrific way to spend quality time together. The experience is inherently enjoyable and there are no distractions from phones, chores, computer games, or television programs. Teaching your teenager to ride and maintain a dual sport can be very satisfying and rewarding.

The possibilities are limited only by your own imagination. A dual sport can provide practical transportation, soul-healing diversion, adrenaline-charged excitement, and access to remote areas—all with the same motorcycle.

2

The Dual Sport Lineup

A good way to start a lively discussion among experienced riders is to ask, "What is the best dual sport?" Some favor light, powerful machines that allow them to travel at near race speeds over gnarly terrain. Some want an "all around" bike that can be ridden everywhere. Others want to travel long distances on highways and still be able to make occasional forays onto dirt roads. The range of options is so wide that veterans may even argue whether some models are really dual sports at all.

This chapter defines dual sports classifications, presents the strengths and weaknesses of each category, and explains how to compare specifications of specific models and determine their best use. It also covers conversions and used bikes.

WHAT IS A DUAL SPORT?

Most roads were still unpaved when motorized bicycles first appeared around 1900. In a sense,

In the beginning, all motorcycles were dual sports.

all motorcycles at that time were dual sports, equally at home on dirt and pavement. Advertisements well into the 1920s depict motorcycles on dirt roads, raising clouds of dust.

By 1940, most roads were paved and motorcycles had become street oriented. However, lightweight motorcycles, equally competent on pavement and dirt, were still desirable. In the 1950s and '60s British manufacturers like Triumph and BSA offered versions of their relatively light street motorcycles with high pipes and called them Scramblers.

Then, in 1968, Yamaha introduced the hugely successful Yamaha DT 1, based on a 250cc two-stroke engine. Other manufacturers soon followed with similar models which they called Enduros. These lightweight machines were good on trails, but only adequate on pavement.

Over the next 20 years manufacturers began producing heavier and less dirt-worthy Enduros based on four-stroke engines, as they searched for better combinations of weight, power, durability, performance, and comfort. These machines were less popular with "real" dirt riders, who began modifying them to create lighter, more competent, trail machines.

Suzuki introduced the DR350 in 1990 and promoted it as a dual sport or "dirt bike with a license plate." The terms "dual sport" or "dualie" were quickly adopted by riders and the motorcycle press.

The search for an ideal combination of specifications—weight, power, comfort, and handling—continues today. Currently, manufacturers' offerings range from near dirt bikes to near street models, and a small after market industry supports riders who wish to improve factory offerings, or convert off-road bikes for street use.

The 1990 Suzuki DR350 was the first motorcycle promoted as a dual sport.

Although riders understand that dual sports are motorcycles that can be operated on both pavement and dirt, manufacturers have not universally embraced the term. Suzuki uses the term DualSport (one word) to describe its products. Kawasaki describes its offerings as dual purpose, Honda lists its entry under off-road, and other manufacturers still describe machines as enduros, or simply list them as model numbers. In addition, European manufacturers offer a few models which they designate as "adventure" bikes. From the manufacturers' perspective, terms like dual sport and adventure bike are marketing terms designed to boost sales, not strict definitions describing specific types of bikes.

This book uses the popular definition of dual sport: any motorcycle that is offered by the manufacturer or converted by the rider for use on both pavement and dirt. Most of the later chapters apply equally to dual sports of all kinds. I will distinguish among them only when necessary to make specific points about suitability, riding technique, and equipment.

DUAL SPORT CATEGORIES

Obviously, there are different kinds of dual sports, but trying to distinguish among them using terms like enduro or adventure bike is difficult because the manufacturers don't agree on these classifications. Instead, this book will classify dual sports by weight—ranging from single-cylinder, lightweight machines with a minimum of bodywork to multicylinder heavyweights with more extensive body panels. The chart below shows some of the characteristics of dual sports in three weight categories.

RANGE OF DUAL SPORTS			
CLASSIFICATION	**Lightweight**	**Middleweight**	**Heavyweight**
Best Use	Trails & Two-Tracks	Paved & Dirt Roads	Longer Road Trips
Weight	250–300 lbs.	300–400 lbs.	400+ lbs.
Power	<20–50 hp	40+ hp	80+ hp
Suspension Travel	10–12 in.	6–8 in.	4+ in.
Ground Clearance	10–12 in.	6–8 in.	4+ in.
Number of Cylinders	1	1	2 or More
Body Coverage	Open	Medium	Full
Wind Protection	None	Some	Good
Wheel Size	21–18 in.	21 or 19–18 in.	Other
Tires	Knobby	Intermediate	Street

Note the wide range of characteristics. Weights have a range of more than 150 pounds. Horsepower ranges from less than 20 to more than 80. Some bikes have no wind protection at all and some have full fairings. Some have dirt-oriented tires and others have near-street tires. Motorcycles at different ends of the spectrum will excel in different applications.

BEST USES OF DUAL SPORTS

By definition, dual sports are compromises between dirt and street performance. Some of the very things that make a bike great in the dirt detract from its street performance.

Great dirt bikes are as light as possible, have aggressive tires, favor a standing riding position, offer a bare minimum of comfort, and trade more maintenance to get more performance. Great street bikes are as heavy as they need to be, have smooth tires, provide high levels of comfort, and run a long time with very little maintenance. It is not possible to get everything in one motorcycle.

People who spend most of their time on challenging trails will naturally gravitate toward lighter, more nimble bikes. Those who spend most of their time on pavement and graded dirt roads will naturally lean toward heavier bikes which offer more comfort, durability, cruising range, power, and the ability to carry luggage. Once a bike is too heavy for trails and shod with street-oriented tires, there is little reason to be overly concerned with shaving ounces, and many riders prefer to add accessories and equipment.

There is a huge selection of clothing, accessories, and equipment available from motorcycle manufacturers and other sources. Chapter 4 covers these options in detail.

While middleweight and heavyweight dual sports may not be the best choice for rugged trail riding, intrepid riders do take them into remote and difficult terrain, all over the globe, on trips of tens of thousands of miles. There is a whole literature of adventure touring recounting many wonderful and amazing feats. However, it is important for you to know where the various weight categories fit most naturally into the spectrum of uses.

The KTM 950 Adventure (left), Husqvarna TE610 (middle), and KTM 525EXC (right) span the dual sport range from heavyweight to lightweight.

The Domain of Lightweights

Agile lightweights are happiest on the trail. A 100-mile outing of mostly single-track trail (just wide enough for a motorcycle), and rough two-track (just wide enough for a Jeep), with occasional stretches of pavement and graded road would be a perfect outing.

Some of the lightweights are designed for riders who just want to enjoy the outdoors and mild sensations of movement. Others are designed for riders who want to travel at near race speeds, but all lightweights are competent on rough trails and two-tracks.

Models obviously change over the years, but general principles of suitability are timeless. Here are some examples of current bikes to illustrate the best uses.

The Kawasaki KLX250 is an example of a mellow lightweight dual sport. It is promoted as an "aggressively-styled, go-anywhere, street-legal motorcycle." Its small, mildly tuned engine is adequate for trails and has just enough power to keep up with traffic on the freeway. Dual sports like this are good choices for riders who just want to have fun without pretending they are racers.

The KTM 525EXC is promoted as a "racer with a license plate." It weighs only 250 pounds, has a powerful motor, and is at home on the roughest single-track trails or pounding across the desert. These bikes are very popular with western riders who like to go fast and who have access to big areas of relatively open public land.

Somewhere around 300 pounds, dual sports cross a divide from lightweight to middleweight. The difference is more relative than absolute; much depends on the motorcycle design, size, strength, and skill of the rider.

However, a 300-pound bike has 20 percent more mass than a 250-pound bike. Other things being equal, it is slower to accelerate, turn, and stop. All riders, regardless of their size and strength, will notice the difference.

The Husqvarna TE610 is an example of a dual sport on the borderline between lightweight and middleweight. It has long-travel suspension, high fenders, a powerful motor, and knobby tires. However, at 308 pounds it is more than 50 pounds heavier than a KTM 525EXC. This bike

At a lithe 250 pounds the powerful KTM 525EXC is extremely popular in areas with access to wide open space and fast single-track.

would be a better choice for fast dirt roads and rough two-tracks than twisty trails.

The Domain of Middleweights

These motorcycles can be up to 100 pounds heavier than the lightest dual sports and are happiest on smoother two-track, graded roads, and pavement. A perfect outing would be 100 miles of mostly paved and graded roads with occasional connecting sections of smoother two-track.

At 308 pounds, the Husqvarna TE610 is happiest on graded roads and fast two-tracks.

At 337 pounds the KLR650 is happiest on smoother dirt roads and pavement. This one has a high windshield, wide seat, and luggage racks for touring.

These bikes need enough power to keep up with highway traffic and not buzz the engine to death. They usually have 600cc or 650cc engines producing between 40 and 50 horsepower.

The Kawasaki KLR650, shown above, has less suspension travel than the best trail bikes, lower ground clearance, and comes with semi-knobby tires. It clearly falls into the middleweight category. The KLR can be operated by skilled riders on short sections of rough two-track or trail, but is not the best choice for a steady diet of these conditions.

The Domain of Heavyweights

At somewhere around 400 pounds, dual sports cross another divide into heavyweights. Here again the boundaries are hazy, but these bikes are biased toward long-range touring on graded dirt roads or pavement. Some have long travel suspension and are promoted as dirt-oriented, but they are about 150 pounds heavier than the lightweights and a real handful on trails. A 200-mile (or longer) trip on highway and graded roads with would be a perfect outing for a heavyweight.

Note that tires are an important feature distinguishing trail and street-oriented dual sports. Knobbies are terrific on trails, but terrible on the street. They wear quickly, give a rough, noisy ride, and have dangerously inadequate grip for panic stops and aggressive cornering. Semi-knobby tires are better on the street, but not great in the dirt. They have inadequate traction on steep hills, in deep sand, and in mud.

SPECIFICATIONS AND USES

New models appear every year and manufacturers' websites provide up-to-date information on all of the offerings. In general, the sites start with descriptions which contain valuable clues about the intended use of the model. Lists of features and specifications contain the detailed information needed to make comparisons.

Definitions of Specifications

Here are some key specifications and their definitions:

MSRP. Manufacturer's suggested retail price. Sometimes dealers will price models at significantly less than MSRP so it pays to shop around before buying. What you will actually pay is an "out-the door" price which includes the dealer's sale price plus applicable setup, taxes, and license fees.

Warranty. One year is common for factory dual sports, but make certain about the terms.

Street legal. Some models are approved for street use as they come from the factory. Some models are approved for street use in every state, but others are not approved for street use in California, which has the most stringent emissions requirements.

Engine type. These days all dual sports offered by manufacturers are four-stroke and all have electronic ignition.

Cooling system. Today, most dual sports are water-cooled, while others are air-cooled. Water cooling can maintain a constant engine temperature if it is properly designed. However, motorcycle radiators are small and some water-cooled models overheat on hot days at low speed. Read reviews and ask other riders about specific models.

Starting system. Most are electric start; some retain the kick starter for backup.

Displacement. 250cc is barely adequate for freeway use; 400–450cc is a good all around size; 500cc and up may be more desirable for heavier, faster riders or highway use.

Transmission. Look for a wide-ratio five- or six-speed transmission. Wide-ratio is the key and should mean that low gear is slow enough for trail use while high gear is fast enough for the freeway. Some racing bikes have close-ratio five- or six-speed transmissions which are not satisfactory for dual sport use.

Wheel (suspension) travel. Shorter travel generally allows lower seats but less ability to negotiate gnarly terrain; 12 inches of travel is about standard for trail bikes. Motorcycles with four to six inches of travel can be operated on smooth graded roads.

Adjustable suspension. A good sign, but not an indication of suspension quality. The best off-road suspensions use carefully designed components that can be adjusted to match the needs of a wide range of riders. You need to read reviews and ask other riders about the suspension of specific models.

Wheel base. 56 inches is nimble on trails, 58 should be more stable at speed.

Brakes. Modern bikes have brake discs that can easily be replaced when worn. Motorcycle brake drums are part of the wheel and are not easily replaceable. Also, drum brakes don't work well when wet.

Seat height. The distance from the ground to the seat at its lowest point (without the rider). For more serious riding, a bike that fits is mandatory. Some dual sports have about 12 inches of suspension travel and high seats. This is not a problem for people with average leg length, but short riders need to pay attention. If you have short legs, test the seat height before you buy. Sit on the bike to compress the suspension and try putting both heels down. If you can't do it look for something else or have the bike lowered.

Ground clearance. 12 inches is adequate for single-track; 15 inches is better—a bike with low ground clearance gets hung up on obstacles. Bikes designed primarily for use on dirt roads can get away with 4 to 6 inches of clearance.

Weight. Light is nimble. Big strong riders can usually manage more weight. In general motorcycles in the 225- to 300-pound range can be ridden on rough trails. Heavier bikes are a handful, even for strong riders, but are more comfortable on long trips.

Fuel capacity. A minimum of 2.5 gallons is desirable for 250cc engines; a minimum of 3 to 3.5 gallons are desirable for 400cc and up.

Rake, trail, compression ratio, and carburetor size. These specifications are more interesting to engineers than to most riders. Try to find some reviews that describe power and handling.

Obviously, models and specifications change every year, so you must prepare your own comparisons. Copy web pages for motorcycles that interest you or take notes and make comparison tables like those shown below. You may already have some idea of the type of dual sport you want and can limit your research to those models which are most likely to satisfy your needs.

At 436 pounds, this KTM 950 Adventure is better suited to highways and smooth graded roads.

Jerry has been all over Nevada on his KLX250S.

Lightweight Specifications

It is difficult to relate tables of lifeless numbers to real-world riding applications without some illustrations of how they are used. Here are some specifications followed by comments about how members of my dual sport club use the bikes. I have included different types of popular dual sports; many other currently available bikes are not included.

Note the wide range of offerings. Even within the classification of lightweights, prices for the selected motorcycles range from $3,949 to $8,299. Engine sizes start at 223cc and go to 510cc. Weights range from 238 pounds to 291 pounds. The figures will change with the years, but the wide ranges are very likely to persist.

Lightweights in Use

Mike has an XT225. He rides it slowly (which he likes) and always finishes club rides. The little XT has been up 10,000-foot mountains, crossed raging spring streams and bounced over rocky trails. He is using it to lay out our club's Ride Reno 200 Dual Sport event this year.

Jerry has a 2006 KLX250S and had a 2002 KLR250 before that. He rides at moderate speed all over northern Nevada. Thousand-mile, multi-day trips, sand washes, rocky canyons, graded roads, and pavement all disappear beneath his wheels. These small KLXs have great gas mileage and stone reliability.

The smallest lightweights usually get a big yawn from magazine test riders who think they are boring, but they are wrong. Morning air is just as crisp, meadows equally green, and lakes

REPRESENTATIVE LIGHTWEIGHT SPECIFICATIONS				
MODEL	Yamaha XT225	Kawasaki KLX250S	Suzuki DR-Z400E	KTM 525EXC
MSRP	$4,199	$4,799	$5,599	$8,299
Displacement	223cc	249cc	398cc	510cc
Cooling system	air	water	water	water
Starting system	electric	electric	electric	electric/kick
Weight	238 lbs.	262 lbs.	291 lbs.	250 lbs.
Transmission	6-speed	6-speed	5-speed	6-speed
Fuel capacity	2.3 gal.	1.9 gal.	2.6 gal.	2.1 gal.
Seat height	31.9 in.	34.8 in.	36.8 in.	36.4 in.
Ground clearance	11.2 in.	11.0 in.	11.8 in.	15 in.
Wheel base	53.1 in.	56.5 in.	58.5 in.	58.3 in.
Wheel travel	8.9/7.5 in.	10.2/9.1 in.	about 11 in.	12 & 13 in.
Suspension	some adj.	adjustable	adjustable	adjustable
Brakes	disk/drum	disk	disk	disk
Warranty	1 yr	1 yr	1 yr	6 mos.

the same shade of blue on the smallest factory dual sports. These little bikes are terrific for exploring new places and enjoying the outdoors.

About half of our club members ride Suzuki DR-Z400s or Kawasaki KLX400s, which are basically the same motorcycle. The engines have enough power for heavier riders and longer rides on the freeway. These bikes can handle rough terrain at faster speeds and have a terrific reputation for reliability. They may be a bit tall and heavy for smaller riders. Otherwise, they are a logical choice for many people.

The dual sports described above are designed by factories as compromises between dirt and road bikes. In general, they sacrifice a little power, gain a little weight relative to their engine size, and lack the ultimate in suspension. In return they offer durability with less maintenance.

Lightweights Based on Racers

Both KTM and Husqvarna offer lightweight dual sports based on their very successful off-road racing bikes. These dual sports are the ultimate trail weapons—powerful, agile, and exciting. They could be entered in any amateur desert race or enduro and be competitive. They are definitely the ticket to adrenaline-charged thrills.

However, their gains on the trail are offset by losses in other areas. They have narrow, uncomfortable seats and require careful attention to maintenance. Their powerful engines shred tires and demand high levels of riding skill. They can be ridden on the street, but that's a bit of a waste unless you need to connect trails or head into a small town for gas.

KTMs merit special comment. They have been the number one candidate for dual sport conversions for several years and are street legal from the factory in 2007.

KTM uses the same frame, suspension, and basic motor with different bore and stroke, to produce 400cc, 450cc, and 525cc motorcycles. This allows them to offer the highest quality components at reasonable cost. Also, dealers can stock fewer parts, but still satisfy most needs for replacement components.

The 525EXC has a battery and electric starter like the DR-Z400 and has a bigger motor, but still weighs 40 pounds less. This is enough to make a

At 250 pounds Don's KTM 400EXC weighs the same as the 525EXC, but its less powerful motor is easier to manage on tight trails.

The lightweight Husqvarna 250 (left) doesn't look that much different from the middleweight Suzuki DR650 (right), but the 250 is much more agile on the trail.

big difference in handling. It is also $2,400 dollars more expensive.

KTMs are extremely popular with the ex-racers in our club and have proven to be quite durable in the role of dual sports where they usually loaf along at a fraction of their full potential. They need frequent oil changes and regular valve adjustments, but our club members have ridden them 10,000 miles and more without serious problems.

Husqvarnas have similar specifications, but their dealer network seems smaller than KTM. We have three in our club and their owners are pleased.

Riders on lightweights and middleweights enjoy riding together on this outing consisting of dry lakes and smooth two-tracks.

This F 650 GS Dakar is competent on graded roads and as good as many street bikes on the highway.

Middleweight Specifications

The following table compares specifications for middleweight dual sports.

Middleweights in Use

Several of our club members have Suzuki DR650s and love them. They have the power for long highway trips and can also be ridden on rough two-tracks, and occasional single-tracks. At 324 pounds they are a good match for larger, stronger riders.

Kawasaki KLR650s have been in production for about 15 years with very few changes. The windshields offer some wind protection at higher speeds on the highway, and appeal to long-distance riders. They have a devoted following and are at home on rough dirt roads, but are definitely not trail bikes.

The 387 pound F 650 GS Dakar is heavy, and relatively expensive, not something you would want to drop in the rocks. On dirt roads and pavement, it is smooth, quiet, and powerful. Larie has ridden his on a few club rides and conquered some rough sections. He also rides long distances with his wife on the back.

REPRESENTATIVE MIDDLEWEIGHT SPECIFICATIONS			
MODEL	**Suzuki DR650SE**	**Kawasaki KLR650**	**BMW F 650 GS**
MSRP	$5,099	$5,199	$7,100
Displacement	644cc	651cc	652cc
Cooling system	air	water	water
Starting system	electric	electric	electric
Weight	324 lbs.	337 lbs.	387 lbs.
Transmission	5-speed	5-speed	5-speed
Fuel Capacity	3.4 gal.	6.1 gal.	4 gal.
Seat height	34.8/33 (adjustable) in.	35 in.	30.7 in.
Ground clearance	8.9 in.	9.4 in.	5.1 in.
Wheel base	58.1 in.	58.9 in.	58.2 in.
Wheel travel	10.2/8.7 in.	9.1 in.	6.5/6.7 in.
Suspension	some adj.	some adj.	some adj.
Brakes	disk	disk	disk
Warranty	1 yr	1 yr	3 yrs./36,000 mi.

Heavyweight Specifications

The following table compares specifications for heavyweights.

Heavyweights in Use

Heavyweights are based on large, powerful street engines and offer the highest levels of durability with an absolute minimum of maintenance. They offer good wind protection and comfortable seats. Five-hundred-mile days in the saddle are feasible and enjoyable.

However, these highway virtues come at the expense of agility. One of our club members rode his KTM 950 on single-tracks for a few months, but most of us regarded him with open-jawed amazement. After numerous crashes he switched to a lightweight dual sport for serious single-track.

A couple of club members have Suzuki V-Stroms and ride them all over the USA, Canada, and Mexico. They are great highway bikes and handle most dirt roads at reasonable speed.

With their powerful engines and long-travel suspension the KTM 950s are dirt road rockets. Two of our club members have them and like them.

These V-Stroms are about halfway through a 3000-mile trip to Mexico. Suzuki calls them dual sports but they are most at home on the highway.

These BMW 1200 GSs are great long distance touring bikes—ready for a trip to Alaska or around the world.

None of our club members has a 1200 GS Adventure; maybe the high price explains it. They are beautiful machines and include many options that would cost extra on other brands. Just looking at them in the shop makes one think of places like Tierra del Fuego or Dakar.

REPRESENTATIVE HEAVYWEIGHT SPECIFICATIONS

MODEL	Suzuki V-Strom 1000	KTM 950 Adventure	BMW 1200 GS Adventure
MSRP	$8,999	$13,998	$16,775
Displacement	996cc	942cc	1170cc
Cooling system	water	water	water
Starting system	electric	electric	electric
Weight	462 lbs.	437lbs.	492 lbs.
Transmission	6-speed	6-speed	6-speed
Fuel Capacity	5.8 gal.	5.8 gal.	8.7 gal.
Seat height	33.1 in.	34 in.	35.2 in.
Ground clearance	6.5 in.	10.3 in.	n/a
Wheel base	60.4 in.	61.8 in.	59.5 in.
Wheel travel	6.3 in.	8.3 in.	8.3/8.7 in.
Suspension	adjustable	adjustable	n/a
Brakes	disk	disk	disk
Warranty	1 year	1 year	3 yrs./36,000 mi.

SOME IMPORTANT THINGS YOU CAN'T FIND IN SPECIFICATIONS

Specifications relate a ton of valuable information, but don't tell the whole story. Here are some other considerations.

Service and Support

A good dealer and service department are highly desirable. Look in the yellow pages and note which brands are available locally.

In general, the Japanese big four—Honda, Kawasaki, Suzuki, and Yamaha—are available almost everywhere. KTM used to be rare and exotic, but they have developed a strong dealer network and legions of satisfied riders in the past few years. BMW also has a very strong dealer network.

Visit the shops and speak with sales, parts, and service personnel. The MSRP is only a starting number and not the price you will actually pay. Ask the dealers about out-the-door prices including tax, license, and any other charges. Tell them you are thinking about buying and ask some questions. Do they have time to talk? Do they listen? Are they helpful?

Experience with big motorcycle shops can range from pleasant to pitiful. The best dealers have well-trained employees who deliver parts and service, as ordered, and on time. The worst take forever and screw things up. Your disabled mount could sit for three to four weeks in a busy service department waiting for overworked mechanics to examine it, get parts, and finish repairs.

A poorly managed dealership shouldn't keep you from riding a good brand, but you will be happier if you know what to expect. If you don't like your area's dealers look for independent repair shops. Maybe you can find one that specializes in dual sports.

Less popular models may look terrific on paper, but use some caution. The dealer may fold or stop carrying them, parts may become scarce, and big tanks and other after-market goodies may not be available at all. If you have a good dealer and some off-road experience, brands such as Husqvarna or Husaberg may be viable options.

Rider Feedback

Some very important characteristics are not listed in specifications. How much does the engine vibrate? Does it have a tendency to overheat? Will it go both slow enough for trails, and fast enough for highways? Is the seat comfortable? Are people having mechanical problems?

To get answers to these questions you need to talk to other riders and visit web forums dealing with specific models. Spend some time on this. It's is fun and can help you avoid costly mistakes. Make notes about out-the-door prices and other information and add them to your comparisons.

USED DUAL SPORTS

GREAT DEAL!

2001 Suzuki DR-Z400, licensed, 500 miles, ICO trip computer, skid plate, more, $3,100. Call for details.

Used bikes can get you riding for thousands less. Many riders purchase dual sports, take them on a few rides and then lose interest. There are always a few of these low-mileage bikes for sale and they can be a good alternative to buying new. Consider a rider who bought a new DR-Z400 in 2003 for $5,500. He rode it about 20 times a year. Now, three years later, this motorcycle has about 6,000 miles on the odometer and will sell for about $3,500. Someone should be able to ride the bike for another three years and sell it for about $2,500 dollars.

Buyer Beware

Disconnecting a dual sport odometer is ridiculously easy, and indicated mileage may be a poor measure of a bike's condition. You must judge the bike from what the owner says and your eyes see.

Here is a story found on the Web:

"My friend purchased a nice 2001 DR-Z400 on eBay. The bike was clean and appeared to have little use. However, it started making a rather loud knocking noise after a few rides. The noise continued to get worse.

Is this used DR-Z400 a beauty or a bomb?

Robert dropped it off for me to investigate the noise. After a quick drain of the oil, it became obvious that he had a major problem. The decision was made to tear it apart and find out what happened."

This fix required a complete teardown of the engine and replacement of several expensive parts—about $900.

The story conveys an important "buyer beware message," but don't let it scare you completely off. Knowing how to buy is the key to success.

How Long Do They Last?

Lightweight dual sport engines usually need an overhaul after 10 to 15 thousand miles. The heavier, more street-oriented models will run much longer. Pistons, rings, and valves are often the first to need overhaul—a "top-end" job—and can be replaced while the engine is in the bike. A top-end job for a single-cylinder engine may cost from $500 to $1,000 at a dealer, including parts and labor. Clutches, electrical components, radiators, and carburetors can also be repaired with the engine in the frame.

Some lightweight dual sports are operated in harsh conditions, so they wear very quickly. Tires, brakes, chains, and sprockets go first. Dirt tires last from 800 to 3,000 miles depending on the tire and conditions. Brakes may last 3,000 to 5,000 miles. A good O-ring chain and steel sprockets can go 8,000 to 10,000 miles. These things are easy to see and easy to fix.

Bottom-end components, such as bearings, crank shaft, connecting rod, and gears usually last a long time on a cycle that has not been raced or abused. The engine must be removed from the frame and completely disassembled to replace them.

Sometimes a motor will have a catastrophic failure. For example, a valve may break while the engine is running. This can ruin valves, head, piston, cylinder, and more. A complete teardown and rebuild may cost $1,000 to $2,000 including parts and labor. Many running bikes sell for less than $2,000 so the catastrophe may cause it to end its life as parts on E-bay or junk.

IS A USED BIKE RIGHT FOR YOU?

Remember that there are three parts to every sale: buyer, seller, and bike. Start with yourself and answer these basic questions:

- Are you willing to wait for the right bike and price?
- Do you trust yourself to spot problems both visible and hidden?
- Are you able to estimate what it will cost to fix any problems you see?
- Are you able to fix problems yourself or willing to have them repaired?
- Do you have friends who can help you and/or give good advice?

If you can't answer "yes" to most of these questions, you should probably buy new until you gain some experience. Another option would be to buy a used bike from a reputable dealer. These bikes are usually sold "as is," but a good dealer will not knowingly offer you a bike with big, hidden problems. A private party who is leaving town may not care about anything but getting your money.

> **PLACES TO LOOK FOR USED BIKES IN YOUR AREA:**
>
> - Ask your friends
> - Check the classifieds
> - Look at Craig's List and E-bay

Shopping for a Used Machine

The first steps are to define your needs and select candidates—the same as buying new.

Know what you want before looking at used bikes. Driving all over town without having a clear idea of what you need is a poor use of time. Also, you won't recognize a screaming deal if you

▶ ## ASK THESE QUESTIONS ABOUT A USED MOTORCYCLE

Let's assume that you find a used bike you want. The next step is to call the seller and verify that the ad is correct.

I have rarely seen a used bike that was not in "good condition," according to the seller. Once I drove 50 miles one-way, to look at a "good" bike that actually had missing turn signals, cracked switches, broken headlight, torn seat, bent wheels, and leaking head gasket. Ask specific questions about the motorcycle:

- Do you have clear title?
- Why are you selling?
- Are you the original owner?
- Who owned it before?
- Can you send me a digital picture?
- What is the odometer mileage; is it correct?
- Where has it been ridden?
- How has it been ridden?
- Are there after-market accessories?
- Have there been any repairs; are there receipts?
- Are there maintenance records?
- What form of payment is acceptable?
- Ask about the condition of tires, brakes, bars, switches, controls, chain, suspension, clutch, motor, and body parts.

Make some notes about the answers, and set up an appointment if the answers satisfy you.

Go prepared to buy, if you like what you see. Have sufficient funds and a way of taking the bike with you. On a couple of occasions I left a deposit and returned to discover that the bike had been sold to someone else, who came later and offered $100 more. ∎

see it. Great opportunities don't sit around forever waiting for you to think about them; someone else will snap them up in a heartbeat.

Go online to the Kelly Blue Book of Motorcycles and get prices for used models. Kelly lists retail (what dealers ask for bikes in good condition) and wholesale (what they will pay for them). A private party will generally ask for something in-between. Remember, these prices are for bikes in good condition.

Another source of used bike prices is National Association of Automobile Dealers, which is also on-line. Their figures seem to be a bit lower than Kelly for the models I cross checked.

The Kelly prices are national averages. Dealers with lots of competition may shave prices on new bikes with a corresponding effect on used. Compare prices listed in your local classified advertisements. Also, you might buy cheaper in the off-season. In some places, used prices fall a little in winter and rise again in spring.

Evaluate the Seller

To avoid disasters, you must judge the seller as much as the bike. Do everything possible to spot liars because you will be relying in large part on their statements. The best option is to buy from a friend you know and trust.

The following are good signs for strangers:

- The bike is clean and ready for sale.
- The paperwork is in a neat folder or envelope, and complete.
- The seller is mature and answers your questions thoughtfully.
- There is an owner's manual, and even better, a service manual.
- The seller has an organized garage with some tools.
- Answers to your questions match the condition and appearance of the bike.

Most of us are pretty good at spotting flakes and a flaky seller is not a good sign. When you meet the seller, ask some of the same questions again to see if he gives the same answers. Now you are ready to look at the goods.

Inspecting the Goods

Note the overall appearance—some scratches are normal. Cracked, broken, missing, and poorly repaired parts are bad signs. Rounded nuts and bolts or ruined screws are signs of incompetent repairs. Dual sports that are operated in the dirt develop a patina of small nicks and scratches which indicate how hard a bike has been used. Those operated on the street won't offer these clues. Look for tool marks on the rear rim that indicate frequent tire changes. Worn brake disks and sprocket, and loose kick starter pivots are also clues to high mileage.

Note things that are out of place. For example, one bike, with an otherwise medium neglected look, had a brand new spark plug cap. The seller mumbled something about the old one being cracked, but the bike actually had a bad coil. It started OK, but missed at high speed. I bought it anyway because the price was right. I replaced the coil, and got four good years of riding from it.

- Note the odometer mileage.
- Make sure the seller has legal title.
- Look at the VIN and match it to the title.

Chapter 11 has a list of things that need periodic inspection. You can also use it to assess the condition of a used bike.

If the difference between new and used is only a couple of thousand, you should expect a creampuff. You want a bike that is like new in every respect. At the other end of the spectrum are bikes that show lots of wear and are priced really low. These can still be reasonable deals if you are willing and able to make some repairs. Estimate the cost of any needed items and deduct it from the price you are willing to pay. Don't hesitate to walk away from a bike that you are unsure of.

Now is the time to bargain if you want to buy. You know what the bike is worth because you have done your homework. Ask for any manuals, tools, or equipment that you may be able to use. Note any flaws in the machine and ask for a price reduction. If the machine is perfect, try an offer of 10 percent less than asked. Most sellers will knock a few bucks off, but the seller should also have done his homework. Don't expect him to give it away.

A used dual sport could be the best option if you have some mechanical skills and the prices of new bikes are more than you want to pay.

DUAL SPORT CONVERSIONS

Many riders prefer to convert an off-road bike to dual sport use. There are several reasons that this could be the preferred approach. It may be cheaper to convert a bike than buy a new or used one—particularly if you already have a dirt bike that you like. It may be possible to build one that matches your riding style better than factory offerings. This is often the case for experienced riders who know exactly what they want in terms of weight, power, and suspension. Or you may enjoy mechanical work and the satisfaction of building something unique and beautiful.

Dirt bikes come in several varieties: motocross racers, off-road bikes, and play bikes. Motocross

▶ **INSPECTION CHECKLIST**

After you have completed the routine checklist described in chapter 11, perform the following tests:

- ▶ Start the engine and let it warm up.
- ▶ Make sure it starts quickly and idles smoothly.
- ▶ Listen to the motor—clicks and whirs are normal, but clanks, grinds, and whines are not.
- ▶ Check the headlight, tail light, brake light, turn signals, and horn.
- ▶ The buyer should let you ride it. Show your motorcycle license, helmet and gloves; offer to leave your car keys.
- ▶ Clutch operation should be smooth.
- ▶ The brakes should work—always check immediately when riding an unknown bike.
- ▶ The transmission should shift smoothly into each gear.
- ▶ The motor should accelerate smoothly and briskly.
- ▶ Now that the motor is hot, look at it carefully for any signs of leaks.
- ▶ Check the oil level and condition. Make sure that it is not some extra heavy concoction designed to disguise serious wear.
- ▶ Sniff the radiators—leaking antifreeze smells like alcohol.
- ▶ Check the brake fluid levels.
- ▶ Rev it up and look for excessive exhaust smoke.
- ▶ Ask about any problems you may not be able to spot.
- ▶ How often did the seller change the oil and clean the air filter?
- ▶ Does the buyer know of anything wrong with the engine, clutch, and transmission?
- • Has the motor been overheated, run with low oil, or submerged in a lake or stream? ∎

bikes trade increased maintenance for the lowest possible weight and highest possible power. They are designed for the track and are not usually good candidates for dual sport use. Off-road bikes are usually a bit heavier, may have less power than motocrossers with similar sized engines, and are usually better candidates for conversion. They are usually equipped with spark arrestors and mufflers that are required in national forests.

The smallest off-road bikes are sometimes called play bikes. They tend to have small engines that appeal to beginning dirt riders. They are usually mildly tuned and could appeal to dual

Conversions like this 525EXC are very popular.

sport riders who just want to putt around and enjoy being outdoors.

The table below illustrates some currently available bikes in each category. It is not intended to be comprehensive, and the models will change each year, but the same principles will continue to apply.

Before you consider any potential conversion, make certain you can license it. Every state has different regulations and some are very restrictive. For example, California has a list of specific motorcycles that can be licensed. Other states merely want equipment such as speedometer, horn, mirrors, turn signals, tail light, stop light, and headlight with high and low beams.

Learn your state's requirements, before you buy a motorcycle for conversion. Several companies, most notably Baja Designs, specialize in conversions and may be able to advise you. Your dealer may also have some good information and be willing to do the conversion for you.

Be aware that motor vehicle employees are not dual sport experts. Conversions are relatively rare and the regulations change constantly. I have converted several different motorcycles in Nevada. Some have gone smoothly, but others have been frustrating. A different employee appears every time I go to the DMV, and each tells a new story. I have learned to be patient, not to argue, and do whatever seemingly stupid thing they ask.

Example of a Conversion

If you are considering a conversion, you should compare the cost with buying a factory dual sport—so gather specifications and costs. Let's follow a typical rider as he goes through the process.

Bud is an experienced rider who has been competing in local desert races where he rides a Yamaha YZ450F. Lately he has been thinking of

EXAMPLES OF YAMAHA OFF-ROAD MOTORCYCLES

	MOTOCROSS	OFF-ROAD	PLAY BIKE
MODEL	YZ450F	WR450F	TT-R230
STREET LEGAL	no	no	no
MSRP	$6,999	$7,199	$3,449
DISPLACEMENT	449cc	449cc	223cc
COOLING SYSTEM	water	water	air
STARTING SYSTEM	kick	electric	electric
WEIGHT	220 lbs.	247 lbs.	246 lbs.
TRANSMISSION	5-speed	5-speed	6-speed
FUEL CAPACITY	1.8 gal.	2.1 gal.	2.1 gal.
SEAT HEIGHT	38.9 in.	38.5 in.	34.3 in.
GROUND CLEARANCE	14.7 in.	14.4 in.	12 in.
WHEEL BASE	58.8 in.	58.5 in.	54.5 in.
WHEEL TRAVEL	11.8/12.4 in.	11.8/12.0 in.	9.4/8.7 in.
SUSPENSION	adjustable	adjustable	n/a
BRAKES	disk	disk	disk/drum
WARRANTY	30 day	30 day	90 day

Off-road motorcycles like this Honda XR650R are good candidates for conversion.

getting a dual sport so he can explore the local area. The dealer has a two-year-old Honda XR650R for sale. Note that this is Honda's off-road model, not the street-legal XR650L. Bud wonders whether he should try to convert it or buy a new bike.

The first thing he does is gather specifications and compare them. He decides to compare the Honda 650R to a street legal Husqvarna TE610. However, the same technique would work for any comparison.

The next thing Bud does is to make a copy of the title and take it to the DMV. He makes absolutely sure that the bike can be licensed and learns that his state requires a speedometer, head light with high and low beams, tail light, and stop light. The stop light must be operated by switches on the front and rear brake levers. The state requires two rear-view mirrors, a horn, and turn signals. They also want a certified mechanic or dealer to inspect the added equipment and brakes, and sign a form. These are typical requirements, but your state could be different.

Now Bud gets an out-the-door price for the TE and prices for all the equipment he must add to the XR. He also goes to the Web to learn all he can about the two options.

Bud will need to add other accessories to both bikes, but at this point he only wants to get a rough idea of relative costs. The next table shows how the comparison might look.

In this example the Honda is a lot cheaper, but it already has 3,000 miles and will probably need repairs if Bud plans to ride it a lot.

Note that this comparison gives Bud costs and specifications, but it does not really tell him which bike to buy. He can only choose after he develops a clear idea of how he will use the bike.

COMPARISON OF SPECIFICATIONS		
MODEL	**XR650R**	**TE610**
STREET LEGAL	no	yes
PRICE	$3,500	$7,299
DISPLACEMENT	649cc	576cc
COOLING	water	water
STARTING	kick	electric
WEIGHT	277 lbs.	308 lbs.
TRANSMISSION	5-speed	6-speed
FUEL CAPACITY	1.8 gal.	3.2 gal.
SEAT HEIGHT	36.8 in.	37 in.
GROUND CLEARANCE	12 in.	11.6 in.
WHEEL BASE	58.3 in.	59.3 in.
WHEEL TRAVEL	11/12 in.	11.8/12.6 in.
SUSPENSION	adjustable	adjustable
BRAKES	disk	disk
WARRANTY	used	n/a

FINAL COMPARISON, CONVERSION VS. PURCHASE		
MODEL	**XR650R**	**TE610**
PRICE	$3,500	$7,299
TAX AND LICENSE	$335	$700
DUAL SPORT EQUIPMENT	$600	n/a
TOTAL	$4,435	$7,999

FINAL THOUGHTS

This chapter has defined three classifications of dual sports and described how they are typically used. It has also explained how to gather information, compare specific models, and relate the specifications to actual use. However, all dual sports are compromises. They give a little here to gain a little there.

The best compromise is the one that fits your needs and that depends on what you will do with the bike. You can't make an intelligent choice until you decide how you intend to ride. The next chapter will guide you through the process of defining needs and making a final selection.

Matching a Dual Sport to Your Needs

This chapter explains how to define a dual sport dream, verify that the dream includes the things you really enjoy, research local riding opportunities, and inventory your personal and financial resources. Based on this information you will be prepared to choose the model that makes your dream a reality.

KNOW WHAT YOU WANT

Most motorcycle enthusiasts enjoy reading the classifieds to see what's for sale. Once or twice a year, I find an item substantially like this:

LIKE NEW!

ABC450. Bought two years ago;
Many extras, Only ridden three times.
$9,000 invested. Will sell for $5,500

The models and details vary, but the story is the same—someone bought a new bike, added a ton of goodies and now wants to sell without ever riding it much.

These ads raise two types of questions. First, what were these people thinking—how could they spend so much money and virtually never ride? Did they have some unforeseen problem or just lose interest and discover a new hobby? Second, could these be good deals?

The answer to the second question is that these bikes are bargains only if they match the needs of the buyer. Otherwise, they could be another costly mistake, just like the seller made.

The right dual sport should be like a good dancing partner—responsive to every lead. The two of you should flow over terrain like Fred Astaire and Ginger Rogers. Your partner should be light-footed and willing, not an ill-mannered beast that fights you all day. You want Ginger, not the Terminator.

You will have no problem finding new and used equipment—the range of motorcycles and accessories is wide. Magazines and web pages are filled with photos and specifications. Full page ads tout the exploits of factory-sponsored racers on various brands. Articles pronounce new offerings to be near perfect, and subsequent articles encourage you to buy $5,000 of accessories to improve them.

All of this is fun to read, but what does it really mean to you? The answer is not much, without knowing where and how you will ride. The challenge is in honestly defining your needs. What you really enjoy, where you want to go, who will be your riding buddies—these issues are much more important than which bike has the lightest weight, or the most powerful motor, or the longest cruising range.

Even experienced riders make mistakes when they are seduced by advertisements that don't match their riding styles. Here are some examples of errors made by veterans:

Bob was a very experienced trail rider. He rode rocky single-tracks on his 250cc and was good at it. Then he bought a tall, heavy 400cc that was better for long trips. He began falling in the rocks because he couldn't get his feet down. His single-track riding got worse. Then he bought a 500cc which was lighter, but just as tall—plus it had a scary fast motor. Now he had two disadvantages: a tall seat and a motor he couldn't control. He wishes he had his 250cc again.

Richard was an experienced street rider who was becoming bored with sitting in traffic jams on a sport bike that was capable of nearly three

Although he is mounted on a very mild 250cc Kawasaki, this rider has enough power to go pretty much wherever he wants to go. His bike is easy to maintain, easy on tires, and above all it matches his vision of what a dual sport should be.

times the speed limit, and wanted to try some dirt. He sold his street bike and bought a heavy-weight dual sport, thinking he would have the best of both worlds. After a few rides on graded Forest Service roads he ventured onto an over-grown logging road, but it soon became too rough, and he had to turn back.

Over the next few months he tried many two-tracks with the same results. His new bike was too heavy and had too little ground clearance for the rocks and logs on the most interesting routes. Now he wishes he had kept the street bike and gotten a more dirt-worthy bike for his off-high-way adventures.

These riders made the mistake of buying what they thought they wanted, instead of what they really needed. Spend the time to clearly define what kind of riding you want to do before buying a dual sport.

THE SELECTION PROCESS

Choosing the right dual sport can be difficult in an environment where slick brochures entice you down multiple, conflicting paths, but the rewards are well worth the effort to clarify your needs. The diagram below shows a process that can help organize your thoughts.

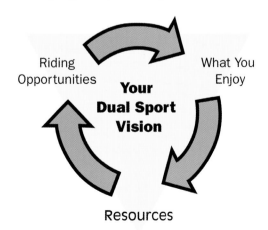

Dual Sport Selection Process

In the center is your dream, a short statement of what will be the most fun and give the greatest pleasure. This dream is surrounded by considerations that shape the actual riding experience and determine whether the dream is realistic. These include riding opportunities, what you most enjoy doing, and your personal resources. The selection process is to define a dream, research your personal considerations, and adjust the dream until you have a clear definition of your needs.

What Is Your Dream?

A dream should include the activities that give you the most pleasure.

Here are some examples of dual sport dreams:

- Dream Number 1 – I want to ride directly from my house to a variety of roads and trails ranging from easy to hard and experience the sheer joy and satisfaction of moving at speed over all types of terrain.
- Dream Number 2 – I want to get away from the traffic and congestion of my area and take day or overnight rides to beautiful lakes, rivers, deserts, mountains, and canyons that see few other travelers.
- Dream Number 3 – Now that the kids are grown, I would like to ride again. I don't want anything too extreme. I just want to have pleasant afternoon rides and maybe make some new friends.

Here are some questions that will help you develop your personal dream.

Is this your dual sport dream?

Questions About Your Dream

- What type of riding do you want to do?
- How many hours will you spend on an average trip? An afternoon? A day? Overnight?
- Do you have a special use or "dream trip" in mind?
- How often will you ride on pavement?
- How many miles on pavement?
- How often will you ride on dirt?
- How many miles on dirt?

Spend some time thinking about these questions and answers. Then write a brief description of your dream.

Places within the red circle can be reached in about one hour by a rider living in Sacramento, and include his most likely riding areas.

What Do You Enjoy the Most?

Now it's time to zero in on the aspects of dual sport that will give you the most pleasure. This is very personal. The questions below are intended to start your thinking, but there may be other considerations that are even more important.

- If you are currently riding a dual sport or off-road motorcycle what do you like and dislike about it?
- What is the most fun you can have on a motorcycle? Is it speed? Surmounting obstacles? Reaching destinations?
- Do you want something that will be admired by your friends and recognized as the best?
- Do you like loud mufflers, and wheel-spinning power?
- Would you be satisfied with a smaller, less prestigious bike?
- Do you want to carry a passenger?
- Do you like mechanical work?

Make a short list of the things that you would most like to do; then compare it with your dream. Is there anything that needs to be changed?

Learning About Riding Opportunities

Most riding will probably be within a couple of hours of where you live because it's relatively easy to squeeze an afternoon or day ride into a busy schedule. There may be enough time for only a few longer trips each year. In any case, it is very important to learn about the types of routes and surfaces you will ride.

Start by getting a map of your area and drawing circles around areas that you can easily reach in a day, leaving some time to explore dirt roads and trails. The map shows an example for Sacramento, California. Places within the red circle can be reached in about one hour. It may be necessary to draw a larger circle to include more distant destinations if there are no riding opportunities within one hour.

If you currently ride dual sport, you may already have a good idea of the types of riding that are available. If not, gather information.

Start by noting whether there is any public land in the area. The US Forest Service administers 193

This well-maintained dirt road is a good route for any dual sport.

Is this a good crossing or a trap? The water could conceal a crossing or bottomless mud.

million acres of land, most of which is well supplied with roads, and possibly trails, that are open to dual sport. The Bureau of Land Management administers another 264 million acres of public lands, located primarily in the 12 Western States. The Forest Service is organized by forest and the BLM is organized by region. Your local office can provide maps and usually has an OHV ranger that can supply valuable information. Be sure to ask if motorcycles are permitted in the areas of interest.

Go onto the Web and search for OHV under the heading for your state. Some states have OHV parks and trail systems.

Gather maps. Most highway maps show only major routes. Read Chapter 13 for information about paper and on-line topographic maps. Also, ask friends and people at the motorcycle shops. Check with local clubs, etc. If you are planning a long trip, see Chapter 14 for sources of information about more distant routes.

Riding Surfaces

Next, learn how to classify dirt surfaces and relate them to the capabilities of different types of dual sports.

The previous chapter described the best uses of lightweight, middleweight, and heavyweight dual sports relative to roads, two-tracks, and single-tracks without describing actual riding surfaces. There are huge differences in suitability to various kinds of terrain that must be considered when choosing a motorcycle. Without getting overly detailed, here are some general descriptions of surfaces and suggestions for which types of dual sports are most appropriate for each.

Maintained Dirt Roads –
Most appropriate dual sport: Heavyweight

- Type of route: Dirt roads, constructed for transportation which receive some maintenance and are passable by two-wheel-drive cars and trucks
- Steepest slopes: 0 to 10 percent (climb 1 foot in ten feet)
- Worst surface: Hard packed, rocks and ruts up to two inches high; with knobby tires add shallow sand or mud

Even good dirt roads can change into muddy challenges when it rains.

Dry roads like the one in the top picture can be ridden at speeds up to 55 miles an hour with street-oriented tires. (It is possible to go much faster, but it takes a very long time to stop a heavy, fast moving bike on dirt. Washouts and oncoming vehicles are ever present possibilities, and prudent riders maintain reasonable speeds.)

Even high quality graded roads may have impassable sections, particularly after rain, as shown in the next picture. Fresh ruts indicate that trucks have been going across without sinking too deeply. This bottom should support a motorcycle, but what if it doesn't? Long sections of slippery, muddy road can reduce your speed to a crawl or cause you to crash.

Strong, determined riders can traverse short sections of difficult terrain, but even the strongest will tire when manhandling heavy machines over miles of obstacles or long stretches of slimy, rain-soaked mud.

**Poorly Maintained Two-Tracks –
Most appropriate dual sport:
Middleweight**

- Type of route: Two-track created by the passage of full size four-wheel Jeeps and trucks; poorly maintained, wide enough for only one vehicle
- Steepest slopes: 10 to 20 percent (climb 1 foot in 5 feet)
- Worst surface: Rocks, roots, logs, or ruts up to four inches deep; with knobby tires add gentle whoops up to 1 foot deep; shallow sand or mud

The pictures show some types of terrain that can be ridden by middleweights.

Middleweights and even heavyweights with knobby tires should have no trouble with this section of two-track. However, the road is for high-clearance four-wheel-drive vehicles and there are no standards for maximum slope nor is there any regular maintenance. Who knows what might be around the next corner?

This picture shows a badly eroded two-track. There is a good surface at the right, but a deep, rocky rut goes straight down the hill and forces the rider to cross it just around the bend. It is relatively simple to ease a middleweight down short sections like this, but doing it for long periods can really sap your energy. Sooner or later the bike will fall and you will struggle to lift it and get going. A few repetitions of this routine can lead to exhaustion on a hot summer day and the motorcycle will suffer some damage.

Here is another section of the same road. It climbs steeply and becomes very soft. There are also some rock ledges near the top. A middleweight should be able to negotiate this section, but a heavyweight could easily lose traction and bury its wheel in the soft sand.

This picture shows a short uphill that is near the limits for a middleweight with dual purpose tires. The surface is hard packed but the hill gets steeper near the top and makes a turn over small rocky rain ruts. The picture was taken in the spring when the ground was still hard. Later in the summer this hill will get loose and slippery.

Single-Track Trails –
Most appropriate dual sport:
Lightweight

- Type of route: Single-track constructed for or created by motorcycles, 40 inches wide or less, often has many tight turns
- Steepest slopes: Greater than 20 percent
- Worst surface: Large rocks, roots, logs, or ruts; severe whoops. Need to pick lines carefully and use special riding techniques. Deep sand or mud. May need to dismount and lift motorcycle over large obstacles

This nice single-track through the sage is perfect for lightweights.

This picture shows a rocky single-track near the limit of rideability for a lightweight. It is barely wider than a tire and the rocks are from one to three feet tall. Even with care and a good skid plate, it is possible to damage the engine cases or frame. A few people have been going through this section, but mostly they avoid it.

Whose idea was this? These riders descended a rocky ridge, only to discover an ugly little ravine at the bottom. After much lifting and pushing, they have reached a trail and are having an energy restoration interlude.

This section of single-track is impossible for most riders to climb and even experienced veterans may dismount to descend. Light weight is a huge advantage in situations like this, but only the strongest and best conditioned riders enjoy a steady diet of terrain like this.

▶ QUESTIONS ABOUT RIDING OPPORTUNITIES

Try to get out and look at some of the routes you intend to ride or ask about conditions. Go to trailheads and observe what types of riders and motorcycles are using them. Then answer the following questions.

- What types of paved roads are available within an average trip?
- What types of dirt roads and trails are within an average trip?
- What types of surfaces will you ride?
- Will you need to lift or drag the motorcycle?
- If you are planning a special trip, what types of roads and trails will you ride?
- Who will be your riding partners?
- What do they ride?
- Where do they ride?
- How do they ride? Fast, medium, slow?
- How far will you travel between gas stations?

Answer these questions and then look at your dream again. Does it match the actual type of riding that will be available? If not you may need to redefine your dream. ∎

▶ ASSESSING YOUR PERSONAL RESOURCES

This is the place to consider things like physical condition, money budget, and time budget.

- Height?
- Weight?
- Leg length?
- Physical condition?
- How much riding have you done?
- What kind?
- How would you describe your riding skills?
- How much time will you spend riding?
- How much money do you want to spend?
- How good are your mechanical skills?
- Do you have health insurance?
- What would happen if you were injured and unable to work for several weeks?
- What dealers and repair shops are in your area? Do they have skilled mechanics and a good selection of parts and accessories? ∎

SIZE MATTERS

For serious riding, a bike that fits you is mandatory. Off-road bikes have about 12 inches of suspension travel and high seats. This is not a problem for people with average leg length, but short riders need to pay attention.

You should be able to sit on the bike and put both feet down, with your heels on the ground. Don't believe sales people who say this doesn't matter; it does. Sooner or later you will need to lower a foot and lift to avoid dropping the bike. A leg that is already straight and barely reaching the ground can't lift anything. You will be trapped, supporting the weight of the motorcycle on one leg, and it will go down.

How tall a seat can you ride? Measure your leg from the bottom of your foot to your crotch and add five inches to get a ball park estimate. The five inches includes suspension sag, plus your boot. If you have a 33 inch leg, a 38 inch seat height would be maximum and a little lower would be better.

Test the height before you buy. Sit on the bike to compress the suspension and try putting both heels down. If you can't do it look for something else or have the bike lowered. Chapter 5 covers setup.

Big, strong people can handle bigger motorcycles. Smaller and weaker riders will be happier with smaller, lighter bikes. You can test this by trying to lift the back of the motorcycle off the ground. Hold it by the handlebar and subframe and lift it back and up, using your knee for extra support. If you can't get the rear wheel off the ground it is too heavy for trail use. See "Assessing Your Personal Resources" at left.

Dual sport riders come in a wide variety of sizes, shapes, and abilities. Be realistic about your conditioning and personal resources. Answer the questions and then look at your dream again. Does it match your resources?

MAKING A FINAL SELECTION

Armed with a good definition of your planned use, you are ready to make a final motorcycle selection. Now is the time to re-read the specifications, visit dealers, sit on bikes, and haggle over prices.

Sooner or later you will have an opportunity to lift—light is good.

It may be possible to find a dual sport that meets your requirements exactly, but more likely you will need to give a little here to gain a little there. This isn't really a problem because dual sports are inherently fun. You need a motorcycle that matches your most important needs not one that is superior in every respect. Just remember, the objective is enjoyment, not perfection.

If you are new to motorcycle riding, you may finish this chapter with some unanswered questions. The obvious choice for new riders is a 250cc or 400cc factory dual sport that can be ridden for a couple of years to gain experience. Look for a dealer who can modify the bike to fit if you are unusually tall or short, and keep accessories to a minimum until you can appreciate them. Hand guards and a skid plate are all the accessories you really need.

There are two options for people living in major metropolitan areas or states where the closest dirt riding opportunities are several hours away: buy a middleweight or heavyweight and ride it on pavement to the dirt, or carry a lightweight on a truck, trailer, or rack to the trailhead and start the ride on dirt.

Harbor Freight offers small folding trailers that can carry two bikes. Several other manu-facturers sell bike carriers that attach to a trailer hitch. Either of these options will cost less than $500 and will work just fine. The most important consideration is how you want to spend your time, riding on the highway or driving on it.

If your dream is to take one or two long trips each year, think carefully about buying versus renting or joining a tour which supplies the motorcycles. It may be safer and cheaper to take the tour, particularly if you envision shipping the motorcycle to another country.

EXAMPLES OF DREAMS AND CHOICES

It might be nice to have a formula that automatically selects the best bike, based on specifications and point values for needs, but riders have too many different priorities. About the best you can do is collect the necessary information, think carefully about your riding preferences, riding opportunities, and personal resources, and make your own choices.

To illustrate how the process works let's return to the three examples of dual sport dreams and follow these hypothetical riders as they make their selections.

A KTM 450EXC fills his need for speed.

Dream Number 1

I want to ride directly from my house, to a variety of roads and trails ranging from easy to hard and experience the sheer joy and satisfaction of moving at speed over all types of terrain.

The correct choice for this rider is heavily dependent on available riding opportunities. He visits websites, studies maps, makes several trips by car into nearby mountains looking at roads and surfaces, and meets with the local OHV ranger to learn more about riding opportunities. The nearby mountains include a good variety of dirt roads, rough two-tracks, and trails.

Next he refines his list of requirements:
- Plan to ride about 2,000 miles per year
- A good selection of two-tracks and single-tracks is available within two hours of home
- Will take the bike to trailheads on a rack
- Will ride short stretches of dirt roads and pavement to connect trails
- Should have enough power for a 200-pound rider
- Want it to look good
- Should not weigh more than 300 pounds
- 38-inch seat height
- Wide ratio transmission and electric starter
- Good suspension; probably need heavier springs for my weight
- Large gas tank
- Want new bike
- Good parts availability

This rider chooses a lightweight, race-derived KTM 450EXC.

Dream Number 2

Get away from the traffic and congestion of my area. Take day or multi-day rides to beautiful lakes, rivers, deserts, mountains, and canyons that see few other travelers.

This rider wants to travel long distances and will need to spend most of the time on pavement. He collects the maps and brochures of parks and attractions in a several-state area, reads a couple of books on adventure touring, spends some time looking at heavyweight dual sports and talks to friends who have similar interests.

Next he refines his list of requirements:
- Plan to ride about 15,000 miles per year
- Long trips on pavement and graded dirt roads
- Want to ride from Denver to Copper Canyon next summer
- Riding companions have big BMWs
- Like to cruise on freeway at 75 mph
- Want it to look good
- Light weight is desirable, but need durability and carrying capacity
- Want good availability of luggage and accessories
- 35-inch seat height
- Good wind protection and hand warmers
- Enough electrical capacity to run a heated vest and other accessories
- Large gas tank
- Want new bike
- Good parts availability

This rider selects a Suzuki V-Strom 1000.

These Suzuki V-Stroms are a good choice for riders planning some serious mileage.

The little DR200SE is a perfect choice for a beginner or someone who just wants to putt around in the woods.

Dream Number 3

I rode dirt bikes many years ago and enjoyed it. Now that the kids are grown, I would like to ride again. I don't want anything too extreme—just want to have pleasant afternoon rides and maybe make some new friends.

This rider asks at the local shops and finds a dual sport riding club in his city. He attends a meeting as a guest, explains his situation and meets a couple of people who have recently retired and started riding. They tell him about local riding opportunities and what they are riding. A couple of them are riding Suzuki DR-Z400s.

Next he refines his list of requirements:

- Low maintenance
- Easy to ride—low seat, not too much power, quiet
- Good dealer support
- Need hand guards and skid plate
- Decent resale value so it can be traded in a year or two

This rider goes to the local Suzuki shop and compares the various models available. He selects a Suzuki DR200SE.

Everyone has different priorities, interests, and skills. Spend some time thinking about what you really enjoy and buy a dual sport to match. Don't be sucked into buying the most powerful, race-oriented bike available if you would really be happier with something else.

This well used Suzuki DR350 satisfies my need for cheap thrills.

EVEN A BEATER CAN BE FUN

Most importantly, do not let all of the options and considerations paralyze you. There is always one more feature for a few more dollars and another factor to ponder.

I am currently riding a 1995 Suzuki DR350 which I got from Harry, who got it from Harold, who used it to lay out a couple of District 37 enduros. Still basically stock, it has mapped, roll-charted and proofed three Ride Reno 200 courses, traveled all over northern Nevada and California in the summer, and chugged through countless miles of mud and snow in the winter.

It matches my dream of a simple, compromise bike that isn't terrific at anything, but competent in a wide range of conditions. It cost me $1,600 and has returned a fortune in enjoyment.

Section 2

RIDING GEAR AND MOTORCYCLE SETUP

All dual sport riders need protective gear and suitable clothing. The off-highway environment is filled with slippery surfaces, rocks, washouts, and overhanging branches. Falling or banging into something is an ever-present possibility. A helmet, eye protection, gloves, and boots are mandatory. You could also be exposed to bone chilling cold, blistering heat, and drenching rain—on the same day. Carefully selected clothing can keep you comfortable and riding at peak efficiency.

Your dual sport needs some setup and accessories to shape it to your body, local conditions, and riding style. The right setup and accessories will make you safer and more comfortable. They will make a new bike into your bike.

What is the best protective gear? What should you look for in clothing? How can you make your dual sport fit better? What tires should you use? What is the right way to adjust suspension? This section has the answers you need.

Protective gear and good motorcycle setup keep him safe in hazardous surroundings.

4

Personal Riding Gear

Dual sport riders can be exposed to a very wide range of riding conditions—from muddy forest trails to freeways. Carefully selected personal riding gear can prevent injuries and keep you safe and comfortable in these diverse environments, and everything in-between.

This chapter provides the information you need to make sound selections based on your riding style and location. It contains explanations of potential hazards, descriptions of gear, and suggested riding outfits.

WHY YOU NEED PROTECTIVE GEAR

The proper place to begin selecting gear is understanding the potential hazards of dual sport.

An intersection on the street is the most dangerous place you will ever ride.

Road Hazards

The Hurt study is still the best source of information about accidents on streets and roads. With funds from the National Highway Traffic Safety Administration, researcher Harry Hurt conducted the definitive study on motorcycle accidents at USC in 1979. His team studied 3,622 accidents and drew many important conclusions relative to motorcycle safety. No follow-on study has been conducted.

Most motorcycle accidents involved a short trip associated with shopping, errands, or recreation, and the accident was likely to happen in a very short time, close to the start. Approximately three-fourths of the accidents involved collision with another vehicle, which was most often a passenger automobile. In two-thirds of these incidents the driver of the car violated the motorcycle right-of-way and caused the accident. Intersections were the most likely place for motorcycle accidents.

Failure of motorists to detect and recognize motorcycles in traffic was the predominant cause of accidents. The driver of the other vehicle did not see the motorcycle before the collision, or did not see it until too late to avoid a collision. Accidents could have been significantly reduced by the use of motorcycle headlamps (on in daylight) and wearing high visibility yellow, orange, or bright red jackets.

Approximately one-fourth of accidents involved a single vehicle, where the motorcycle collided with the roadway or some fixed object. In single-vehicle accidents, motorcycle rider error was the accident precipitating factor in about two-thirds of the cases, with the typical error being a slideout and fall due to overbraking or running wide on a curve due to excess speed.

Most motorcyclists involved in accidents were essentially without training; 92 percent were self-taught or learned from family or friends. Motorcycle rider training experience reduced accident involvement and was related to reduced injuries when accidents occurred. Riders with dirt bike experience were significantly under-represented in the accident data (had fewer accidents).

Riders showed significant collision avoidance problems. Most overbraked and skidded the rear wheel, while underbraking with the front wheel, greatly reducing collision avoidance. The ability of the rider to countersteer and swerve was essentially absent. Almost half of the fatal accidents showed alcohol involvement.

The most deadly injuries to the accident victims were injuries to the chest and head. Use of a safety helmet was the single most critical factor in the prevention or reduction of head injury. Heavy boots, jacket, gloves, etc., were effective in preventing or reducing abrasions and lacerations, which are frequent but rarely severe injuries.

In summary, the Hunt Report concluded that most street accidents were caused by drivers who failed to see motorcyclists. Accidents and injuries can be reduced by measures to make riders more visible, rider training, and by the use of protective gear.

Dirt Hazards

There is no corresponding formal study of off-road accidents, but my experience tells me that single vehicle incidents are the most frequent type.

Dirt bikes are operated on steep slippery terrain where falls are common. Most mishaps occur at low speed, and resulting injuries, if any, are minor. Falls from higher speeds can result in serious tissue damage and broken bones. Much of

The typical off-road fall is a tipover at low speed. The rider of this motorcycle lost control in the snow and fell over. This incident happened at low speed and did no damage to bike or rider.

this danger can be avoided by riding at speeds that match your riding abilities with the terrain. Collisions with other vehicles are more common at popular riding areas and are usually caused by inattention and excessive speed.

Types of Injuries

The main injury risks faced by all motorcycle riders include: abrasion, striking injuries, twisting injuries, and excessive deceleration.

Abrasion occurs when the rider falls and slides along the ground or pavement. The rough surface cuts through clothing like sandpaper and removes skin and flesh.

Striking injuries occur when body parts hit hard surfaces like pavement or rocks. They cause injuries close to the point of impact such as bruises, gashes, broken ribs, and chipped teeth. Fortunately, abrasion and striking injuries can be minimized or prevented by protective gear.

Twisting injuries occur when a foot, leg, arm, etc. is held or pushed more than its joint will allow. The result is a sprain, hyperextension, or

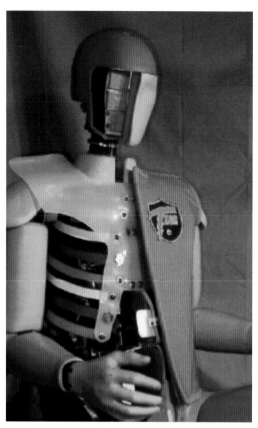

This crash test dummy is used to measure deceleration force.

dislocation. Riders can wear braces for ankles and knees, but they are not without risks. If the joint can't move all of the force will be transferred to the bone, possibly causing a very nasty spiral fracture. Braces are often used by riders who have prior injuries and need extra protection.

Excessive deceleration occurs when the rider strikes an immovable object at speed. The leading part of the body—the chest for example—stops instantly but the mass behind including ribs, lungs, and spine, has momentum and continues to travel. The resulting force can break bones and rupture organs. Automobile fenders and frames crush several feet upon collision, absorbing part of the deceleration and drivers are further protected by seat belts and air bags. Motorcyclists absorb the entire force with their bodies. To state it graphically, the tremendous internal forces of deceleration can rupture hearts, lungs, spleens, and brains. No amount of surface body armor can prevent this type of damage.

Helmets are designed to reduce head injuries from deceleration, but only up to a point. A body colliding with a car, and stopping instantly from a speed as low as 30 mph, will be subjected to a force more than 180 times the force of gravity. Fatal or critical injuries are highly likely.

Fortunately, dual sport riders have several built-in protections from serious injury. First, they are often riding in areas with few cars or no cars and thereby avoid the number one cause of most serious accidents. Second, the mental attitudes, judgment, and skills they develop in the dirt put them in a class far above the abilities of most casual street riders allowing them to avoid many "rider error" and "failure to avoid" accidents. Later chapters will cover these aspects in detail.

Heat, Cold, and Dehydration

The right gear can extend the riding season by several months and greatly increase your potential for fun.

However, there are many and often conflicting claims about garments. This one is moisture absorbing and that one is moisture wicking. That one is vented and another is waterproof and breathable. How do you match the right garment to your expected riding conditions? Should you try to get by with one outfit or do you need several?

Riding comfort is about much more than just feeling all right. It is also about maintaining peak mental and physical abilities, and avoiding injuries caused by exhaustion or confusion. It is easy to stay comfortable if you only take short rides on pleasant afternoons. However, riding in all seasons and all types of weather requires careful selection of appropriate garments, particularly if you combine vigorous exercise on trails with long periods of seated riding on roads. The closer you get to extremes of temperature the more you need to think about appropriate clothing.

The table below summarizes the most important considerations and the paragraphs that follow describe them in detail.

Normal core body temperature is about 98.6°F and even small deviations have serious detrimental effects on performance. For example, a core temperature of 102°F will cause severe

CLOTHING STRATEGIES FOR MAINTAINING PEAK PERFORMANCE

	TEMPERATURE RANGE		
	Below 50°F	50°F to 70°F	Above 70°F
Moisture Control	Move sweat away from skin	Move sweat away from skin	Allow sweat to evaporate near the skin
Wind Control	Very wind proof	Wind proof	Loose weave or vents
Hydration	Important	Important	Critical
Color	Darker	Dark or light	White or very light
Insulation	Heavy	Light	Minimal

sweating, flushed appearance, fast heart rate, impaired judgment, and possibly exhaustion.

Core temperature is maintained by "burning" fats and sugars in body cells. When the air temperature is about 70°F you feel comfortable—neither hot nor cold—but your core is nearly 30°F hotter than the surrounding air. Heat from the core passes through layers of muscle and radiates into the air. At temperatures above 70°F, you start to feel warm and the skin begins to sweat, cooling itself by evaporation. High levels of humidity reduce evaporation, causing the body to sweat more. At temperatures below 70°F you start to feel cool and put on clothes, which slows the rate of heat transfer.

Muscle temperatures rise about 6 to 8°F during exercise. Hotter muscles slow heat transfer from the core to the air, resulting in profuse sweating.

Riding at speed blows lots of air past the body and promotes evaporation, but exposes you to another risk: dehydration. Symptoms generally become noticeable after your body loses two percent of normal water volume. Initially, you experience thirst and discomfort, and may also suffer a loss of up to 50 percent of your physical potential. You must replace the fluids lost by sweating. A sports drink designed to help athletes replenish electrolytes, sugar, and other nutrients, is recommended.

During the day, the sun continuously transfers solar energy to the air. Air is colorless and there is a lot of it, so it warms slowly. Black reflects about five percent of solar energy and absorbs 95 percent; white reflects 80 percent and absorbs 20 percent. *The surface of a black helmet or jacket can easily rise to 100°F even though the surroun-*

ding air temperature is only 80°F. The surface of a white shirt under the same conditions will only rise to 84°F. Almost everyone knows that black absorbs heat, but many riders foolishly dress in black on hot days.

The correct strategy for staying cool on hot days is to wear white or light colors, allow sweat to evaporate on the skin, move at a good rate of speed, drink plenty of liquids, and refrain from strenuous exercise. On really hot days you may need to soak your garments in water.

Lowered core temperature is equally detrimental to performance. A decrease of your core temperature to 95.0°F will cause intense shivering, numbness, and mental confusion. Wind chill is the apparent temperature felt on exposed skin due to a combination of air temperature and wind speed. In still air, the body warms a thin layer of surrounding air, and then loses heat through it. Wind blows away the surrounding layer, thereby increasing the rate of heat transfer. The body loses as much heat at 40°F and 60 mph as it does in still air with a temperature of 25°F.

Air temperature falls about two or three degrees for each 1,000 foot rise in elevation. If it is 50°F at 3,000 feet it could easily be only 35°F at 9,000 feet, and you could get dangerously cold.

The correct strategy for staying warm on cold days is to wear dark colors, wind-proof garments, and insulating layers; reduce speed; get more exercise; and move sweat away from your skin. Exercise will cause sweating, even on cold days, so be sure to drink lots of fluids. On really cold days you may need electrically-heated garments.

No one ever died from wet skin alone, but air blowing through soaked clothing can significantly reduce your body temperature on cold days. Waterproof garments are absolutely essential when you are riding in a cold rain.

Pay attention to the weather forecast and dress appropriately. Take layers of clothes if you expect a wide range of temperatures. Carry them in a backpack or tie them around your waist when they are not needed.

There are limits to how much you can accomplish with clothing. When you become really uncomfortable your body is trying to warn you. Listen and take appropriate action.

SIMILARITIES AND DIFFERENCES BETWEEN DIRT AND STREET GEAR

You can get some good clues about what to wear by looking at professional racers. At first glance it may seem that dirt and road racers wear radically different protective gear, but there are many similarities.

Off-highway competitors are often standing on the pegs and absorbing big impacts with their legs and upper bodies. Other times, they lift or push through difficult sections. Off-road racers

Are we having fun? This intrepid rider is pressing on in foul weather, but he may be overdoing it. One patch of ice at speed on the pavement could put him in the hospital.

wear jerseys made of cotton or synthetics, heavy boots with shin guards, knee and elbow guards, chest protectors, gloves, goggles, and helmets.

In contrast, street riders are often seated for hours at high speed. Road racers wear one-piece suits of leather or Kevlar with protectors on shins, knees, elbows, shoulders, and back, plus boots, gloves, and full-face helmets with face shields.

The main difference between dirt and road racers is that the off-roaders choose jerseys and helmets that allow them to exercise vigorously while the road racers choose abrasion-resistant suits. Both groups agree on boots, body armor, gloves, helmets, and eye protection—gear that protects them from abrasion and striking injuries.

HELMET, GOGGLES, AND GLOVES

Helmets perform two functions. First, they protect your brain in case of a crash. Second, they keep you more comfortable by keeping your head warm and blocking wind noise. However not all helmets are created equal. As of this writing they range in price from as low as $50 to more than $500.

Types of Helmets

First, it is important to understand the basic types. Open-face helmets have no protection for

Every ride should start with basic protective gear. The range of available protective gear and clothing is truly vast with new options appearing each year. Catalogs and stores often have separate sections for street and dirt items, but dual sport riders can choose from either street or dirt clothing to match expected riding conditions.

the lower face and are not recommended for dual sport use. Motocross helmets have chin bars, large eye ports to accommodate goggles, and a visor to keep the early morning or late afternoon sun from blinding you. However, the visor lifts the helmet at high speed on the highway and can become a nuisance.

Street helmets have a chin bar and a transparent viewing window that flips up. They can fog badly when you start exercising and breathing heavily. They are not suitable for serious off-road use.

Helmet Construction and Certification

All helmets have a hard outer shell made from plastic or layers of material like fiberglass, a foam liner of the same material used in ice chests, and an inner liner of cloth and foam rubber. The purpose of the "ice chest" foam is to compress during a crash.

When we think of helmets most of us picture the hard shell, but it's the "ice chest" foam, expanded polystyrene, that does much of the protecting. When the skull stops suddenly—as it does when it hits something hard—the brain keeps going and has its own collision with the inside of the skull. If that collision is too severe, the brain can sustain any number of injuries, from shearing of the tissue to bleeding in the brain. The foam compresses under impact from the skull, and slows the speed of impact between the brain and skull. This prevents injury—up to a point.

Replace any helmet that has been crashed. The expanded polystyrene may be compressed and unable to protect you the next time.

Helmets are tested by dropping them and a head form inside the helmet, from a given height onto a test anvil bolted to the floor. By varying the drop height and the weight of the head form, the energy level of the test can be easily varied and exactly repeated.

The head form has an accelerometer inside that precisely records the force, showing how many Gs the head form took as it stopped, and for how long.

Each G is equal to the force of gravity; if the brain is subjected to too many Gs it will be injured. The Department of Transportation and

This Fox Motocross helmet has a chin bar and visor.

A street helmet with flip-up chin bar like this HJC is great for riders who wear glasses. This one has a single-button release which allows the chin-bar/ face shield to be opened with one hand. It is easy to get into this helmet when wearing glasses.

Snell Memorial Foundation both publish slightly different standards for testing helmets and how many Gs are measured in the head form.

Don't even consider buying a helmet that does not at least meet the DOT specification. Many inexpensive helmets also meet the Snell specification. More expensive helmets offer long-lasting lining materials, superior fit, and features like removable, washable pads.

After the technician finishes his preparations, this helmet will be tested by dropping it onto the anvil below. Photo courtesy of Snell Memorial Foundation.

These Scott goggles have scratch resistant, replaceable lenses and generous foam venting to prevent fogging. These goggles are designed to be worn over glasses. They are useful even if you have perfect vision, because you can wear dark glasses under them. Dark glasses help you see much better when the sun is low in the horizon.

Helmet Fit and Comfort

A very important consideration is how well the helmet fits. Put it on and shake your head vigorously. The helmet should move with your head, not slide around independently. It is common for the inner foam to collapse a bit with use so a snug fit is okay when the helmet is new.

Some helmets are reasonably quiet while others amplify wind noise so they are louder than riding with no helmet at all. If at all possible, test the helmet by riding on the freeway before buying it, or make sure you can return it.

Even with a good helmet, loud exhaust and wind noise can permanently damage your hearing. If the noise level is uncomfortable, it is probably too loud. Use earplugs whenever you ride. This is no joke. Continued exposure to loud noise can cause you to lose your hearing.

Goggles

You must wear goggles with motocross-type helmets. Protect your eyes at all times. A branch, rock or even a bee at speed could permanently damage your vision.

Summer dual sport rides can be very dusty and it may be impossible to wait for all of the dust to settle before following someone. Dusty goggles can seriously reduce your vision. I often see newbies trying to ride with lenses so dusty they can barely see. This is dangerous. Stop as often as needed to clean your lenses. For really dusty conditions, apply a thin coating of baby oil to the foam surrounding the lenses. This will reduce the amount of dust that gets through the foam and into your eyes.

Gloves

Gloves are made for motocross, cold weather, hot weather, wet weather, and muddy conditions. For dual sport, I recommend that you have summer gloves and winter gloves. Any good lightweight motocross gloves will work in the summer. An insulated glove is necessary below about 40°F. Make sure that gloves fit well and have no blister-causing seams or bulges in the palm or inside the fingers. Simple leather gloves from the hardware store also work well for dual sport use in the summer.

Winter days are more fun with MSR Cold Pro Gloves. These winter gloves feature a waterproof lining with thermal insulation. A comfortable inner liner gives you a positive grip and makes it easy to put your gloves on over wet hands.

The Firstgear Mesh Tex 3.0 Motorcycle Jacket includes a vented ballistic poly-mesh shell, CE-approved armor in the shoulders and elbows, EVA foam back pad, perforated nylon lining for maximum air flow, and a removable windbreaker liner.

A lightweight shell like this Fox Jacket can be worn over a jersey in summer or over layers of clothes in winter. It has removable sleeves that can easily be stored in the inner pocket.

GEAR FOR YOUR UPPER BODY

Clothing can make you visible, keep you warm, dry, or cool, and protect against dehydration. Good riding apparel can help you maintain normal body temperature and increase your endurance. Some garments also contain body armor. It may be possible to find one jacket which will satisfy all of your dual sport needs if you only ride occasionally, and stay on paved and dirt roads.

Garments are made of leather, natural fibers like cotton, and synthetics. Manufacturers describe clothing that is not made of leather as "textile"—flexible material composed of a network of natural or artificial fibers made by weaving, or pressing the fibers together. The synthetics can be engineered to have a wide range of desirable characteristics.

Features and Considerations

Comfort and Fit. Garments from different manufacturers are cut differently; as a result some garments and some of the armor may feel uncomfortable. The best way to get a good fit is to visit a well-stocked shop and try things on.

Color can do a lot more than make you look sharp. If you accept the findings of the Hunt study, increasing your visibility on the street should be an important consideration in selecting a color. The American National Standards Institute (ANSI) has defined high visibility colors for people who must work near traffic. These luminous colors are fluorescent yellow-green, fluorescent orange-red and fluorescent red. There are also standards for reflectivity to make the garments visible at night. Color also controls the amount of solar energy that will be reflected and absorbed—as described earlier.

Unfortunately, clothing manufacturers sell many products as fashions. As of this writing, black and gray, which offer virtually no contrast when viewed against pavement, are the colors most frequently offered. You should be able to find some reds or yellows and may want to

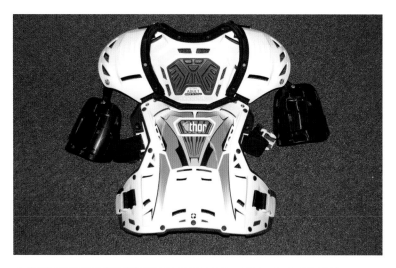

A chest protector like this Thor can be worn under or over a jacket.

This SixSixOne ballistic jersey provides all-in-one protection for the upper body.

SixSixOne guards protect the elbow joint and forearm.

consider a separate high-visibility vest for rides around town, which expose you to a large number of intersections. Note that it is the front of your upper body that will be most visible to oncoming motorists.

Abrasion Resistance. Leather has good abrasion resistance, synthetics can be designed to have good abrasion resistance, and natural fabrics like cotton have little abrasion resistance.

Body Armor

Manufacturers have two approaches to body armor: incorporate it into the garment or provide it separately. Except for cruiser-style jackets most street jackets include removable armor for elbows and shoulders; some include back protectors.

Some street armor is described with terms like dual-density or hard plastic. Other armor is described as CE approved. The CE Mark (an acronym for the French "Conformité Européene") certifies that a product has met the health, safety, and environmental requirements of the European Union. All manufacturers must meet CE Mark requirements, where applicable, in order to market their products in Europe.

Virtually all apparel armor is removable. Some resides in pockets within the garment while other armor attaches to the outside.

Off-road riders often prefer separate armor that can be worn with a jersey. Chest protectors spread the force of impact over a large area and can prevent punctures and broken ribs.

Protectors come in several varieties. The one shown here (top left) has a hard plastic front and back. It opens like a clam shell. In the closed position, it is held in place with side straps. These protectors are offered with and without upper arm guards, but guards are highly recommended. Elbow guards that combine hard plastic cups with a short length of elastic sleeve are also available and offer good protection.

The next photo (top right) shows a protector that attaches armor to a mesh, pullover shirt. It includes molded polyethylene impact areas on the chest, shoulders, back, and elbows and an easy-to-adjust, double-closure kidney belt. This item provides great upper body coverage. Wearing one of these, a friend of mine took a really ugly fall in a rocky stream crossing and bounced up completely uninjured.

Clamshell protectors can be worn under or over a jacket; the mesh shirt should be worn under a jacket. Decide how to wear your protector and buy a jacket to fit.

Wind Protection, Moisture Control, and Insulation

There are two ways of getting a satisfactory combination of wind protection and insulation. Layering uses a windproof outer shell over one or more inner layers of underwear, shirts, sweaters, and vests. Combination garments use zip out linings under the outer shell.

Wind Protection. Leather and tightly woven materials prevent air molecules from penetrating the garment, providing a windproof barrier. Insulating materials can then trap air close to your body, surrounding it with a layer of air that is close to normal body temperature.

Moisture Control. Both rain and sweat can transfer moisture into the insulating layers until they become soaked and useless. Some raingear is made of nylon coated with plastic; it keeps out the rain, but does nothing to let sweat escape. These coated products work well enough for seated riders, but you need something better for exercise.

Waterproof, breathable fabrics allow perspiration to escape while preventing rain from entering. The most famous of these is Gore-Tex, but other companies have their own brands. Gore-Tex has an informative website (gore-tex.com) that explains their product.

Gore-Tex is composed of a fabric, usually nylon or polyester, to which is bonded a thin, porous membrane with a urethane coating. The membrane has about 9 billion pores per square inch, each of which is approximately 20,000 times smaller than a water droplet, making it impenetrable to liquid water while still allowing the smaller sized water vapor molecules to pass through. The outer fabric is treated with water

Micro pores in Gore-Tex allow water vapor to escape and prevent drops from entering.

A waterproof shell like this Moose Racing XCR Jacket is comfortable in a wide range of conditions. It is advertised as being highly waterproof and breathable.

The Tour Master Transition jacket has a long list of features.

repellent and seams are sealed to prevent water leakage through pinholes caused by sewing the fabric. The resultant product is breathable, waterproof, and also windproof.

Waterproof, breathable fabrics work pretty well, but don't expect miracles. I have tried gear designed for motorcycling, hiking, bicycling, and snowboarding; all of it keeps me dry for short periods when sitting, even in heavy rain. On long rides, water invariably finds a seam, zipper, or gap and then wicks into wide areas of clothing underneath. Sustained, vigorous exercise always leads to the same result: I sweat and get soaked inside the rainproof clothes.

Venting. Some garments feature large numbers of vents, but you really only need a few. A jacket with generously-cut arms plus wrist closures, a front zipper, and underarm vents works well in a wide range of situations. With the zippers closed it conserves heat. There will be a good circulation of air with the front, wrists, and underarm vents open. The quality of the zippers is very important. They should be easily operable with a gloved hand without having to struggle.

Garments with vents are essential for riding in hot weather, but they often leak in the rain. Also, rain gear loses its effectiveness with time. Most manufacturers recommend regular spraying with a product like Scotchgard Ultra Water Repellent.

Combination Garments

Many of the suits, jackets, and pants combine several desirable features. For example the Tour Master Transition jacket, pictured here, claims the following features:

- The Three-Quarter Length 600 Denier Carbolex® and 600 Denier Ballistic Polyester shell incorporates reflective Phoslite® material panels for strength and increased nighttime conspicuity.
- A waterproof and breathable Rainguard™ barrier allows dryness without perspiration buildup.
- Collar anchor snap eliminates flapping while collar is open.
- Waterproof zippered chest vents combine with sleeve vents, rear exit vents, and the pipeline ventilation system, providing flow-through ventilation.
- Durable main zipper closure with dual wind flap seals out the elements.
- One-inch-wide reflective strip across the back, reflective sleeve piping, Phoslite™ material panels and Tour Master's signature reflective rear triangle help to increase nighttime conspicuity.
- The Micro fiber-lined collar and cuffs are soft, yet durable.
- Adjustable sleeve take-up straps at the forearm help to secure elbow armor and material.
- Removable, CE-Approved armor at the elbow and shoulder with an articulated Triple Density back protector.
- Zip-Out Quilted liner of 100G polyfill insulation.
- Vertical zippered chest map pockets, zippered hand pockets with flap closure, internal media pocket, dual zippered fanny pack, and sleeve key pocket.
- Adjustable waist belts with TPR pulls help to fine tune the fit.
- Includes a jacket/pant zipper attachment with the pant side included.

This product combines many terrific features, but remember that zippers break, cloth tears, and seams unravel. One good-sized tear in the outer fabric could render the whole garment unusable.

Be aware that there are some really strange combinations of features on the market. One jacket with body armor is made of black material which does nothing to make its wearer more visible to motorists—the main hazard. Its mesh torso promotes cooling airflow, but the black color absorbs heat. Its waterproof layer is under the removable lining—ensuring that the wearer will be dry, but surrounded by a thick layer of near freezing water on cold rainy days.

Evaporative Vests

For really hot weather, evaporative vests are available, or you can soak a long-sleeved cotton shirt and wear it under a light vented jacket. The vest is thicker and holds more water, but both work the same—hot air evaporates the water and cools your body.

Electric Garments

Equipping yourself for extended trips in all seasons and weather is the ultimate challenge. Experienced travelers recommend against jeans and cotton clothing, in favor of lightweight, quick-drying synthetic shirts and pants which can be washed in a sink and dried in your room overnight. They use fleece and electric garments, with a substantial reduction in weight and bulk.

Widder Lectric offers heated vests, heated chaps, and heated gloves. Make sure that your motorcycle electric system will handle the load before buying. The Widder website at widder .com has a lot of valuable information.

GEAR FOR THE LOWER BODY

The same considerations—abrasion resistance, color, moisture control, etc.—also apply to pants, but to a lesser degree. Legs are less visible to motorists and have less influence on core body temperature.

Pants

Knees are the most critical area to protect. Many riders wear jeans or similar pants around town, but combination pants made of waterproof/

Cortech Textile pants offer good protection for the lower body.

breathable fabric with built-in knee armor offer better protection.

The Cortech pants shown above feature:
- Armor-Link III mesh abrasion resistant material
- Aqua-Therm® 2-stage removable, waterproof insulated liner
- Leather impact panels at the knees
- Hip pads and CE-Approved armor at the knees
- High padded back panel and pant-to-jacket zipper for attaching pants
- Three position knee armor alignment system and adjustable belts with TPR pulls to fine tune fit

Double-front cotton Carhartt pants are cool in the summer and offer good protection from brush.

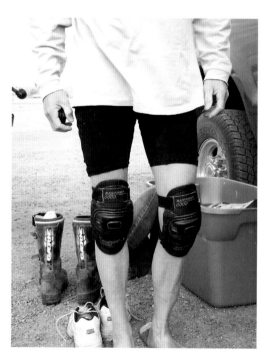

This rider is protecting his knees with skater's pads from a sporting goods store and will wear them under his pants.

Most riding pants like these come in small, medium, large, and extra large. If you are large around the middle and short in the leg, you could be walking around with an extra six inches of material bunched around the ankle. Many of the pants have zippers in the bottom making it very difficult to shorten the legs. Try before you buy.

Most synthetic fabrics melt quickly when they brush against hot exhaust systems. The head pipe near the cylinder is the hottest and it will melt pants in an instant. Make sure that your pipe is well-shielded with factory or aftermarket guards.

For dirt riding you may want two pairs of pants, one for hot weather and one cold, rainy conditions. Summer pants should be a light, heat-reflecting color and allow air to flow through. You can buy motocross pants or use Carhartt double-front cotton pants which offer adequate protection from brush and abrasion and provide comfort on hot days. For winter you need waterproof, breathable pants.

Separate Knee Guards

Knees often hit rocks when you fall in the dirt; trailside bushes and branches attack them constantly. Hard plastic cups with padding are essential. Knee armor may be included in street pants, but dirt riders wear separate knee guards which attach firmly to your knee and can not be knocked aside.

Many of the available knee guards are made to be worn under boots and pants. Straps secure the guard to your lower leg and your boots and pants hold the shin guard and knee cup securely in place. Other guards can be worn over pants, but these may slide around your knee under impact and expose the joint to injury.

Boots

Feet are especially vulnerable to injury. On the street, they are often the first thing to hit the ground, even if you manage to stick your leg out and prevent a fall. In the dirt, they are only a few inches away from all manner of hazards including rocks, roots, and logs. When the foot does hit something, whether pavement or dirt, it is liable to catch and be flung backward against the motorcycle, injuring your ankle bones in the process.

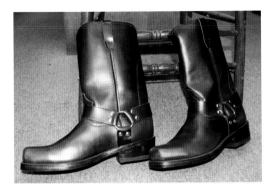

Classic biker boots have no armor for ankles and shins.

Tour Master Response boots offer some protection for the ankles.

Heavy motocross boots like these from Gaerne offer full off-road protection for feet, ankles, and shins. These boots are made from a combination of leather, plastic, and metal parts. The buckles and straps are replaceable and the toes, ankles, and shins are protected with plastic. Boots like these offer good protection and comfort on the trail.

The best protection would be a hard plastic shell covering your entire foot, ankle, and shin, but then you would be unable to walk. Street and graded-road riders need to seek a compromise between protection and walking comfort. Trail riders need protection above all else.

The classic "biker boot" at top has no padding around the ankle and offers very little protection for the foot. Boots like this are not good choices for dual sport.

The Tour Master boots shown in the next picture offer more protection. They are constructed from waterproof leather and include a waterproof/breathable membrane with sealed seams. They have hard molded toe cups and circular molded ankle bone protectors. Boots like these can provide a good combination of protection and walking comfort. Even insulated high-top hiking boots provide better protection than street shoes or biker boots.

For trail riding you need motocross type boots. They are not good for walking, but provide absolutely essential protection for energetic off-road riding. Don't skimp on dirt boots; go for a heavyweight boot with good padding and armor around the toes, ankles, and shins. Check to ensure that replacement straps, buckles, and toe clips are available.

OTHER ITEMS

Dust Mask

Paper dust masks that fit over your nose and mouth are an effective way to reduce inhalation of small airborne particles. There are two types of paper masks: rated and unrated. Rated masks are approved for use in workplaces regulated by the Occupational Safety & Health Administration. They meet federal standards for use in specific applications such as painting, welding, or grinding.

Non-rated masks do not meet OSHA standards and are often described as hobby or comfort masks. They are cheap, easy to find, and trap about 90% of airborne particles—which should be good enough for occasional dusty rides. Breathing into the mask can cause goggle fogging and you may need to experiment to get a satisfactory combination of clean air and clear lenses.

Masks can also keep your lips from freezing in cold weather and protect your face from the sting of rain drops as you hit them at 50 mph.

Hydration packs are available in a variety of sizes and configurations. Some include cargo pockets.

Hydration

You need a way to carry water. Some riders still use canteens, but virtually everyone else has switched to hydration packs. Guard against dehydration on hot days. It can sneak up, robbing you of coordination or even kill you. Drink when you are thirsty; don't put it off until you finish another few miles. In summer, you can carry water purification tablets and refill from streams.

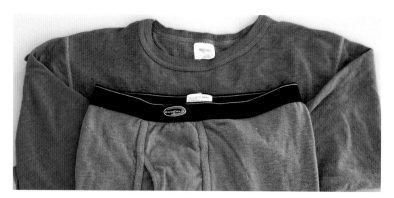

This Duofold two-layer underwear makes a good base layer for cold weather. It has an inner polypropylene layer that moves moisture away from your skin. The outer layer blends Merino wool with quick-dry polyester. This shirt provides no-chill comfort, even in damp conditions.

Underwear

Underwear can be as simple as a cotton T-shirt and briefs for a warm day. For cold weather, long woolen or moisture-wicking synthetic underwear makes a good foundation. Wool keeps you warm, wet or dry. Some synthetics like polypropylene wick sweat away from your skin. Avoid cotton long underwear which absorbs sweat and holds it next to your body, making you cold and miserable. Buy from a sporting goods store that caters to backpackers or hunters.

Long days in the saddle may cause your butt cheeks to rub together, producing a painful condition known as monkey butt. I don't really want to explain it here, but you will understand if you look at the affected area in a mirror. Some riders prefer padded bicycle shorts which reduce chafing.

Bicycle-style shorts with padded hips can provide additional protection.

Socks

Heavy calf-length socks of wool or synthetic material should be worn under boots. You can get suitable socks at any sporting goods store.

Most new boots start out waterproof, but after a few thousand miles they begin to leak. SealSkinz waterproof socks are the solution. They are thin enough to fit into boots over thin wool socks. SealSkinz are great in winter and early spring when splashing through cold puddles and streams. The boots can get completely soaked, while your feet remain dry. A combination of SealSkins and wool socks is unbeatable.

COMMUNICATION

Two-Way Radios

Two-way radios are useful for reassembling groups of riders who become separated on the road or trail. The Family Radio Service (FRS) is a low-power option limited to 500 milliwatts in the U.S. The General Mobile Radio Service (GMRS) can transmit up to 50 watts although most consumer radios actually have from one to five watts. Higher power equals longer range. Manufacturers claim up to ten miles from one-watt radios, but transmission is heavily dependent on terrain and can be blocked by hills and mountains. An

A fanny pack like this MSR will carry emergency tools and spares.

FCC license is needed for GMRS, but enforcement is rare.

Cell Phones and Satellite Phones

Cell phone coverage is spotty or non-existent in many remote areas, but most riders carry them always. Satellite phones are prohibitively expensive for casual use. Do not make the mistake of taking extra chances because you have a phone. Safety depends on gear, attitude, preparation, and skill. Lying by the side of the trail with a dislocated shoulder is not an acceptable result—no matter how many phones you have in your group.

Avoid filling inside chest pockets with cameras and radios. The whole point of wearing a chest protector is to shield ribs from rock impacts in case of a fall. Putting hard objects inside a protector is like carrying your own rocks.

FANNY PACK

You need a way to carry wrenches and tire repair tools. The best accessory is a small fanny pack with a bare minimum of essentials. Backpacks, tank bags, or fender bags are also used. Some dual sports are so festooned with bags that you can't tell whether they are bikes or bag ladies, but use whatever works for you.

Fanny packs are convenient because they are out of the way and attach to your body, which gives them a degree of shock absorption. However, they add to the weight supported by your legs in the standing position. Carefully choose what you carry and keep things organized so you can find them easily—all of the tire repair stuff in one pocket, all of the tools and mechanical things in another.

> ## MY RECOMMENDATIONS FOR WHAT TO PACK:

- Trail snacks
- Tow strap
- Good tools to fit spark plug and all nuts, bolts, Allen heads, screws
- Pliers, knife
- Spare nuts, bolts, sparkplug, fuses
- Duct tape, soft wire, quick epoxy like JB Stick Weld (to repair a cracked case)
- Spare front tube (will also work in rear)
- Axle wrench
- Tire irons, pump, inner tube patch kit
- Band aids, toilet paper, lighter, rag
- Aspirin, stick of sunscreen (can also be used on lips), antiseptic ointment
- Coins for phone, credit card, cash
- License, proof of insurance, registration
- Compass always; map and GPS when finding new routes
- For night, add flashlight, headlight bulb

For overnight in a motel add a backpack with comb, toothbrush, toothpaste, underwear, hat, socks, shirt, pants, light shoes. ■

Always carry a fanny pack, canteen, and tool kit when riding off-road.

TODAY:
Brisk with rain developing this morning, mainly north of highway 50.
Then scattered snow showers in the afternoon.
Snow accumulation up to 2 inches.
Highs 34 to 44.
West winds 10 to 20 mph with gusts up to 30 mph.

▶ SUGGESTED RIDING APPAREL

Fashion police will not jump out and bust you for inappropriate dual sport attire. Your primary concerns should be protection and comfort. Here are some suggested combinations. Watch the weather forecast and dress accordingly.

LAYERED APPROACH FOR DIRT AND SHORT TRIPS ON PAVEMENT

Various combinations of layers will allow you to ride in a wide range of conditions. Here is a list of gear that can keep you comfortable in temperatures from the high 90s to the low 30s. Choose what you need to match expected temperatures.

- Briefs and T-shirt. Many long distance riders recommend padded bicycle shorts.
- For cold days:
- Wool or moisture-wicking long underwear
- Wool or moisture-wicking sweater or shirt
- Fleece vest (and possibly pants)
- Balaclava or face mask
- Waterproof, cold-weather gloves
- Waterproof, breathable pants and jacket with vents
- For hot days:
- Light-colored cotton shirt and pants
- Light gloves
- Always: Helmet, boots, knee protectors, elbow protectors and body armor.

Some of these layers can serve double duty. You can sleep in the long underwear on overnight trips and go to dinner in the vest.

It is important to stay dry when it rains. Getting wet is no problem with temperatures in the 60s or higher. Getting wet and riding for hours in the 40s or 50s could lead to hypothermia.

SHORT TRIPS ON PAVEMENT AND GRADED DIRT ROADS

A brightly colored jacket, sturdy shoes, gloves, jeans, eye protection, and a helmet are basics for casual street riding. A motocross helmet and goggles will work for short jaunts, but you will be more comfortable on long street rides with a full-coverage street helmet.

Add some thick socks under high-top hiking boots, plus some knee and elbow guards, and you will also be ready for easygoing rides on graded roads. Set limits. Do not start on the graded road and then start to explore rough two-tracks and trails. You will soon bang your foot into something and possibly injure it. Wear motocross boots for rough terrain.

LONG RIDES ON PAVEMENT

The gear listed below will serve you well on long pavement rides with short excursions onto graded roads. Choose what you need to match expected temperatures.

- Briefs or bicycle shorts and T-shirt
- Long, wool or moisture-wicking underwear
- Quick-drying pants and shirt
- Heated vest and pants
- Waterproof, breathable jacket and pants with removable liner and body armor
- Balaclava or face mask
- Heavy or light gloves

This outfit should be comfortable into the 30s and lower for short distances.

You may be able to ride in cold weather with fleece vest and pants rather than electric garments.

Good riding gear is the key to winter comfort.

The contents of your fanny pack may determine whether you can finish a ride when you break down. Use your emergency tools and equipment regularly in the garage so you know they work; keep everything light and small.

There are many styles of bike-mounted bags, but all are exposed to the full pounding of the bike. Metal tools and tire irons will survive the beating; all other materials will eventually be reduced to fragments or goo so pack accordingly. Rear fender bags can make it hard to swing your leg over the back and are poor choices for short riders with tall bikes.

FINAL NOTE ON GEAR

Always protect hands, feet, head, eyes, and critical joints. Eventually, you will fall or run into something, and the riding gear will be the only thing standing between your soft, tender skin and mean, ugly rocks or pavement. Get the right gear and use it always. Never go for "just one little ride" without a helmet or "just a few miles" without your gear.

You can spend a fortune on riding gear, but it's not really necessary. Good, serviceable boots plus knee guards and thin leather gloves will protect your extremities. Mid-priced goggles and a low-priced, DOT-certified helmet will protect your head. Add a chest protector, light jacket, and fanny pack and you have the basic necessities to have fun on pleasant days.

Don't let all of the options and high prices scare you away. The picture below was taken on a wonderful winter day of damp sand and deep canyons, under a brilliant blue, cumulus accented sky. The boots are very old, the pants are denim over knee guards, and the rider has been having a terrific time.

This rider is equipped for low-budget fun with old boots and knee guards inside his jeans.

5

Setup and Accessories

Some careful adjustments and well chosen accessories will turn a good dual sport into a great one. This chapter covers basic adjustments and motorcycle accessories for day rides and longer trips.

SETUP IN ACTION

The old road from Slater Mine twists down a rocky ravine in the shadow of Mt. Siegal. We have been to Smith Valley and are heading back to the fairgrounds in Gardnerville. The Suzuki and I are hustling along, dodging rocks and protruding branches of juniper and nut pine. This road

Rides to great places like this are safer and more comfortable with a good setup and some accessories.

hasn't had any real maintenance in 40 years and each summer four-wheel drivers reroute it to pass downed trees and rock falls. I go straight for 30 feet, turn tightly around a tree, go straight for 50 feet, and turn again. All of the corners are blind and filled with rocks.

The bike is talking to me, and isn't happy. Wheels deflect from unseen rocks and I get little thrills saving myself from falling. In younger days, I would have ridden the adrenaline wave and gone faster, but crashing into rocks hurts. Experience counsels a different approach. Rather than carrying speed into the corners, I accelerate harder on the short straights and brake more before the corners. Now I'm going faster in the fast places and slower in the slow places. The Suzuki is happy again, and I am back in my comfort zone.

I flow with the sections—pick a line, twist the throttle, scan the next turn, hard on both brakes, feel the front start to go and ease off, pivot with the rear brake as the corner reveals itself, pick a new line, back on the throttle again, alternate between sitting and standing. The road absorbs my attention as I focus on the next turn, and the next, and the next. I ride instinctively and well.

Riding like this requires more than experience. It also requires a good setup and some basic accessories. Controls must be positioned for use without clumsiness or delay. Tires must grip and suspension must flow with the ground. The bike must be protected from occasional rock hits; fingers must be safe from encroaching branches. A bike that is properly set up and equipped becomes an extension of your body, shielding it from whoops, rocks, ruts, and roots while you glide above, enjoying the elation of speed in harsh conditions.

If necessary, loosen the pinch bolts and position the fork tubes at the factory setting.

Setup includes all the things that shape a motorcycle to your size, weight, and riding conditions—simple adjustments, bolt-on accessories, and modifications. It includes basics that everyone can and should do, but may also include more difficult things best left to professionals. Tires are so important they have their own chapter. Advanced suspension tuning is covered in Chapter 7. Let's look at the simple stuff.

SUSPENSION ADJUSTMENTS

The place to start is with your owner's manual. Read it to determine which suspension adjustments can be made on your model and what settings the factory recommends. Check everything mentioned below to ensure that some bonehead has not messed with things.

First, adjust the chain tension. The chain must be loose when the suspension is uncompressed because it pivots around the countershaft sprocket which is in front of the swing arm pivot. This causes the chain to tighten as the swing arm approaches the center of its swing. The manual should cover this. A tight chain interferes with suspension travel, wears faster, and can cause damage.

Check wheel travel by pushing down on the forks, and then on the rear suspension. Both should move freely on compression, and when you release them, they should return to approximately the same position from which they started. There should be no problems with a new bike, but a used machine could have suspension parts that are bent or worn. Any serious sticking or limitation of travel must be diagnosed and fixed before proceeding further.

Make sure that the fork tubes are in the factory specified position in the triple clamps. The tubes may be raised and lowered in the triple clamps by loosening the pinch bolts on the clamps.

A small change of three to five millimeters can impact how the bike turns. Raising the tubes lowers the steering head and makes the steering angle steeper. This may cause the front end to turn in too quickly and catch in deep, sandy turns. Going the other way causes the front wheel to turn in more slowly and push though turns. If you are new to dirt riding, neutral steering that neither turns in too quickly nor pushes is desirable. Experienced riders can adjust tube height to get the steering characteristics that work best for them.

Now Check the Ride Height

Start by placing a pencil mark on the rear fender and then pull up on the rear of the bike to completely extend the suspension. Measure the vertical distance from the top of the axle to the pencil mark and record the result.

Put on all of your riding gear. This is important because a complete set of off-road gear—boots, water, and fanny pack—can easily add 20 to 30 pounds to your riding weight. Prop one handlebar against a wall so the bike can't fall, but so the rear suspension is free to move. Sit near the seat/tank juncture and have someone measure again from the pencil mark to the top of the axle. Write down this measurement.

Subtract the second number from the first. The difference is called "laden sag," also known as ride height, and it affects steering as well as comfort. Compare your measurement with the figure in the owner's manual. Most bikes with 12 inches of rear wheel travel specify about four inches (100 millimeters) of laden sag.

Measure sag from the top of the axle to a mark on the fender or frame.

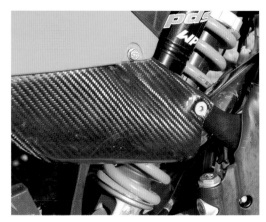

Adjust rear suspension preload (and ride height) by turning the threaded adjuster at the top of the spring.

Note that a lower rear end rotates the fork tubes back, increasing the steering angle. This has the same effect as raising the steering head; it causes the front end to push.

Set the laden sag to the recommended amount by turning the threaded preload collar on the rear shock. Then measure the unladen sag (without the rider). It should usually be about 1.0 to 1.5 inches.

The purpose of measuring both the unladen and laden sag is to help determine whether the spring is right for your weight. Let's say the book calls for four inches of laden sag and you weigh 190 pounds with gear. Dial in the laden sag to whatever the book says and then get off the bike and measure the unladen sag. If the rear sags less than one inch you may need a stiffer spring because a lot of preload was necessary to get the correct ride height. Conversely, if the unladen sag is more than 1.5 inches you may need a softer spring.

Remember that ride height is the most important measurement as it will affect steering. Unladen sag is only a clue indicating whether the spring is too soft or too stiff. You need to ride the bike to make the final determination.

Companies like Race Tech and Eibach offer springs matched to your weight.

If you are a casual rider and not terrifically heavy or light, you can probably get by using only the preload adjuster to dial in the proper ride height. This may not be optimum, but you will be riding instead of wrenching.

Clicker Adjustments

Good suspension settings are critical at more aggressive levels of riding, but don't spend all your time adjusting the suspension if you only plan to ride a few times each year. Dial in the factory recommended settings, stay on smoother surfaces, and enjoy yourself.

Modern bikes have clickers to adjust compression and rebound damping on both the rear shocks and front forks. Set the clickers according to instructions in your owner's manual. Factory settings are usually near the middle of the range. It is possible for air to accumulate in the forks as they move up and down resulting in a harsh ride. Some bikes have air valves on top of the forks to relieve pressure. Release the air and close the air valve.

At this point everything will be at factory settings and you should ride for a few days. This is essential on a new bike because the suspension

The rebound clicker on this KTM fork is located on top.

This Enduro Engineering seat is taller and softer than the seat that came with the bike.

will break in and become more compliant as you put on some miles. After a few hundred miles you will know whether you can live with it.

If you are not satisfied with the ride, you can adjust the suspension clickers to suit your style and riding conditions.

Less compression damping will often cure a harsh feel on choppy ground. Starting with the factory settings, ride over the same ground repeatedly, making small changes as you go.

It is often difficult for new riders to relate ride quality to the proper adjustments. People often stop and give things a few clicks without really knowing what they are doing. Soon the suspension is worse than ever. Experiment with harder and softer settings to see what they do. Do this in the field where you can get immediate feedback, not in the garage after the ride.

It may be impossible for you to get good results with the clickers. If so, there is a thriving industry of suspension tuners. Chapter 7 has more information on suspension tuning and services.

MAKE SURE IT FITS

Suits, skis, and golf clubs are made in different sizes to fit different people. Motorcycles come in only one size per model. Manufacturers design each to fit some hypothetical average, possibly someone who is five feet nine inches tall and weighs 165 pounds. You may be that size, but chances are that you're not. The next task is to make the bike fit you. Average-size people should ride for a few hundred miles to get a feel for the bike. Unusually tall or short people may need immediate corrective action.

Seats

Start with the seat because many of the other adjustments will use your seated position as a reference. Sit near the seat/tank junction, dressed in riding gear, and check the height. You should at least be able to get both your heels on the ground.

Riders with short legs may need to lower the seat and/or suspension. Tall riders may have the opposite problem. Try moving from the sitting to standing position. If this feels like deep knee bends, you may need a taller seat.

One way to lower the seat height is to use a rear tire with a smaller diameter. Check to see what you have and whether there is a smaller tire available. For example, the bike might come with a 100/110 rear tire. Going to a 100/100 would lower the rear about ½ inch. Be aware that this change to a smaller rear tire will also increase the steering angle and lower the overall gearing.

Racers spend most of their time standing and use seats only when turning. Even then, they are likely to be perched on the edge of the seat and weighting the outside peg rather than sitting normally. They like firm, narrow seats. Dual sport riders spend most of their time sitting and therefore need broader softer seats. You need a seat that will support your buttocks, not push your shorts through your ears. If the seat feels like you are sitting on the sharp edge of an ax, have it modified or buy another seat designed specifically for dual sport.

Companies like Travelcade, Ceet, Guts Racing, and Enduro Engineering offer seats with a variety of styles and thicknesses. Corbin offers a seat with a narrow front and wide rear so that you can get more support by moving back. They also use special foam which is claimed to have more resiliency without crushing down like stock foam. This gives a lower seat height without sacrificing comfort. At $299, it's expensive and the shape is more suited to long road trips than single-track.

Handlebars

The most important requirement for handlebars is a good fit. Most steering input comes from weighting and body position, but riders depend heavily on the bars to maintain position and

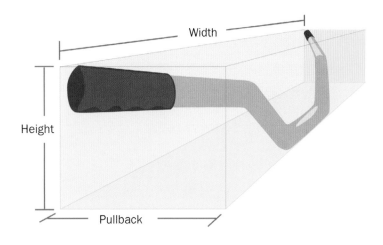

Some manufacturers give the exact dimensions of their bars. This diagram shows how handlebars are measured.

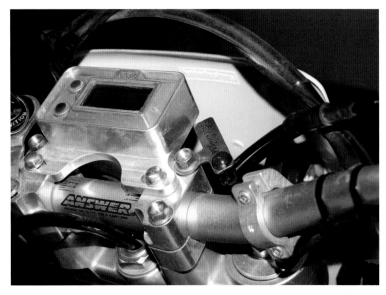

This bike has Answer fat bars and an ICO trip computer.

balance. Experienced riders may already have preferences; new riders should ride a while before making major changes.

Loosen the bar clamps and then sit forward on the seat with your head over the steering stem. Rotate the bars to a comfortable position (some models also allow you to move the bars forward or backward). Then stand on the pegs with knees slightly bent and let your hands drop to the bars. You should be able to grip them without bending forward excessively. If it is not possible to get the bars adjusted right, you may need bars of a different shape, taller bars, or spacers to raise them.

Some motorcycles have steel bars which bend easily. For greater strength replace them with Renthal aluminum bars which are much stronger, lighter, and better able to absorb vibration.

Manufacturers name various bars after motocross stars, but width, height, and pullback are what really matters, not namesake. You can measure the dimensions of your bars with a long straightedge and ruler. The height and pullback are measured from the center of the clamped area, but you can measure from the outside and then adjust for the center. Here is a diagram showing the dimensions.

To let you research the range of available handlebars, companies like Renthal and Pro Taper publish charts showing the dimensions of their products. Another approach is to take your bars to a well supplied dealer and compare them with bars they have in stock. Some woods riders who like riding between trees cut their bars to about 30 inches wide.

Handlebars come in two varieties: 7/8 inch constant diameter, and tapered. Before 1991, all bars were a constant 7/8 of an inch in diameter. Then Pro Taper introduced tapered bars which were said to be stronger and better at absorbing vibration. These bars are 1 1/8 inches thick in the center and 7/8 inch thick at the hand grips. Now tapered bars are very popular, offered by several manufacturers and available on some bikes as original equipment. Adding tapered bars to a bike that came without them requires special handlebar mounts to accommodate the extra thickness.

Dual sport handlebars can become crowded. Hand guards, levers, switches, mirrors, GPS, roll-

Space can become hard to find when you mount multiple accessories on the bars.

chart holders, and speedometers all find their way onto bars. It is not rocket science to mount these items on straight-walled bars; just find a vacant spot and clamp them in place. Mounting accessories to tapered bars is much harder because the taper fights every attempt.

Hand Grips

A wide variety of hand grips is available from companies like Scott USA, Smiths, and Pro Grip. Some emphasize comfort and vibration damping while others emphasize the gripping pattern. Gripping pattern is most important in wet or muddy conditions. A waffle pattern works well.

Manufacturers recommend that the grips be glued onto the bar ends as this is undoubtedly the most secure method. However, the glue makes it hard to change grips. If you replace grips often and don't want to spend hours doing it, clean the bar end and throttle tube with contact cleaner and spray the inside of the grips until soaked. Then, the grips will slide on easily. After the contact cleaner dries, safety wire them in place and then you will be able to quickly remove them when they need replacement.

To safety wire the grips wrap 18-gauge steel wire around them in the center and at both ends. Then twist the ends to tighten the wire. Finally trim the ends and push them down into the grips.

Grip Heaters

Hand warmers can significantly extend your riding season in cold climates. It is possible to dress warmly enough to ride into the high 20s (°F), especially when you are moving around on the bike and getting a lot of exercise. However, your hands may get so cold and stiff they can't use the controls. Grip heaters will keep you functioning comfortably when temperatures are low.

The best ones are small heating elements enclosed in plastic tape. They stick onto the bar end and throttle; then the hand grips slide over them. Moose makes a nice kit that includes wires and switches. Depending on the capacity of your bike's charging system, you may not be able to run a headlight and the grips at the same time. If that is the case, install a switch to turn off the headlight when you need maximum hand grip temperature.

Hand Levers and Controls

Adjust all of the levers, controls, and switches so you can reach them easily from both standing and sitting positions. Hands and feet should fall naturally to the controls.

You must be able to use levers with one or two fingers without shifting your grip on the bars. Picture yourself climbing a rocky trail. You slow to climb a ledge and the engine bogs. You need to

Position the levers so that you can easily reach them with one or two fingers.

This lever has been cut so it can be pulled all the way to the bar with one finger—without hitting the others.

slip the clutch, but can't unwrap your fingers because rocks will tear the bars out of your hands. The engine coughs and stops.

Now picture it another way. The levers are adjusted so that you can reach them with one finger without releasing your grip on the bars. You squeeze the clutch with a finger, slip it, and continue on.

Look at pictures of motocross stars railing berms or sailing over jumps. They have one finger on the clutch and/or brake lever. What works for them will work for you. You will be riding mostly in a seated or neutral standing position. Rotate bars forward and levers slightly down so you can easily reach them from these positions.

Levers attached to cables must have some free play before they start pulling the cable (about 1/16 of an inch is usual). The cable has an outer flexible tube and an inner cable. The outer tube causes the cable to follow a longer path when it bends as you turn the front wheel. Free play provides enough slack to compensate for bending the cable. Make sure there is still free play when the wheel is turned.

Some people cut levers to a shorter length—just long enough to reach with two fingers. Then they can pull the levers all the way back to the hand grips without touching the fingers that are wrapped around the bars.

Levers attached to hydraulic lines usually have a screw that adjusts the position at which the lever starts to push on the master cylinder. Be careful to allow some free play between the end of the adjuster and the piston. Without this free play, fluid will accumulate in the piston and the brakes will lock (or the clutch will slip).

Make sure the throttle is properly adjusted. First, set the idle speed. There is usually a screw adjuster on the side of the carb. Set the idle just high enough to resist stalling on tight trails.

Most modern motorcycles use two throttle cables. One opens the throttle and the other closes it. Such a throttle turns easily because it has a light return spring, without risking that it will stick open. Adjust the closing cable so it just pulls the slide down onto the idle adjustment screw. You should hear the throttle slide click against the adjuster as it closes. Then adjust the opening cable so it has about 1/16 inch of free play.

Footpegs

The shock of a million rocks and ruts will travel up through the footpegs and hammer your feet, making them sore. Wide footpegs, which are available from several manufacturers, spread the impact better.

Big, wide dual sport gas tanks make it hard to stand (particularly when leaning forward on hills) because the tank is in the way. Modifying your pegs by adding an inch to the back of the pegs may allow you to stand more to the rear and place your knees in the narrow juncture of seat and tank.

Foot Levers

The gear shift lever is mounted on a splined shaft. You can move the lever up or down by removing it and changing its position on the splines. Set the lever position so you can reach it both seated and standing while wearing riding boots. You may need to bend or weld the lever to get it just right.

The rear brake usually has two adjustments: one that adjusts height and another that adjusts when the lever starts to push on the master cylinder. Adjusting the lever downward is the same as stepping on the brake. Compensate by changing the other adjustment or the brake will always be on. Be careful to allow some free play or else fluid will accumulate in the piston and your brakes will lock.

Set the lever height so that you can reach it from the standing position with your arch on the footpeg. This is very important. You must be able to use the brake from the standing position. Do not set it so high that you drag the brakes (either standing or seated), but get it high enough to apply firm pressure with a natural foot movement while standing.

From the seated position it may then be hard to use the lever when you slide forward on the seat. This is normal. Learn how to lift your foot from the peg and then use the lever as described in Chapter 9.

Take some test runs with the new adjustments. Make sure that you can easily reach the clutch and brakes from the standing position. Be sure you can use them instantly without having to sit before you can reach them. Readjust as necessary.

These Fastway footpegs are wider, give better support, and distribute impact over a wider area.

The nut on the left adjusts the point at which the brakes start to engage; the one on the right adjusts pedal height.

Lift your heel off the peg and brake with your toe when seated far forward on the seat.

Modern bikes have pretty good brakes. Replacing a rubber brake line with an aftermarket steel braided line may improve feel. Brake pads made of Kevlar tend to absorb moisture and lose efficiency when wet. Sintered metallic or carbon graphite pads are recommended for wet conditions.

ESSENTIAL ACCESSORIES FOR DAY RIDES

At this point the bike should be adjusted to fit you. Now you can begin to add some necessary accessories.

Street Legal Equipment

You need a horn, headlight, taillight, stoplight, mirror, turn signals, and whatever other equipment your state requires. Factory dual sports come with the necessary equipment but several suppliers offer conversion kits for off-road bikes.

The best known name in dual sport conversion kits is Baja Designs. They have been developing high-end aftermarket lighting systems and other adventure products for the off-road industry for 14 years. They claim the following features:

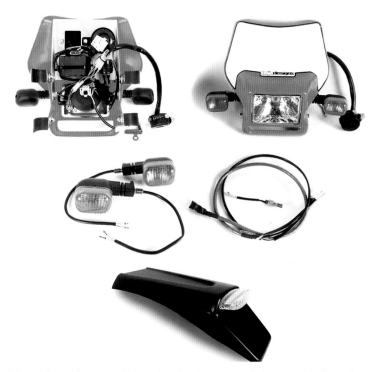

Baja Designs kits have all the electrical components to convert off-road bikes to street legal.

Complete Kits. Halogen headlight, turn signals and taillight, OEM style handlebar switch assembly with push-to-cancel turn signal button; and integrated high-beam indicator.

Quick Release. Incorporate multi-pin connectors in the wiring harness at the front of the bike and under the seat. Once installed, removal and reinstallation of the kit can be accomplished in just a few minutes without having to identify any individual wires.

Easy Installation. All front accessories (headlight, turn signals, horn, flasher relay, etc.) are pre-attached and pre-wired, eliminating the need to identify and connect most individual wires. A small NiCad battery and rectifier/regulator are included for bikes without batteries.

All states require DOT tires; some states have additional requirements such as a speedometer/odometer, mirrors, etc.

Trail Tech offers a complete line of trip computers which include a speedometer function. They offer kits including the computer, integrated speed sensor, cable, mount assembly, handlebar mounting hardware, and instructions. An aluminum protector is sold separately.

Converted off-road bikes may not have enough electrical charging capacity to run all of the required lights. A high beam is usually 60 watts, a tail light is 15 and a stop light is 35. This adds up to 110 watts minimum, plus whatever it takes to run the horn and turn signals. Read the owner's manual and find out how many watts your alternator produces. Ricky Stator offers a complete line of lighting coils and stators that can increase your electrical charging capacity.

A stator produces electricity when magnets on the flywheel spin past wire coils. The amount of electricity produced in the coils can be changed by changing the thickness of the wire or the number of turns in the coil.

Good hand guards protect knuckles and levers.

Most bikes have 55/60 watt halogen headlights which are adequate for casual off-highway use at night. Some people try to run 100 watt bulbs to get brighter light, but they run hotter. The added heat can damage the bulb or the headlight housing. A better solution for occasional moonlight rides is to use a high efficiency 60-watt bulb. These trade shorter service life for more light. A Bilux 37R bulb available from an auto supply store gives near daylight visibility on nighttime dirt roads. PIAA also makes a line of high efficiency replacement bulbs.

Rear View Mirror

Acerbis makes nice plastic framed, dual sport mirrors. They are very light and can be folded out of the way for off-highway use. Another option is to use a small metal framed mirror mounted below the hand grip.

Hand Guards

A dual sport needs decent hand guards. Dual sports are often operated near branches and limbs that really hurt when you bang against them at 30 or 40 mph. The need to protect your fingers should be obvious. Hand guards also prevent bike injury. In the old days we always carried spare levers because we fell and broke them every few rides. With hand guards it is unusual to break a lever.

Each hand guard must clamp to the handlebars in front of the levers and loop around to another attachment at the end of the bars. Plastic brush deflectors should be added to the guards to protect your fingers. Moose and MSR are two well-known suppliers of hand guards. Clamps are made for specific handlebars. Make sure you settle on handlebars before buying hand guards.

Brake Protector (Shark Fin)

Rear brake rotors are highly vulnerable to rock damage. You can usually place the front wheel precisely, but the rear doesn't always follow. The rock you avoided with the front wheel may clip the back. Brake rotors are expensive and it is impossible to ride with one that is badly bent. A "shark fin" is a metal guard that is outside of, and slightly larger than, the rotor. It takes the hits and prevents damage.

Scotts make a very nice 3/8-inch thick billet aluminum shark fin. It incorporates the brake carrier as an integral part. This means the axle passes through the shark fin making it very strong. It's a beautiful piece of work.

This Scotts shark fin is a well-designed accessory to protect the rear brake disk.

A strong chain guide helps keep the chain on the rear sprocket. This one shows some serious dings.

A case saver on this KTM protects the engine from damage if the chain breaks.

This well used skid plate shows dents from hundreds of rock hits, any one of which might have damaged the engine case.

A well constructed skid plate protects the engine and frame tubes. Many manufacturers offer skid plates. Here is one from Utah Sport Cycles.

Chain Guides

The chain guide is equally vulnerable to damage. A bent or broken guide can derail your chain and destroy the center cases of your motor, costing big bucks. Don't take the gamble, it's very cheap insurance.

Several companies sell case protectors that can prevent a broken or derailed chain from munching the aluminum. The pictured item is from KTM.

Skid Plates

Many dual sports have 13 to 15 inches of ground clearance and 12 inches of suspension travel. Thus, the engine is only one or two inches above the ground when the suspension is fully compressed. A rock could easily puncture your engine cases, the oil could leak out, and the engine could destroy itself. This picture of a well used skid plate shows evidence of countless rock attacks.

A sturdy plate will protect your engine and frame tubes from damage. Look for one that wraps around the front of the cases and has an oil drain hole. Some models come from the factory with skid plates, but they tend to be weak and ineffective. Be aware that big hits on rocks can drive the skid plate into the frame tubes and flatten them. Take it easy in the rocks.

Radiator Guards

Most modern dual sports have water cooling and their fragile radiators need protection. Some gas tanks wrap around the radiators and offer decent protection. They are a good option, but can also be wider, resulting in a "knees out" position when sliding forward on the seat.

Several companies make radiator braces, but some of them are rather weak. They attach to the frame and radiator shrouds, but the shrouds are flimsy plastic, the braces are thin aluminum, and the radiators have no strength at all.

Gearing

Some dual sports are operated in rock washes at a crawl and on freeways at 70. Test your bike by riding it at about 6 mph. It should run smoothly and accelerate to higher speed without needing the clutch. Now take it to the freeway and test the top (legal) speed. You should be able to cruise comfortably, keeping up with traffic. Note: Smaller or larger rear tires will change the overall effective gearing. Make sure that you settle on a tire size before testing the gearing.

If your bike is geared too high for both the low and high speed tests, you can lower overall gearing by changing the sprockets. The EXC450 is an example of a bike with gearing that is too high. It goes about 90, but needs excessive clutch in tight rock washes. Gearing it lower is no problem.

A smaller front sprocket lowers top speed in each gear; a smaller rear sprocket raises top speed in each. There is usually enough adjustment in the chain to add or subtract one tooth to either sprocket. Bigger changes require longer or shorter chains.

The change in speed is proportional to the change in the number of teeth. Let's say your bike has a 15-tooth front sprocket and won't go below 7 mph in low gear with the clutch out. You change to 14 teeth. The proportionate change is 1 tooth divided by 15 teeth = .07. The bike will now go 7 mph times .07 = .49 mph slower.

You could accomplish the same thing by adding teeth at the rear sprocket. Let's say your rear sprocket has 50 teeth. Then .07 times 50 equals 3.5 teeth so you would change from 50 teeth to 54 teeth.

If the bike passes one test, but not the other (low speed or high speed), think about your riding conditions. Gear for freeway speed and stay out of rock washes if you ride primarily on pavement and graded dirt roads. Gear for low speed and ride in the slow lane if you like gnarly stuff.

A 15-tooth front sprocket might be good for cruising on the freeway, but may force you to use the clutch excessively in really gnarly terrain. You can change the overall gearing by switching from a 15-tooth sprocket to 14 in about 5 minutes. If you really want the right gear for every occasion, bring an extra sprocket.

Steering Dampers

Many dual sports are now equipped with steering dampers. They are essentially small shock absorbers that mount between the steering head and frame. Dampers resist forces from rocks and

A big, wrap-around gas tank offers some protection to the radiators in case of a crash.

Here are some good looking KTM braces made of steel tubing that mount to the frame. The radiators mount inside the tubes.

A properly chosen rear sprocket and some front sprockets with different numbers of teeth provide gearing for any situation.

This Scotts steering damper absorbs impacts that would otherwise cause the front wheel to deflect.

This KTM, equipped with a big tank, has just finished a long desert race.

ruts that would otherwise push your front wheel to one side or the other. With a steering damper, big hits won't rip the bars from your hands. Other benefits include less fatigue from fighting the bars, and controlling wobble on bikes with steep steering angles.

On the negative side steering dampers are not cheap and they complicate mounting and adjusting the bars. A tall Dust Devil complained that his back killed him in the whoops. I suggested he raise his bars up higher with spacers, but he said the steering damper prevented it. Recently, I saw he had bar spacers and a damper that mounts under the bars. Make sure everything is going to fit before buying.

Big Gas Tanks

Larger gas tanks are a popular addition. IMS and Clarke make tanks for most models. They mount well, fit perfectly, last for many years, and come in translucent plastic that shows how much gas is left.

One disadvantage of a larger gas tank is the added weight. Gas weighs about six pounds per gallon and adds the weight high on the bike where it has the biggest effect on handling. Gas mileage varies significantly from bike to bike and according to riding conditions. Determine your range under various conditions and buy a tank that matches your actual needs.

Even with a larger tank, there may be times when you need to carry an extra gallon. Some riders carry extra gas in an antifreeze container. They fill it just before a long section, wrap the container in a plastic bag, put it in a backpack, and empty it into the tank as soon possible.

PERFORMANCE MODIFICATIONS

Riders who want to improve the performance of their dual sport engines will find a wide range of aftermarket companies ready to assist.

Carburetion

Motorcycles burn a mixture of vaporized gasoline and air. The ratio should be about 15 parts air to one part of gasoline when the engine is running at normal speed. Starting and acceleration require relatively more gasoline to air.

A big gas tank can give you the range you need when the next available gas is 96 miles away.

Some dual sports have fuel injection, but most still use carburetors. A carburetor controls mixture and flow with a variety of passages and nozzles (jets). There are different paths for starting, idling, and accelerating which should have been correctly chosen at the factory for some hypothetical conditions. However, the density of air changes with elevation, temperature, and humidity. Racers choose their jetting very carefully to match expected conditions.

Dual sport riders are more tolerant. They need motors that start easily, run smoothly at different speeds, produce reasonable power, and get decent mileage. Some carburetors fail even these simple criteria. Here are some tests you should make.

Follow the instructions in the manual and start your bike. It should start quickly whether you kick it or press a button. It will probably need some choke at first and then settle down to a steady idle. Let it warm up and go for a test run. The motor should pick up speed smoothly when you twist the throttle. Acceleration should be brisk and the bike should maintain speed without surging when you hold the throttle steady. There should be no detonation (pinging) on hard acceleration.

Get the motor hot, then turn it off and restart. It should start promptly. Blip the throttle; the motor should return quickly to idle when you close the throttle. Failure to return to idle could indicate an air leak between the carburetor and engine.

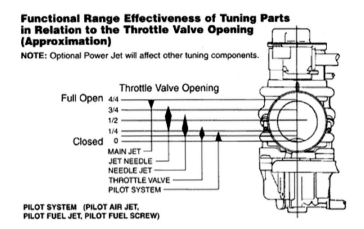

A carburetor tuning guide will show you which jet does what. Sudco and Carburetor Parts Warehouse are good sources of information and parts.

If the bike fails these tests, the carburetor may not be properly jetted. Jetting a carb is not rocket science, but you must correctly diagnose the problem, change the jets, and retest. This can lead to another round of adjustments and tests … and another. Several companies specialize in jetting. You should call them if you suspect a problem with your carburetor(s). They provide jets and instructions that usually get things sorted out quickly.

Get a carburetor manual if you decide to tinker (Haynes publishes an excellent one). Adjust the starting circuit first, then the idle circuit, then the needle and/or slide cutaway, and last the main jet. Each circuit provides some gas and some air and they are all in play at wide open throttle. Start at the beginning and get the starting circuit right before making final adjustments to the idle mixture; get the idle right before you make needle adjustments, etc.

Special note on CV carburetors: Some factory dual sports have constant velocity (CV) carburetors. Twisting the throttle opens a valve in the carburetor that creates a vacuum in the carburetor body. This vacuum then acts on a rubber diaphragm that lifts the slide and needle. The spring that closes the slide is matched to the vacuum and is relatively weak. Bouncing across whoops

At the top is a Mikuni main jet calculator used by tuners pursuing horsepower at different elevations and temperatures. Below it is a JD jet kit with needles and main jets to tune Keihin carburetors for a variety of conditions.

may cause the slide to bounce up and down, causing erratic performance. The solution may be an aftermarket carburetor.

Exhaust Systems

Factory dual sports must meet federal standards for noise, which is measured in decibels. A decibel (dB) is the basic measurement unit for sound. Decibel measurements are made on a logarithmic scale, which means that an increase of three decibels approximates a perceived doubling of the noise level.

The US Forest Service requires an approved spark arrestor in good working condition. They have also established noise limits for motorcycles. Your vehicle must measure 101 dB(A) or less if it was manufactured before January 1, 1986 or 96 dB(A) if manufactured later. Pro Circuit, Leo Vance, and FMF make mufflers that comply.

An FMF Q2 muffler meets Forest Service requirements for low noise and spark arrestor.

Several manufacturers market aftermarket mufflers on claims of increased power. However, the purpose of a muffler is to reduce noise, not increase power.

Think carefully before buying a "lighter, more powerful" aftermarket muffler. Few factors contribute more to misunderstanding and prejudice against the motorcycling community than excessively noisy motorcycles.

The power and weight benefits may be barely noticeable on the trail, but the noise will be obvious to everyone. Loud bikes are the biggest single cause of complaints and trail closures. They also cause rider fatigue and hearing damage.

In any case, the intake and exhaust work as a system. A change to the exhaust that allows substantially more air to flow will require re-jetting the carburetor.

Engine Modifications

There are endless and often confusing modifications which claim to increase power. Sometimes it helps to oversimplify things, so let's start with the basics. Internal combustion engines burn hydrocarbons (gasoline). Assuming an engine in good condition, the amount of power is proportional to the amount of gasoline burned—more gasoline equals more power. The amount burned can be increased by removing a bottleneck, spinning the engine faster, or making it bigger.

Bottlenecks are things like carburetors that are too small or mufflers that excessively choke the flow of exhaust. Federal and state mandated levels for emissions and noise continue to change and manufacturers sometimes achieve compliance with band aids rather than well-conceived solutions. Some even go as far as installing screws that prevent the throttle from opening more than halfway.

Magazines and websites have information about bottlenecks and many companies supply solutions. However, removing a bottleneck may render your bike non-compliant with whatever law the bottleneck addressed. The best solution is to do your research before buying and get a bike that meets your needs without modification.

The next steps beyond removing bottlenecks are to spin the motor faster or bore it to hold a larger piston. Modern four-strokes are already operating near the limits of rotational speed. Things like hot cams, stiffer valve springs, and polished ports are best left to racers who can afford frequent engine rebuilds. Water-cooled engines do not usually have enough room in the cylinder for a bigger piston. Also, when you are 70 miles from the nearest services you don't care about extra power, you just want to keep your bike running until you are safely back in town.

The easiest, best, and cheapest way of increasing power is to buy a dual sport with a bigger engine. For example, a DR350 with a bigger aftermarket carb, extra holes in the air box, free flow air filter, careful jetting, and a bigger piston is still slow. A 450 KTM with no modifications whatsoever is a rocket. Buy a bike that matches your riding style and spend any extra money on suspension tuning, where it really counts.

ACCESSORIES FOR THE HIGHWAY AND LONG TRIPS

There is a huge selection of clothing, accessories, and equipment available from motorcycle manufacturers and other sources.

Sources of Equipment

Companies like BMW, KTM, and Kawasaki offer a wide range of factory accessories that bolt on with a minimum of hassle. If you buy a new bike, you may be able to bargain and get these accessories included in the purchase price.

Dozens of smaller manufacturers offer similar equipment plus many other items. In some cases, they are the source of the manufacturer's offerings.

The Web has a great selection of sites that will help you research various destinations and gear. Spend some time browsing and profit from others' experience.

Most products are well made and fit properly. However, there is always the possibility that you will need to grind, file, or bend something, particularly if the item is designed for use on a variety of machines. Start early and give yourself time to adjust or return items. Avoid installing new accessories the night before you leave on a long trip.

Armor for Your Bike

A skid plate and hand guards belong on all dual sports. For middleweight and heavyweight bikes you can also buy crash guards that protect the sides of the engine and radiator from crash damage. They are a good idea. Sooner or later you will fall, hopefully on the dirt at low speed. Even a low speed tip-over could damage the engine or radiator if the bike lands on a rock.

A long trip represents a considerable investment of time and money. Why take an unnecessary chance that your trip will end with the bike in a crate or a long wait for repairs. Also, crash bars look very "adventure."

Electrical Considerations

You may wish to equip your steed with additional lights, GPS, and radar detector, in addition to electric riding clothes. Make sure there is enough

These crash bars on a V-Strom offer wrap-around protection from damage.

electrical charging capacity to power everything. The owner's manual or service manual should indicate how many watts are produced by the alternator at a specified rpm, which is usually in the cruising range.

Add the wattage of all the stock lights and accessories. For example, the high beam might be 60 watts, the tail light might be 20, and the instrument lights another five. You will intermittently need more watts to run the turn signals, horn, and stop light. Make an allowance of about 20 percent for these items. Subtract the total used plus the allowance from the total available. The remainder can be used to power additional accessories.

Take this seriously. Any excess of the accessories over the capacity of the alternator will be drawn from the battery until it goes dead, possibly leaving you stranded in the dark in the middle of nowhere.

Accessories can be powered from this electrical receptacle on a KTM.

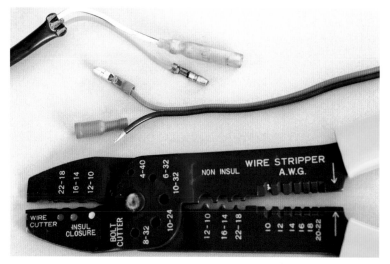

It is difficult to fabricate good quality wiring with hand tools and connections from local sources. The picture shows a short segment of factory wiring at the top and a hand-crimped connection, and crimping tool below. The factory bullet connector is crimped both to the wire and also to the insulation. It was applied by an expensive machine which squeezed with just the right amount of pressure, onto wire specified by engineers to be flexible and strong. The connectors below it come from a local electronics supply and aren't even close to the factory items. There is no way of precisely controlling the pressure applied by a hand crimping tool. No one at the store knew anything about the flexibility and strength of the wire.

PIAA has a good, long standing reputation for quality lighting. The PIAA light pictured above produces as much light as a 60 watt bulb from 35 watts of power. It has mounting brackets and a stone shield and is available in long range, or wide beam light patterns.

Vibrations of off-road riding will attack and possibly destroy any shoddy connections, wire routing, or mounts. Don't spend your vacation trying to repair the damage caused by a short. It may be best to have a skilled technician install a fuse and accessory receptacle.

Think carefully before undertaking extensive rewiring projects on dual sports operated on trails and rough two-tracks. It is extremely difficult for the average home mechanic to create truly durable wiring.

It is possible to work carefully and produce nice looking work, but it will probably not last as long as a factory wiring harness. If you do your own wiring, use ample wire gauges, and route everything where it can't rub through the insulation. Make a neat diagram of your work and keep it for future reference.

Lighting

Accessory lights are a popular addition to middleweights and heavyweights that are operated primarily on highways. However, experienced dual sport enthusiasts avoid riding at night in remote areas. It is hard enough to see hazards in daylight without assuming the added risks of seeing them in the dark.

The quality of light produced depends on the entire package—bulb, reflector, and lens. It is best to buy from long established manufacturers like PIAA or Cibie who offer a wide range of well accepted products.

Be aware that certain accessory lights are not approved for highway use. Enforcement is lax, but you could get into big trouble by blinding an oncoming motorist and causing an accident. Understand what you are getting before you purchase.

Windscreens

Great rider protection is an advantage of touring bikes like the Honda Gold Wing. Their large windscreens and fairings create pockets of comfortable, dead air and protect against the continual blast of on-rushing wind. Windscreens also deflect rain and cold leaving you warmer and drier.

Long rides on my completely unprotected DR350 become pretty unpleasant when I try to

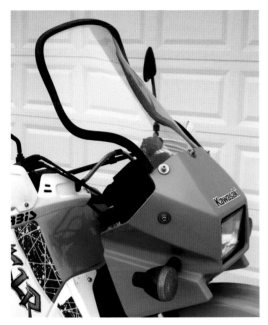

This tall windscreen on a KLR offers excellent wind protection.

keep up with street riding friends. It's not bad poking along at 55, but 70 is a different story. The wind buffets my body and pulses against my helmet. After a few hours, enjoyment lapses into an overwhelming desire to go home. It's not practical to fit full fairings to dual sports, but a properly fitted windscreen will do much to enhance rider comfort.

There are two approaches to getting a good windscreen if your bike came with one that is too low or does not have a windshield at all. You can buy a replacement from a company like Rifle that matches the mounting points of your stock windscreen, or you can use a universal clamp-on type designed for a cruiser.

The latter approach may be less than aesthetically ideal, but the added comfort on long trips will be worth it. I went to Alaska with two friends who used the clamp-on method and teased them without mercy about their "ugly screens." After a few cold rainy days, my scorn turned to envy.

Looking through glasses, a face shield, and a windshield may reduce visibility. Add some rain and reduced vision could become a real problem. The ideal height for a screen is *just below* the line of vision. This means the top edge should be somewhere between your nose and Adam's apple, whichever makes you more comfortable.

(You should be able to see the road, over the windshield, about 20 feet in front the bike.)

To determine the proper height of your windscreen, sit on the bike and look at a point on the road about 20 feet in front of the bike. Ask a friend to draw an imaginary line between your eyes and that point on the road, and measure its distance above the headlight housing. You can then calculate the ideal windshield height.

Compare this height with the actual height of your windscreen if you already have one. The goal is to have good vision while the wind passes over the top of your helmet. The shield is too low if wind buffets your helmet.

Be careful with windscreens. I still remember riding my friend's bike and trying to wheelie it over a bump. The wind screen came up and banged me hard across the nose.

Bungee Caution

Bungee cords stretch. Anything that stretches can allow your load to shift and possibly fall off. Attach loose gear with tight nylon straps whenever possible.

Years ago, I rode cross country on a street bike. I was traveling light and everything was packed into one small airline bag on the rear fender, secured by bungees around the bag and rear frame loops. Somewhere near St. Louis the bag shifted and one small corner, no bigger than a quarter, came in contact with the spokes. The spokes wore through the bag and began unraveling clothes and sucking them one thread at a time through the hole and wrapping them around the wheel.

At the end of a long day I pulled into a motel and discovered that my wardrobe had been magically transformed into a loom of doom. There was nothing in the bag except waist bands, shirt necks and a zipper. All of the remaining fibers were woven intricately through the spokes in an attractive but unwelcome pattern of cotton and denim. Even the contents of my shaving bag had been partially converted, leaving half a tube of toothpaste, and a plastic razor with no handle.

It could have been much worse. Underwear and Levis are cheaper than riding jackets and an unwoven tent would be a real disaster on a cold, wet night.

A cold morning in Death Valley requires several layers of bulky garments.

Overload Caution

Check your owner's manual to find out the gross carrying capacity of your motorcycle and stay within it. The bulk of the luggage weight should be placed low and as close to the center of the motorcycle as possible. Distribute the weight evenly on both sides. Stay within the weight recommendation for bags and mounts. Make especially sure that any attached load does not block lights or turn signals, or interfere with your steering, braking, shifting, or other control of the motorcycle.

It is possible to get away with almost anything for a short time, but overloading will eventually bite you. Luggage takes a terrific pounding on rough roads; sooner or later something will break or crack.

Racks and Luggage

Your trip planning will indicate how much luggage capacity is needed. Winter riding requires warm clothes; riding gear alone can consume a lot of luggage capacity if you want to shed some layers.

Most experienced riders counsel taking as little as possible. Everything you bring is a potential problem and a huge load of junk will negatively affect both handling and stability. At the end of the day it's your stuff and your bike, so bring whatever you want, but at least pack it properly.

Pack only what you will actually, positively need. Every added bag multiplies the number of zippers that can jam or leak, the number of straps that can loosen or break, and the amount of weight that must be balanced, turned, and stopped.

This KLR has luggage properly attached with straps, but think about the consequences of filling all these bags with stuff. This bike weighs about 330 pounds dry. Its six-gallon tank holds 36 pounds of fuel. The tank bags could easily hold 25 pounds of gear and the rear bags could hold another 60 pounds. Imagine trying to control all of this weight on a muddy, slippery road for several hours at a time.

Luggage Specifications

Luggage can be described in several different ways:

Construction. The three main types are soft bags, plastic trunks, and aluminum trunks.

Soft bags are made of nylon, cordura, or similar materials. They are usually coated with something to make them "waterproof," but most are likely to leak in heavy rain as they age.

Truly waterproof bags are available from Seal Line.

Plastic trunks come in a wide range of quality. The cheapest are pretty flimsy and leak around the lid. More expensive models have good locks and weather seals.

Aluminum trunks are the most durable and expensive option. The best ones are welded from aluminum plate and have good weather seals and locks. Securely attached trunks of good quality offer the best protection against the elements, and highest level of security for contents.

Picture yourself heading into an urban area to eat or visit a museum. Will you feel comfortable leaving soft luggage on the bike in a parking lot or on the street. If not, hard, locking trunks may be the way to go.

Trunk liners are soft bags that fit inside trunks. At night, you can pull them out and carry them into a motel room like normal luggage.

Location. The main locations for luggage on the motorcycle are front fender, tank, and rear. Front fenders won't support much weight and fender bags should be small enough to permit normal operation of the headlight.

Soft saddlebags like these from Cortech may be all you need for overnight trips. The top and tank bags could be added for longer trips.

This KTM is equipped with luggage racks and good quality, removable plastic trunks.

Seal Line bags are completely waterproof.

This Suzuki V-Strom has a sturdy rack and aluminum panniers made by Happy Trails.

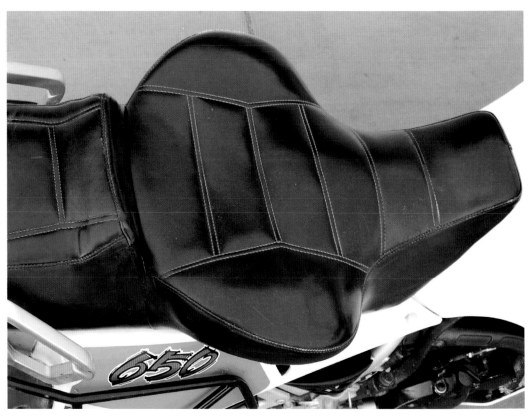

This wide custom seat on a KLR promises all-day comfort.

Tank bags and rear luggage may either sit on top or hang along the side (panniers). Hard trunks mount on the top and sides in the rear. It is possible to create more luggage space by switching to a short seat. keep in mind that the best location for the added weight is low and near the center of the motorcycle. A rider can also carry some gear in a backpack or fanny pack, but they can become uncomfortable on long trips.

How much the luggage will hold. This is usually given in cubic inches or even better in the actual height, width, and length of the item.

Method of attachment. The two methods are straps and bolt-on racks. Soft bags attach directly to the motorcycle or rider with straps and can also be mounted on racks. Luggage that is attached directly to the motorcycle will probably damage the finish over time as dirt works itself under the bag and rubs against the paint. Plastic and aluminum trunks mount on dedicated racks. Some have a provision for a locking quick release.

Cost. Soft bags start at around $100 dollars. Plastic trunks start about $100 and go up to about $600 for a pair of panniers. Aluminum trunks start at around $500 for a pair of panniers and can go much higher. Luggage racks are extra and start at about $100 and go up.

Seats

Middleweight and adventure seats are luxurious compared with the hard, narrow boards found on lightweights. However, you will be spending a longer time sitting and your butt can use all the help it can get. Companies like Travelcade and Corbin offer replacement seats which are potentially more comfortable.

Gel seats use a special type of foam that conforms to your body, eliminating pressure points that cause poor circulation and discomfort. You can buy complete gel seats or gel pads.

It is also possible to order thicker or thinner seats, better matched to your height, for most models.

Suspension and Fork Braces

Good suspension that maintains contact between the wheels and ground is just as important for heavier dual sports as for lightweights. Dirt roads place fewer demands on suspension than whoops and rock fields, but tires must stay on the ground to accelerate, turn, and stop. Hard jolty suspension will also pound your body, bike, and accessories.

Suspension principles apply equally to all dual sports. Read Chapter 7 to learn more about suspension tuning. Suspension travel on heavier bikes is usually shorter, but springs and shocks work the same way, and you can use the same techniques to diagnose problems and get a better ride.

Some middleweight and heavyweight suspensions have minimal adjustments and you may need to rely on selection of spring rates to get an improvement. Companies like Race Tech and Progressive Suspension offer springs. Race Tech offers valve kits; Progressive Suspension and Works Performance build complete shocks.

Fork braces clamp onto the fork tubes and prevent them from flexing, resulting in better control. Raise the front end off the ground and vigorously shake your handlebars from side to side. Note whether the front wheel moves quickly with the bars or feels more like it is connected to a spring. If it feels springy, the forks are flexing and a fork brace may cure the problem.

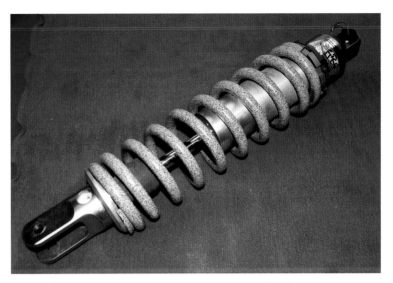

Progressive Suspension offers replacement shock absorbers for many popular dual sports.

Miscellaneous Accessories

This chapter has covered the basics, but there are many other things that can be added to a dual sport: centerstands, heat shields, electronic gadgets. Look thorough a good catalog or surf the Web to see the many possibilities.

6

All About Tires

Dirt tires wear quickly, so it's no small effort to keep good rubber on a bike. However, tires are critically important when negotiating treacherous surfaces at speed. You are balanced on two narrow rubber hoops and must rely on them absolutely. Careful attention to tire selection and condition will increase your enjoyment, improve your riding abilities, and prevent falls.

This chapter has the information you need to make sound decisions about tires, including:

- Tires in Action
- The Importance of Tires
- Tire Characteristics
- Basic Principles of Tire Selection
- Tire Specifications
- Tubes, Rim Locks, and Balancing

TIRES IN ACTION

We are riding to Panamint Springs in Death Valley. The early autumn cold bites thorough jackets and pants as we climb Cerro Gordo road to the old mine and pause in a small saddle below the peak at 8100 feet. To the west, above Lone Pine, the Eastern Sierra spine sweeps in a splendor of granite crags and glaciers partially masked by cumulus. To the northeast lies an equally spectacular view of the Saline Valley flanked by ranges of granite and Juniper, stretching beyond a high tilted plain to endless ranges in Nevada.

The perfect moment sours as I descend the steep canyon below, heading for Saline Valley Road. The rear end fishtails under braking into soft turns and the front skates across small loose rocks, frustrating every attempt to hold a line. I fight at first, but soon slow and resign myself to being mostly out of control. Suspension tuned for more aggressive riding starts to pound and deflect; the bike chooses its own lines; I react rather than direct.

The Sierras above Lone Pine make a perfect backdrop for dual sport.

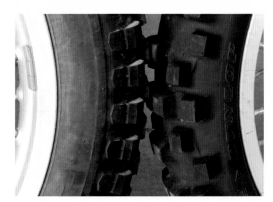

The Continental Twinduro (TKC80) on the right is popular with long-distance riders. The Dunlop 739 on the left is an intermediate motocross tire with sharp handling, but it wears quickly.

The performance of your tires is what keeps your body away from the rocks on slippery off-camber curves like this.

After ten minutes, I reach the bottom feeling dissatisfied. The descent was a clumsy encounter of fumbling strangers rather than the usual graceful dance of man and machine. There are similar descents around Reno where the rear end tracks straight into soft turns. There, I know exactly how the bike will respond and the front holds any chosen line. One of the world's great views, should have been followed by an equally exhilarating descent.

The difference is explained in a single word— tires. Today, my Suzuki is shod with Continental Twinduros rather than my usual Dunlop 739s. The 739s are full knobby racing tires that wear quickly. The Twinduros have less aggressive tread, are oriented more toward street riding, and last much longer.

THE IMPORTANCE OF TIRES

Tires play an important part in safety. Many riders buy the most expensive helmets and body armor but run worn out tires or constantly change tire brands to get them on sale. Protective gear only starts working after you crash; good tires prevent crashes. The importance of selecting the right tires and replacing them when worn should be obvious.

Picture the tires as you enter a loose, rocky turn traveling 40 miles an hour over rough ground. The combined weight of rider and machine is precariously balanced on two contact patches smaller than the balls of your feet. Everything you feel is transmitted through the tires. Your ability to anticipate how the bike will react to changes of weight and balance is determined by your knowledge of what the tires did in the past. Everything you do to control the bike is transmitted back to the ground through them. Good and consistent tire performance must be among your major goals.

Now picture the tires as you push them down a twisty mountain highway. You are still perched on two small patches, and dependent on them to transmit your inputs to the pavement, but now you are going much faster. It is always possible that a car is speeding toward you, half into your lane, around the next blind corner. Your ability to stop or change direction quickly may affect your very survival.

TIRE CHARACTERISTICS

It is relatively easy to create a dual purpose motorcycle. Add lights and mirrors to any machine that handles well in the dirt and it will be adequate for occasional use on pavement. However, tires are more specialized; those that work well on dirt may be dangerous on pavement. Those that work well on pavement are likely to be ineffective on dirt.

I haven't tested every tire on the market, but I have ridden quite a few, including several different types of Dunlop, Pirelli, IRC, Maxxis, and Bridgestone, plus at least one type each of Cheng Shin, Kenda, Metzler, Continental, and Avon. my goal has always been the same: to find one tire that combines terrific handling in the dirt with long wear and safety on the street.

I keep trying different tires and always arrive at the same disappointing conclusion: there are some really good dual purpose bikes, but there aren't any really good dual purpose tires. Street tires and dirt tires are two separate breeds.

Several characteristics determine the performance of tires, and most are compromises between one desirable feature and another. Here are some examples:

The 21-inch front tires above range from street to dirt. On the left is a Maxis Promax street tire, in the middle is a Twinduro, and on the right is a full knobby Dunlop D739.

Rubber Compound. Soft rubber gives better traction on hard surfaces, but wears quickly. Harder compounds wear longer, but don't stick as well.

Tire Profile. Rounded profiles keep gripping at high lean angles, but wear the center quickly when ridden upright. Flatter profiles work better upright at the expense of reduced cornering grip.

Tread Pattern. Street tires aim to get the maximum amount of rubber on the road with a few rain groves and virtually no tread. They are pretty useless in deep sand or mud.

Off-road tires have deep, knobby treads that dig into loose or slimy surfaces, but have only half as much rubber in contact with pavement. They could slide dangerously in panic stops. Semi-knobby tires like the Twinduro accelerate and cruise just fine in the dirt and may encourage you to go fast, but they don't have the bite for aggressive turns and panic stops. Experiment in a safe place when using a new brand of tire to get a feel for stopping and turning, and ride accordingly.

BASIC PRINCIPLES OF TIRE SELECTION

Tires are described by specifications which must be matched to your needs, but the specs don't tell the whole story. Let's cover some basic principles of selection first.

Manufacturers usually list the intended use of their offerings. Dual sport tires are often shown as 70 percent on road and 30 percent off-road, or some other percentages, but these are just marketing descriptions without any objective measures. They certainly don't mean that the tire will be really good in the dirt for the 30 percent of the time you use it there. A tire rated as 50 percent on and 50 percent off is likely to be half as good as a street tire on the street and half as good as a dirt tire in the dirt—pretty bad everywhere.

A quick glance through any catalog will show that there is no standard design for dual sport tires. A manufacturer can apply the term to virtually any tire. Some are very close to street tires while others are full knobbies.

It is up to you to select a tire that meets your needs. To guide you in making your choices here are some principles based on experience:

Principle 1: Choose Tires for Your Primary Use

Choose a tire that is excellent for your primary use and either tolerate it the rest of the time or change it. Do not stagger through most of your rides on a tire that's designed for something you do only occasionally.

When I lived in San Francisco most of my riding was on the street, and I was riding very aggressively in traffic. I ditched the OEM dual sport tires that came with the Suzuki and mounted some real street tires. I was still able to ride the occasional dirt road and was much, much safer in traffic. When we headed for the mountains or desert every summer, I changed to dirt tires. It was a bit of work, but the street tires saved my butt on many occasions.

The difference was dramatically illustrated after I purchased another DR350 and tried to ride it on the street with the same OEM tires I had previously ditched. On the very first day, I turned a sharp corner at my usual lean angle and nearly lost the front end as the tire rolled up unto its

DOT-certified Dunlop 606s are a good choice for a 3000-mile trip in Mexico.

These riders spend most of their time on unimproved desert roads and have chosen dirt tires that grip well on a wide variety of soft surfaces.

shoulder and lost traction. A couple of days later it happened again and those tires went into the trash.

Now the situation is reversed. Living in Nevada, I ride mostly in the dirt. Consequently the bike uses real dirt tires most of the time. When I take long pavement rides, I switch to real street tires.

Some people buy another set of wheels so they have one set with dirt tires and another with street tires. I did this a few years ago and can swap wheels on my bike in about 10 minutes, which is far quicker than changing tires. However, new wheels are expensive. A set of new wheels from KTM with brake discs and a rear sprocket costs about $1,100. It is sometimes possible to find wheels for your bike on E-bay for considerably less.

Your goal is to maximize fun and minimize risk. Think about what you want to do and buy tires to match. The key is to have a good vision of the type of riding you will actually do. If you only ride occasionally on good roads, the tires that come with the bike may be adequate. If you want to explore gnarly terrain, get tires to match. Here are some examples of choices made by others.

John and Bill bought KLRs two years ago to explore back roads. They have been to the Lost Coast and Death Valley and are planning a trip to the Modoc Plateau. They aren't aggressive riders and don't ride often enough to develop advanced skills so they are still running the original OEM dual purpose tires.

Don rides more than anyone else in our club (possibly the world). He is planning a three-thousand-mile trip, mostly on rough dirt roads in Mexico. Durability and traction are what he needs and he mounts some good, hard compound, DOT-certified, full knobbies with a reputation for long mileage.

Ty is an experienced trail rider who clocks occasional highway mileage on back roads, but dirt performance is his main goal. He chooses intermediate motocross tires and rides cautiously on pavement.

The Department of Transportation (National Highway Traffic Safety Administration) certifies some tires for highway use. These are tested for strength and endurance and have a DOT symbol on the sidewall. Tires which have not been certified are marked "Not for Highway Use." You can get a ticket for using these tires on the road.

Most cops have better things to do than read tire labels, so some riders choose to ignore the certification, and run tires that work best in local conditions. However, a rider in full motocross regalia who screams past the highway patrol on an incredibly loud bike may find non-DOT tires added to a list of his infractions.

Tire labeling is primarily a legal and marketing thing. The fact that a tire is labeled "Not for Highway Use" means only that it has not been DOT-tested and certified. It does not imply

These three tires are DOT-certified. The tire on the left is an IRC GP1, the middle tire is a Pirelli MT21 and on the right is a Dunlop 606. The IRC with closely-spaced knobs is more oriented to street riding.

anything about the actual performance of the tire. Many off-road tires have been proven in the most extreme racing conditions while some DOT tires have no more rubber on the ground than intermediate motocross tires. Off-road racers do not need the certification and may even believe that a DOT tire is less race-worthy. The important things for you to remember are that tires with knobs have less traction on pavement, while smooth tires have less traction in dirt.

If you are just starting out and want to gain a sense of what tires to try, go to some local cross country races or dual sport rallies and see what others are using.

The right dirt tires will "feel right." Here are some characteristics of good ones:

- Light and responsive steering
- Track straight and true under throttle and braking
- Hold precise lines in turns
- Follow the ground without deflecting on every rock and bump
- Slide predictably when you want them to
- Feel settled and stable in rocks and ruts
- Perform well on a variety of surfaces: hard, soft, sandy, rocky, and muddy

Good tires do what you want without constantly correcting their mistakes. You can forget them and concentrate on the terrain.

Principle 2: Stick with Tires that Work

If you are serious about riding, find tires that work for you and stick with them. Every hour you ride builds your knowledge of how tires react. This knowledge then shapes thousands of subconscious decisions that keep you safely on course. Constantly changing tire brands and types interrupts the learning process and keeps you physically and mentally off-balance.

To ride well and safely you must be mentally ahead of the bike, setting up for the next section as you ride the current one. This is possible only when you know exactly how the tires will react to brake, throttle, and balance. Otherwise you will be riding behind the bike, reacting to unanticipated things that have already happened.

Imagine that you have a worn rear Dunlop 739 before the big weekend and go to buy a new one. The dealer is out of 739s, but has a special on Michelin MH3s. You say, "Why not?"

On Saturday morning you are shod with the new tire riding a familiar trail, but the bike acts like a stranger. The tire tread is different, the rubber compound is different, and the feel is different.

By the end of the day you are more comfortable, but think about it. You have just spent a full day erasing your Dunlop knowledge and replacing it with Michelin knowledge.

This rider has chosen intermediate-terrain motocross tires to explore dirt roads in Death Valley.

Ride Dunlop, Michelin, or Bridgestone; the choice is yours, but stay with one brand unless you have a good reason to change. Give yourself every chance to build knowledge on a stable base. Do not get into the position of needing a tire at the last minute. Make sure you always have at least one spare tucked away.

Principle 3: Replace Worn Tires Promptly

Worn street tires are pretty obvious, but worn dirt tires may not be. Street tires usually last for many thousands of miles. They start with about an eighth to a quarter inch of tread depth and are worn out when the tread depth is 1/32 of an inch. This is the minimum tread required to channel water away from the contact patch, but at this point they will look almost bald.

Dirt tires wear quickly. A racer can destroy a new knobby in less than 100 miles. In our rocky area, I can usually get about 800 miles of relaxed dual sport riding on a rear dirt tire and about 2500 miles on a front. Rear dirt tires begin with about 12 to 16 millimeters of sharp, square-edged knobs. After a few long rides the knobs will be rounded, half as tall, and less than half as effective. Front tires wear more slowly, but the process is the same. The knobs on front tires can become rounded and torn while there is still quite a bit of tread remaining. Experience will allow you to judge when they will begin slipping. Replace them before you fall, not after.

Replace your tires before they start sliding dangerously. For example, Dunlop 739 rear tires

Measure the tread height when you first install new tires, then monitor the height periodically to track its wear. Record the height at which they begin slipping.

feel a little squirmy on hard ground for the first hundred miles, then have about 600 or 700 miles of good consistent feel. After that, they begin sliding, because the knobs are too worn to grip. They will start to slide badly when the tread in the center of the tire is 5 mm. Measure the center knobs and replace them at 6 mm.

Don't assume that a rear dirt tire is still good just because the knobs on the sides are long. The center knobs wear fastest. When they get down to a few millimeters, the center of the tire will begin riding on the casing instead of the knobs. Then, it will appear that the tire isn't wearing much. It isn't wearing because the casing is in contact with the ground as much as the knobs. By this time, the rear end will be sliding a lot and the danger of crashing will rise dramatically. Don't make the mistake of buying knobbies for their superior dirt traction and then running them until the center knobs have worn down to nothing.

Replacing worn knobbies is very important for two reasons. First, riding on worn tires completely destroys the process of learning. You will be forced to compensate and you will begin to develop a completely different riding technique. Your speeds will be slower, lines will be different, and your confidence will diminish. You will be riding behind the bike, reacting instead of anticipating. This is even worse than changing tire brands because instead of training to ride different tires you are now training to ride bad tires.

Second, worn tires are dangerous. Picture yourself coming into a corner a little too fast. You hit the brakes, the rear starts to fishtail, and now you are still going too fast but with less control. You compensate by squeezing the front brake lever and down you go. I have seen this happen too many times to count.

This summer some club members went out to check our dual sport roll charts for the Ride Reno 200. One appeared with a badly worn rear tire and I said something about running a baldy. He said the tire was okay because he could still climb hills. On the way back he slid into a nothing turn, grabbed the front brake and went down. When we got there he was looking at the front tire with a puzzled expression, but his problem was in the back, not the front. Fortunately, he only had a bruise.

Tires talk to you every minute you ride. Listen and learn. When they start sliding excessively, note the condition of the knobs and measure their height. Next time replace the tires before they become that worn.

Replacing tires is expensive and time consuming, but so is buying gasoline and checking the oil. It is part of the price of riding, and money well spent. You can buy 30 or 40 tires for the price of one trip to the emergency room.

TIRE SPECIFICATIONS

Most manufacturers provide detailed specifications on their websites. Here are the most common and what they mean.

Intended use. It would seem that there is a tire for every occasion. Bridgestone has dirt tires for hard, hard-to-intermediate, intermediate, soft-to-intermediate, soft, and muddy conditions. A hard-terrain tire has more knobs of softer rubber to grip hard surfaces while a soft-terrain tire has fewer knobs of harder rubber to dig into the surface while resisting the occasional rock that might tear them from the tire. In addition some tires are dead and resist bouncing, a highly desirable trait. Street offerings are equally diverse.

Hard-to-intermediate dirt tires are a good place to start for off-road riding. Try a soft-terrain tire if you ride mostly in mud or sand.

Tire size. Motorcycles are designed to work best with specific tire sizes. Changing sizes will affect handling and, in the case of the rear, overall gearing. Stick with the OEM size unless there is a good reason to change.

In the metric system the first number is the width of the tread, the second is the aspect ratio. For example a 110/100 is 110 millimeters wide and 100% as tall as it is wide. Thus, the actual dimensions are 110mm wide and 110mm tall. The alpha system uses letters followed by the aspect ratio to designate tire size. The inch sizes shown above are as wide as they are tall. A different series of numbers like 3.60, 4.20, and 4.25 indicate low profile tires.

Tire manufacturers appear to have made every effort to make sizes confusing, as shown by the chart. However, all you really need to remember is to use the size that came with the bike.

Rim size. Most dual sports have 21-inch front wheels and 17- or 18-inch rear wheels. Obviously the tires must match the wheel diameters and rim widths.

Inflation pressure. Correct inflation pressure is very important. Lower pressure gives a more comfortable ride. Higher pressure resists flats caused by banging into rocks, and overheating caused by excessive flexing of the tire carcass. Eighteen pounds of pressure is recommended for rocky desert and mountain terrain.

Short trips on pavement at speeds up to 55 mph should not be a problem at 18 psi, but always increase pressure for longer, faster trips. Manufacturers usually recommend about 22 psi, front and rear for lightweight, dual sport, highway use.

Heavier bikes need much higher pressure to avoid excessive flexing of the sidewall. Low pressure causes overheating, rapid wear, and possible tire failure. Always use the pressure in your owner's manual for highway use.

Speed rating. This is a letter on the sidewall indicating the highest recommended sustained speed. The letter M is equal to 81 mph and each

DUNLOP MOTORCYCLE TIRE SIZES

FRONT TIRES		
METRIC	**ALPHA**	**INCH**
80/90	MH90	2.50 to 2.75
90/90	MJ90	2.75 to 3.00
100/90	MM90	3.25 to 3.50
110/90	MN90	3.75 to 4.00
120/90	MR90	4.25 to 4.50
130/90	MT90	5.00 to 5.10
REAR TIRES		
METRIC	**ALPHA**	**INCH**
110/90	MP85	4.00 to 4.25
120/90	MR90	4.50 to 4.75
130/90	MT90	5.00 to 5.10
140/90	MU85/MU90	5.50 to 6.00
150/80	MV85	6.00 to 6.25
150/90	MV85	6.00 to 6.25

Running low tire pressure and hitting rocks at speed will quickly cause flats. Use at least 18 psi.

letter is 6 mph apart. For example, N is equal to 87 mph and O is equal to 93 mph. Many dirt tires have an M rating. Exceeding the speed rating can cause the tire to overheat and fail.

Load rating. This is a number following the speed rating indicating how many pounds of load the tire can carry. The total load capacity is the sum of both the front and rear tires. Weight should not be a problem for light dual sports, but could be for heavy adventure bikes, particularly if carrying a passenger. Replace tires with at least the same load rating specified by the motorcycle manufacturer.

Tread depth. Usually given in millimeters or thirty-seconds of an inch. Tall knobs dig into soft surfaces, but squirm on hard pack.

TUBES, RIM LOCKS, AND BALANCING

Tubes come in normal, heavy, and extra-heavy weights. They may be listed as street, motocross, and motocross-heavy. The heavy ones are 3 mm thick and weigh a lot. They are also hard to mount and add unsprung weight. Thin street tubes blow out after high-speed rock encounters, but regular motocross tubes are satisfactory for dual sport use.

A rim lock prevents a tire, which has been inflated to low pressure, from spinning on the rim and tearing the valve stem from the tube. A rim lock will also hold a flat tire on the rim while you ride a few miles. If you ride too far, too fast, the tire will flex, get hot and destroy itself. I saw someone finish the Greenhorn Enduro on a rim with no tire at all. He tried to run a flat too far and it melted. If possible, repair flats immediately.

It may be possible, on 250cc and 400cc bikes, to run without rim locks when tires are inflated to 18 psi. If you want to experiment, take some short rides while frequently checking the rear valve stem. If the stem moves from a vertical position to an angle, the tire is slipping and rim locks are definitely needed.

Rim locks weigh a few ounces and seriously unbalance wheels. You may not feel it on rough dirt trails, but it will really hammer you on the street. It is essential to balance rim locks with weights when dual sports are operated on highways.

Even if you don't run rim locks, it is better to balance tires that are run on the highway. Either have the dealer do it or do it yourself with stick-on lead weights. Place the axle between two supports. The wheel will then rotate until the heavy part is down; mark the place. Add weight to the opposite side until the wheel no longer goes to the heavy point, indicating that the weight you have added has canceled the imbalance. Use carpet tape to hold the weights in place and reuse them.

FINAL THOUGHTS ON TIRES

Tires have a huge impact on your safety and riding abilities. The wrong tires can throw you down on surfaces that could easily be ridden on the right tire. Select a tire type that is appropriate to the type of riding you do most frequently.

It's okay to experiment with different tires to find some that work for you, but after you are satisfied with a brand, stick with it. Check tire pressure and wear frequently. Replace your worn tires before you start sliding in every turn.

Suspension Tuning

This chapter is for those who have been riding a while and can appreciate good suspension, or for new riders who are curious about how everything works. Good suspension is the indispensable foundation to riding at higher levels, but don't get bogged down in suspension details if you only ride a few times each year.

This chapter covers:

- Suspension in Action
- Suspension Components
- The Forces of Nature
- Absorbing Bumps
- Testing and Tuning
- Final Adjustments
- Professional Tuning Services

Good suspension settings keep the wheels in contact with the ground through this rocky section.

SUSPENSION IN ACTION

Picture yourself riding a dual sport with well-tuned suspension. You hustle up a dirt road strewn with egg-size rocks. Your butt is on the seat in total comfort, while the bike absorbs the chatter. Now the eggs give way to grapefruit sized rocks and you stand in a relaxed position and flex your knees as the bike flows over the terrain.

You slow and begin picking lines more carefully while the bike dodges boulders and climbs ledges, precisely following every input. You crest a ridge and descend by a twisty sand wash to the desert below. The bike accelerates, brakes, and pivots with precision in a rushing, flowing duet of bike and rider.

The wash opens onto a desert trail with two-foot whoops. You raise your focus and accelerate to 40, then 50. You are straight and true, in complete control, and loving it.

Now picture the same scenario on a bike with poor suspension. The egg-size rocks jolt your wrists, jar your butt, and blur your vision, forcing you to stand. Wheels deflect in the grapefruit and it is impossible to hold a line. You slow to a crawl and begin dabbing with your feet.

You stall climbing a ledge and barely avoid falling. The bike is nearly unmanageable in the sand as its front wheel plows into every turn. You slow to force it around and the rear wheel spins and wanders when you try to accelerate. The suspension begins bottoming as soon as you gain speed in the whoops. The front dives and the rear kicks sideways. The best you can do is slow down and roll over each whoop individually.

Suspension has a huge impact on riding comfort, safety, speed, and endurance. The most powerful motor can't accelerate or climb without

Motocross jumps require very different settings from those that work well on rocky roads.

traction. The best cornering technique will be wasted if the wheels are skipping and unable to generate turning force. The strongest brakes won't stop if knobs can't grip. Bad suspension will knock the wheels from under you and sap your strength.

Time and money invested in suspension tuning is guaranteed to pay big dividends. Suspension that shields you from the impacts of small rocks and ruts, but resists bottoming on big hits, is the holy grail of off-road riders. There is no perfect setup that works everywhere. Your settings will, necessarily, be compromises between wheel control, plush ride, sharp steering, and stability. However, they will be *your* settings, carefully chosen to match *your* needs, not some generic adjustments chosen to please an average stranger.

You should make suspension settings to your dual sport that work well for your area and your riding style. Focus on optimizing the bike for the type of riding you do most often. If you spend most of your time in sandy whoops, tune for them and don't be alarmed when they jolt on an occasional rock. It may be necessary to change the settings when you go to a different area.

Suspension tuning is still an art and good riders experiment to find settings that work well. Always start with the factory settings and make only small adjustments as described in Chapter 5. If you are not satisfied with the results, read on.

SUSPENSION COMPONENTS

Suspension includes tires, springs, and shock absorbers. Let's start by forming a clear picture of what they do.

Tires

Tires absorb many of the impacts from rocks and ruts. As noted in the previous chapter, dual sport tire pressures should be set to at least 16 to 18 psi to protect against flats and rim damage caused by rocks. This produces a relatively rough ride and increases demands on springs and shocks.

Springs

Springs allow the wheels to travel up and down over bumps. They come in different spring rates (stiffness). For example, 20 pounds per inch means that the spring compresses one inch under a load of 20 pounds. In general, springs of heavier wire and with fewer turns per inch are stiffer.

Some springs have more coils at one end than at the other. These springs are said to be progressively wound and get stiffer as the spring compresses.

Most dual sports come with springs for "average" riders who weigh about 165 lbs. Heavier and/or faster riders need stiffer springs; lighter and/or slower riders need lighter springs.

Suspension compresses when you sit on the bike; the height of a bike with a seated rider is

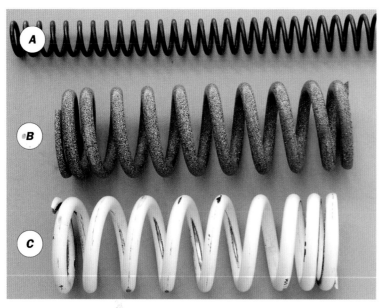

Springs should be chosen to match your weight and riding style. Spring A is a KTM fork spring; B is a stiff spring for heavy riders available from Progressive Suspension; C is a progressively wound KTM shock spring (note the difference in its coil spacing).

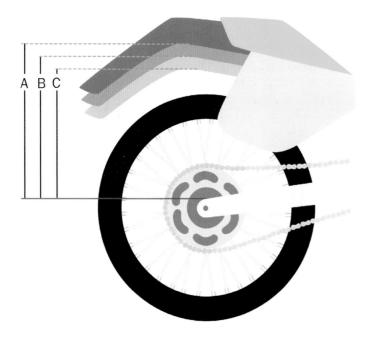

A = Height of fender above axle when suspension is fully extended.

B = Unloaded weight: height of fender when spring supports bike.

C = Ride height: height of fender when rider sits on seat.

(A – B) = Unladen Sag

(A – C) = Ride Sag

called "ride height." Most dual sports with 12 inches of suspension travel are designed to sag about four inches in the rear when a rider wearing full gear sits on them. Bikes with more or less than 12 inches of travel should sag about one third of the total available travel. The amount of sag is adjusted by compressing the spring (preload). The rear spring is preloaded with a rotating collar which is easily accessible, but the front preload is usually adjusted by spacers inside the fork.

Set the ride height properly and then measure the unladen sag (without the rider). It should usually be between one and one and a half inches. Chapter 5 covers ride height in detail.

Manufacturers do not usually provide a recommendation for front sag, but it should be about one to one and a half inches.

Increasing preload to adjust the ride height reduces unladen sag. Too little unladen sag is a clue that the spring may be too soft because it took a lot of preload to get the proper ride height, but you should test it with actual riding. The tests described later will allow you to make a final determination about spring stiffness.

Note that ride height is the most important measurement. Factories design dual sports to be stable at speed, and to turn well, at a specified ride height.

Shock Absorbers

The front shock absorbers are inside the forks and are simply called forks. The rear shock absorber sits in plain view in the rear. It is often connected to the swing arm by a link that changes leverage on the suspension. The lever increases shock and spring travel, relative to wheel travel, resulting in progressively stiffer suspension and better ability to resist big impacts.

Shock absorbers control suspension travel by forcing oil through small holes to reduce unnecessary movement. This is called damping. Without shocks the suspension would bounce up and down several times after every bump.

Shocks consist of a metal cylinder containing oil, and a piston which is attached to a shaft. Forks are partially filled with oil and the remaining space is filled with air. The rear shock has oil and nitrogen under pressure. The purpose of the

Shock absorbers control the speed of wheel travel and help keep the wheels on the ground. This disassembled unit shows the shock body on right and the shaft, piston, and valving on the left.

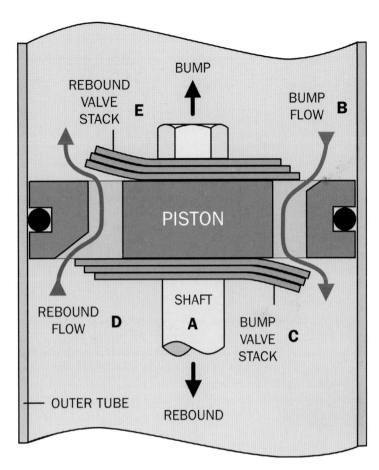

The rate of suspension compression and decompression is controlled by oil which moves through passages in the valve. In response to a bump the shock shaft A moves upward and oil B flows through holes in the valve. On sharp bumps, the compression shims C bend to allow more oil to flow. On rebound the direction of oil flow D is reversed and the rebound shims E bend. There are many variations of shock design and yours may not work exactly as shown.

pressurized nitrogen is to eliminate air bubbles which would otherwise form in the fluid.

Full compression of the shock is called "bottoming." A rubber bumper at the bottom of the shock shaft prevents metal-to-metal contact when the shock bottoms.

Oil flows through passages, called valving, as the piston moves in the shock absorber. Small passages and thick oil result in slow movement; larger passages and thinner oil result in faster movement. Actual shock movement depends on oil thickness, valving, bump shape, and motorcycle speed.

Most modern shocks use a set of thin spring washers called shims in the oil passages. Hard impacts cause the washers to flex and more oil flows. The shock can be tuned to riding conditions by carefully choosing the size and stiffness of the shims.

Dual sport shocks usually have adjustments—"clickers"—for compression and rebound. These control the amount of oil flowing through other small passages which bypass the valving. Adjusting the clickers makes small changes which may allow you to adjust the shocks to suit your riding style.

Compression damping controls the upward travel of the wheel and should be adjusted to your riding conditions. Rebound damping controls downward movement and should be adjusted to match the stiffness of the spring. The goal is controlled travel which smoothly absorbs irregularities in the road surface.

This picture shows components of aftermarket fork valving. The unit on the bottom is the complete assembly; the parts on the top are from a disassembled unit. The shims on the right and left flank a part called the valve. This one is a Race Tech Gold Valve which offers greater oil flow and better adjustability through changing the shims. Race Tech installs the parts and chooses shims that match your riding style. They also offer kits which you can install yourself.

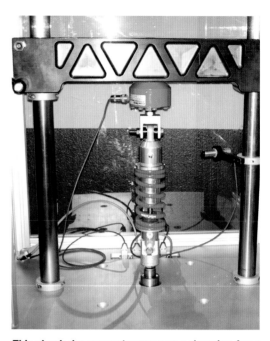

This shock dynamometer measures damping force at different shaft speeds. A motor below the table forces the shock through its stroke and the apparatus at the top measures force.

All of the suspension components interact with each other; some types of adjustments require disassembly of the forks and shocks. This is why there is a thriving business for people who tune suspensions.

The Relation Between Shocks and Springs

Because shock absorbers resist motion, they also help springs absorb bumps. More compression damping is similar to stiffer springs. However, springs and shocks have different functions. Springs allow the wheels to travel up and down; shocks control the speed of wheel travel.

Trying to compensate for springs that are too soft with stiff compression damping may produce a jolty ride. Suspension settings that prevent good tire contact are uncomfortable and can be dangerous.

THE FORCES OF NATURE

Motorcycle suspension must be tuned to balance mass, inertia, momentum, acceleration, and weight. The mass of a motorcycle is determined by the number and structure of its atoms. Mass determines inertia, momentum, and weight.

Inertia is the tendency of mass to remain in one spot unless moved by force.

Momentum is the tendency of a moving mass to continue moving in the same direction, at the same speed.

Acceleration is a change in velocity per unit of time.

Weight is the effect of gravity acting on mass. It is what causes the suspension to sag.

Dual sport suspension travel is caused by acceleration and momentum. Wheels, brakes, rear sprocket, and part of the forks and swing arm are unsprung because they are supported by the ground. They total about 20 percent of the mass of a 250 pound dual sport. The rest of the package—frame, motor, gas tank, and rider—is sprung, because it is supported by the springs.

The sprung mass is free to travel on its suspension, but its substantial momentum resists movement as the ground pushes against the wheels which have less momentum. As a result, the wheels make big movements while the rest of the motorcycle makes small movements.

It is wheel acceleration, not mere movement, that causes suspension to compress or expand. Slowly rolling a motorcycle up a long ramp hardly moves the suspension at all, because upward wheel travel per unit of time is low. This slow, constant upward motion allows the motorcycle to rise at the same rate as its wheels.

In contrast, sharp bumps cause rapid wheel movement. Now, the momentum of the sprung mass resists upward forces coming from the wheels and the suspension moves.

Shock damping force increases as the speed of up and down wheel movement gets faster. The rear wheel is attached to the shock shaft through the swing arm. As these parts rise they push on the shock shaft, which in turn pushes the piston up forcing oil through the valving. The rate at which the shaft travels is known as shaft speed.

High shaft speeds push more oil through the valving, but there is a limit to the number of oil molecules that can flow through a given size valve. The faster the shaft moves, the more the oil resists it. On sharp bumps the wheel wants to move faster than the shock will allow and the entire motorcycle, rather than just the wheel, will be forced upward. This is felt by the rider as a sharp jolt. By carefully choosing the valve shims so they bend with increasing shaft speed, manufacturers attempt to keep the oil flowing and prevent jolts.

Some of the shock oil bypasses the main valving and the clickers allow you to adjust the amount of this flow and dial in the suspension for various riding conditions. However, there is a limit to what you can do with clickers. Even when fully open, they may not allow enough oil to flow to prevent jolts. Conversely they may allow the suspension to become too loose to adequately control wheel movement. It may be necessary to change the valve shims to get the ride you want. Note that this explanation has used the rear wheel as an example. The same concepts apply to the front, but some of the components are different.

Large rounded bumps produce a lot of wheel travel, but relatively slow shaft speed. Small square edged rocks produce less wheel travel, but high shaft velocity. This makes it difficult to get suspension settings that work well everywhere—particularly for dual sports that are operated in conditions ranging from big sand whoops to high-speed rocky roads.

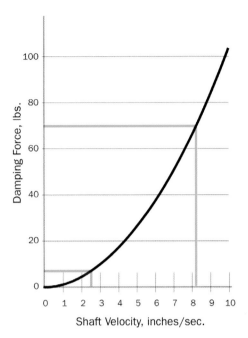

The graph shows damping force versus shaft velocity. The vertical axis shows damping force and the horizontal axis shows shock shaft speed. Resistance actually increases as the square of shaft velocity. Note that damping increases with shaft speed, not the amount of wheel travel.

THE CHALLENGE OF ABSORBING BUMPS

Highways are smooth and place few demands on suspension. The springs on cars and trucks are chosen to support the vehicle. The shocks are chosen to match the springs—and that's the end of it.

However, dual sport damping is much more complex. Here are some factors that must be taken into account when setting up a dual sport suspension.

Bump shape. Rounded bumps move the suspension slower than square bumps.

Bump height. Taller bumps move suspension farther.

Bike speed. Higher bike speeds move suspension faster.

Bump spacing. Closely spaced bumps give suspension less time to return to a neutral position.

Large, rounded bumps give the suspension plenty of time to react, but they may also fully compress the spring resulting in bottoming. Small sharp bumps give suspension very little time to react and produce jolty, skipping action.

▶ CONTROLLING WHEEL TRAVEL OVER A BUMP

Imagine a wheel hitting a three-inch square-edged bump at 30 mph.

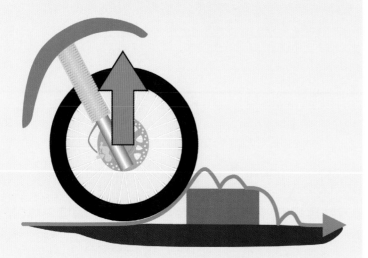

Here is the sequence of events that occur in about one-hundredth of a second:

- ▶ The tire slams into the edge of the bump and deforms.
- ▶ The wheel rolls up to the top of the bump.
- ▶ The suspension tries to move upward at about 22 feet per second, but compression damping limits the speed of travel.
- ▶ The bump then forces the entire motorcycle up because the suspension can't react fast enough, and the rider feels a jolt.
- ▶ The wheel and attached suspension weigh about 25 pounds and acquire their own upward momentum.
- ▶ They clear the top of the bump and bounce off the ground.
- ▶ On the other side of the bump, gravity and the spring force the wheel down, and rebound damping slows the rate of descent.

Now imagine a motorcycle equipped with "magic" shocks. They reduce damping for the fast up-stroke allowing the spring to absorb the jolt. At the top of the bump, the magic shocks increase damping and prevent the wheel from leaving the ground. Finally, they rebound quickly to return the wheel to the ground on the back side of the bump. In this scenario, spring and shock work as a team to completely isolate the rider from the bump. In the real world, suspension tuners seek compromises which match the terrain and motorcycle speed. ∎

Large rounded bumps give the suspension plenty of time to compress, but smaller, square-edged bumps can move wheels faster than shock absorbers can react.

Compression and Rebound Settings

Compression settings must match the ground. Good compression settings prevent bottoming on big bumps, and also prevent wheel bounce on small, sharp bumps. However, excessive compression damping doesn't allow springs to move far enough.

Rebound settings must match the springs. Good rebound settings allow wheels to return to neutral position between bumps. Too much rebound damping reduces downward travel and causes suspension to "pack" in the up position. Too little rebound damping causes the motorcycle to float away from the wheels.

Imagine a motorcycle with too much compression and rebound damping. The first figure on the next page shows its wheel traveling over a bump. The gray area is the ground and the green line is the path of the wheel. On the up-stroke, excessive compression damping causes the wheel to plow into the face of the bump (the red area) rather than climbing over. This will feel harsh and the wheel may start to deflect to the side. Excessive rebound damping prevents the wheel from following the bump on the other side.

The next figure shows insufficient damping. On the up-stroke, momentum carries the wheel past the top of the bump and it flies off the ground as shown by the red area. This makes the bike feel plush, but also vague and unstable. Too little rebound damping allows the wheel to return quickly to the ground after the bump, but the motorcycle does not move in harmony with the wheel—also producing a vague feel.

Excessive damping causes the wheel to plow into bumps and deflect. Because the suspension can't move fast enough to follow the terrain, it transfers force to the bike and rider causing a jolting ride.

Insufficient damping allows the wheel to skip off the ground. This keeps the tire from gripping the surface and makes it difficult to accelerate, turn, and stop.

In summary, both compression and rebound settings should be adjusted to keep the wheels in good contact with the ground and the sprung mass moving at slower speed, and in harmony with the wheels. There are infinite possibilities for size and spacing of bumps. What works well in one area may work poorly in another and it may be necessary to alter the clicker settings to match changing conditions. For example, use one setting for rocky roads in the mountains and another for sandy areas in the desert.

TESTING AND TUNING YOUR OWN SUSPENSION

Suspension tuning can be confusing and time consuming. I recently bought a used bike that was designed for racing, but did not work for my style of dual sporting.

It shook its head on choppy straights, turned in too quickly in the sand, and bottomed in the whoops. In back, I cured the problem with a lower profile rear tire to increase the steering angle, plus stiffer springs, softer valving, and less preload. In front I used stiffer springs, less preload, and thinner oil.

This project got me out of the house on many cold winter days, but it was not something most people would enjoy. I made the mistake of too much fiddling without enough thinking and it took nearly 1,000 miles of testing before I got it right.

When you decide to set up your suspension, the first big question is whether you can get

▶ **TIPS TO GUIDE YOUR SUSPENSION TUNING**

- ▸ Quickly make bold changes to evaluate the suspension. If you pass the tests, make further small adjustments to get everything balanced.
- ▸ Make notes about the settings and results. They will save you time now and in the long run. Keep them in a safe place for future reference. Don't give suspension a few clicks in the garage. Do the adjusting on the trail where you can immediately test the results.
- ▸ Suspension breaks-in as you ride. Use the factory settings and ride a few hundred miles before fine tuning.
- ▸ Settle on tires and air pressure before any serious suspension adjusting. The tires and suspension work together and changing tire brands or air pressure will affect your ride. ∎

satisfactory results with factory components or whether you need professional help. The turning test, spring test, rebound test, and compression test provide the needed information.

The Turning Test

After you have chosen tires and air pressure, and ridden a few hundred miles with factory settings, the next thing to do is test the steering geometry. Any changes you make to the preload or springs will change ride height and affect steering geometry. Start by making sure that ride height is properly adjusted and the damping clickers are in the factory recommended positions as described in Chapter 5.

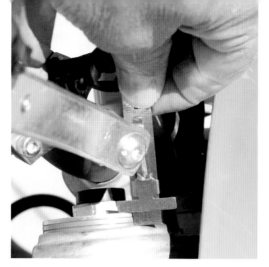

Experiment with different amounts of fork tube height in the triple clamps, and determine where your bike steers best. A few millimeters can make a noticeable difference.

Find a section of choppy road or trail and ride through it several times, gradually increasing your speed into your comfort zone. (Here, comfort zone refers to the riding speed at which you feel in good control of the bike, not the way the suspension feels.) If you have a steering damper set it to full loose. The bike should track straight and true without headshake.

Next, find a turn with a small soft berm. Ride through it several times, gradually increasing speed into your comfort zone. Experienced off-road riders have well-established preferences for how a bike should steer. Some like to dive into turns and slide the bike sharply around the corner with the rear wheel; others prefer to carve smooth arcs. The important point is that the bike should steer the way you want it to without having to fight it all day.

Make some notes about what you feel. If the bike has head shake and/or your front wheel turns excessively to the inside your steering angle is too steep. Any further adjustments that lower the front or raise the back will make the problem worse.

You may be able to compensate for headshake with the steering damper, but the bike still may not turn the way you want it to turn. Dropping the fork tubes in the triple clamps or switching to a lower profile rear tire may cure both problems.

Riding fast with headshake could put you down. If needed, go to the dealer and get advice on how to cure the problem before testing further.

The steering angle is not steep enough if the front wheel has a tendency to push outside on turns. Any further adjustments which raise the front or lower the back will make this problem worse. You may be able to correct pushing by raising the fork tubes in the clamps.

Small changes can make big handling differences when raising or lowering fork tubes to correct steering problems. Experiment in 5 millimeter increments and test again.

When steering is acceptable, you are ready to move on.

The Spring Test

It is very important to get the spring rates right before making further adjustments to compression and rebound. Find a test section of straight whooped trail. Two-foot whoops about 15 feet apart are perfect. If there are no whoops available, find a two-foot dip.

Ride through the whoops or dip in the standing position using the techniques explained in Chapter 9. Start slowly and increase your speed gradually on successive runs until you are in the comfort zone.

You should feel the suspension compress without bottoming hard. Bottoming will feel like the suspension has stopped compressing—it has—and the bike has come down hard against the ground. You may also start to deflect from your chosen path.

These sharp, closely spaced whoops would make a good location for a whoop test.

The front and back should compress about the same amount. Don't try to go faster if you start to bottom hard or if the front end dives severely. Trying to go faster could cause a crash.

Make notes about what you felt. For example, "The front end dove and bottomed" or "The bike traveled level and tracked straight as fast as I wanted to go." If one or both ends start to bottom before you reach your comfort zone, the springs may not be stiff enough. If you never bottom, no matter how fast you ride, the springs could be too stiff. The ideal is to bottom a little on the biggest whoops or dips. More compression damping may prevent bottoming, but is likely to cause a harsh ride in the next test.

As the forks compress they also compress the air above the shock oil. Within limits you can add or subtract oil. High oil levels leave less air in the fork tubes and this has the same effect as a stiffer fork spring.

If you bottom excessively, check with the dealer or one of the companies that specialize in suspension to determine the proper spring rate for a person of your weight, riding dual sport. While you are at it, ask what they know about setting up suspension on your model. If you change springs, you will need to remove the rear shock and disassemble the forks. It might be a good idea to send them to an expert now, and get everything fixed at once.

If you replace the fork springs yourself, be sure to set the fork oil level at the proper height. The owner's manual should show how to do this.

At this point I will assume you have the correct springs and fork oil level.

Rebound Test

Starting with the factory recommended rebound clicker settings, ride through the same section you used for the spring test and note how the bike feels. Too much rebound damping will prevent the springs from recovering before the next dip. Too little rebound damping will cause the front to have a high, floaty feeling and the rear to slap you in the butt. You should apply as little rebound damping as possible without inducing the high, floaty feeling. On bikes with stock springs this is likey to be very near the factory recommendation.

This suspension, which works well in rocky conditions, is too soft for whoops. Going faster will cause the bike to deflect sideways and could lead to a fall.

Try reducing the rebound damping if your bike does not feel floaty or slappy. Start from the factory setting, go one half of the way toward minimum rebound damping, and test again. If it is worse, go back halfway toward the recommended setting. Work in halves either up or down until both front and rear ends feel good. Do not change these settings again during these preliminary tests. Stiffer springs and more preload may require more rebound damping, but leave the settings alone for now.

Compression Damping Test

Now find a section of straight road or trail strewn with egg-size rocks or small choppy ruts. We'll call this the chop test. Starting with the factory recommended compression clicker cettings, ride in a seated position using the riding techniques explained in Chapter 9. Start slowly and increase your speed gradually on successive runs until you are in your comfort zone. The suspension should absorb the rocks without causing your vision to blur.

Try turning on a rough surface. The wheels should follow the ground and generate good turning force. Your goal is to find a good balance between a plush ride and good wheel contact.

If the bike feels good, you are finished with testing. A few final clicks will let you find the ideal ride.

The most frequent complaint from dual sport riders is harshness. Dual sports are often operated at high speed on choppy or rocky roads. If the ride is harsh, try to determine whether the

This road would make a good location for the chop test.

Forks must be partially disassembled prior to setting the oil level. Preload is often adjusted by adding spacers above the springs, but some bikes have external adjustments.

problem is in front, in back, or both. The front will hammer your wrists and the back will pound your butt. Make notes about what you felt.

The following adjustment instructions apply to harshness caused by too much compression damping. Use the same procedure, but adjust in the opposite direction if you have too little damping.

Work on one end at a time—front or back—and make notes as you go. Start with the end that feels the worst. From the factory setting, go one half of the way to minimum compression damping. For example, if the forks have 20 clicks of total adjustment and the factory setting is 10 clicks, go 5 clicks softer. Now test again.

Continue working in halves, either softer or stiffer, until it feels better. For example, if it now feels too soft, go two clicks harder.

Then go to the other end of the bike (front or rear) and repeat the process.

Stop if you get within a couple of clicks from minimum without curing the problems. In this case fiddling with the compression adjusters will not cure the problem.

Be aware that a problem that appears to come from one end of the bike may actually start at the other end. Also, note that you need enough compression damping to prevent excessive wheel bounce and maintain good ground contact.

You can reduce the rear preload a turn to see if it cures a harsh rear end, but if it doesn't, your shock may need revalving. The shock is filled with pressurized nitrogen and needs the attention of a qualified technician.

Do-it-Yourself Forks

If adjusting the clickers doesn't cure harshness, you can make further adjustments to the forks. To do so may require you to remove the wheel and fork tubes every time. This can easily get into a lengthy cycle of experiments. It may be better to send the forks to a specialist who can make all of the right moves in one pass.

Here is what to do if you have harsh forks on the chop test with minimum compression damping. Reduce fork preload 5 mm, lower oil height 10 mm, and change to a lower viscosity oil all at one time. If this does not cure a harsh front end, you probably need revalving.

If you now pass the chop test, repeat the whoop test to make sure you are not too soft. Proceed with caution, working from low speed to higher. It may take more than one attempt to get everything balanced.

FINAL ADJUSTMENTS

The tests described above are designed to determine quickly whether your suspension can be adjusted satisfactorily using the factory supplied springs and valving. If not, you need professional help.

Even if you get good results it will probably be necessary to make final adjustments and to change them as conditions change and your skills improve.

Your objective is to get the wheels and motorcycle traveling in unison without excessive harshness. Magazine shootouts often talk about plush suspension, but that is not the only consideration. You must be able to feel the ground through the suspension in order to judge correctly how to accelerate, stop and turn.

When wheels move downward, the full weight of the motorcycle should follow. Imagine entering a turn and deciding to use the side of a small rut to hold your line. You need to feel wheel contact with the rut and, simultaneously, the motorcycle must actually settle into it. A motorcycle that is wallowing on loose suspension settings, rising when it should be falling, will not stay in the rut or any other place you want it to go.

Suspension settings are always compromises. Do not focus on a single characteristic. Always seek a balance of comfort and feel that works best for your riding conditions.

PROFESSIONAL TUNING SERVICES

If these adjustments don't work, it is time to seek professional help. Suspension tuners offer three basic services.

Oil Change. Suspension oil loses viscosity (becomes thinner) and accumulates metal shavings over time. Damping deteriorates as the oil changes its character.

Racers change suspension oil very frequently, but dual sport riders are less demanding. I ride about 10,000 miles a year and change shock and fork oil annually. My suspension always feels better after an oil change.

Rebuild. The suspension is disassembled and any worn or damaged parts are replaced in addition to replacing the fluid.

Revalve. The oil control shims, and possibly the springs, are changed to match riding conditions. The tuner selects the proper oil and level, and specifies initial settings for the clickers.

There are many approaches to suspension tuning. Race Tech is very scientific. They do extensive testing and offer training to owners and shop technicians.

Following their basic premise that stock oil passages are too small, Race Tech offers Gold Valves, which are said to increase oil flow. The valves come with an instructional video describing how to install them, but you can also have a technician install them. Race Tech products have worked well for me on several different bikes and their website is very informative.

Some suspension modification are easy for owners to make, but for more complex changes you should consider working with suspension specialists, such as these two companies.

Precision Concepts modifies the stock suspension components while other tuners work primarily with valve shims, oil viscosity, and height. All suspension tuners recommend initial settings and most offer after-service advice. Some say that they will revalve if you are not satisfied.

The classified section of Cycle News always carries several ads from suspension tuners; more can be found on the Web. I have recently found a local guy who does good work with short turnaround times; ask at the shops if they know someone in your area with suspension expertise.

Different combinations of spring rates, oil height, viscosity, and valving may give similar results. Try to find someone who has experience setting up your model of bike for dual sport. Ask questions and compare answers before deciding whom to use.

After you have selected a tuner, you must remove the components, take or ship them to the shop, wait for the work to be finished, and reinstall them. Send a copy of your notes with the shocks and make sure the technician knows what you want. You will still need to make final adjustments when you get the suspension back from the specialist. Use the tests and adjustments described above to get it perfect.

Section 3

RIDING, MAINTENANCE, AND TRAILSIDE REPAIR

Dual sport can be an intimate, addictive union of man, machine, and terrain. As one long time rider put it, "I think of nothing beyond control of the motorcycle in the present. Work, chores, money, problems, sense of time, and even family recede in my dust. I am totally immersed in the experience of speed and control. Road riding, touring, and cruising don't offer anything close."

No other form of motorized recreation covers a wider range of terrain. Nowhere does the rider exercise more physical control with subtle shifts of weight and balance. No other machine is as versatile and responsive.

The very things that make motorcycling so exciting and absorbing can also lead to serious injury. Pages of motorcycle magazines are adorned with pictures of professional racers displaying incredible skill and bravery—road racers at insane lean angles, motocrossers jumping huge obstacles, and cross country racers pounding through the rocks at night. However, the same publications are also filled with stories about injuries—the popular favorite out for the season; the star returning after a long rehabilitation; and the

people raising money for a young boy whose prospects are doubtful.

Guts and glory are the very essence of professional racing, but have little to do with dual sport. There are no big salaries for stars, no prizes, and no championships. Dual sport is about fun, companionship, exploration, and adventure. The goal is to maximize enjoyment and satisfaction while avoiding injury and equipment damage. The keys are safe practices, basic skills, and preparation.

Safety starts in your mind. Concentration, focus, and the right attitude are the primary defenses against injury. Dual sport riders must develop basic skills to deal with commonly encountered terrain and obstacles. We must understand how to use the controls, where to look, how to choose good lines, and how to ride in seated and standing positions. Because dual sports travel at high speed, successful riders must always be mentally ahead of the bike, anticipating rather than reacting to situations.

A well-maintained motorcycle is another key to successful dual sporting. It is possible to fix a bike on the trail, but why would anyone want to do

Success on a trip like this depends on good riding skills and a well-prepared machine.

it there? Good maintenance keeps your bike young, minimizes emergency repairs, and keeps you smiling, not wondering how to get home. Despite the best maintenance, bikes will still have problems—flat tires, boiled brakes, and lost bolts. Basic mechanical knowledge and a few tools will usually get them running again quickly.

How can you develop a safe attitude? What is a good seated riding position? What is the right way to use the controls? How can you spot safe lines? What is the quickest way to fix flats? What should you do when the bike stops running?

Section 3 has the answers you need.

Put Your Mind in Gear

Chapter 4 covered helmets and body armor, but your brain is a much better defense against injury: it can keep you from hitting things. Putting your mind in the right place and keeping it there are the most important keys to safe riding. This chapter covers:

- Mental Attitude
- Concentration
- Focus
- Anticipation

Our focus here is on dirt techniques; there are many good sources of information about street riding that you can find elsewhere. The Motorcycle Safety Foundation has excellent courses that teach the basics. They are available in most cities and well worth the cost; take one if you are new to street riding. Read the *MSF Guide to Motorcycling Excellence*. Their website is at msf-usa.org.

Your most important safety device is inside your helmet.

MENTAL ATTITUDE

Humans have marvelous bodies, adapted to thrive in risky environments. We have the coordination, balance, and reactions to fly stunt planes, kayak spring runoff, surf big waves, and ski steep chutes. We can use these wonderful abilities to manage the risks of dual sporting. Good mental attitude is the place to begin.

I have a little ritual of getting dressed before rides and I always do the same things in the same order—socks, riding pants, and then boots. While dressing I reflect on the day's priorities to get my mind in the right place. These priorities are always the same: return home alive, avoid injury, and don't damage the bike.

All other considerations are secondary. The objective is always to maximize the fun, adventure, and comradeship of dual sporting while minimizing its potential danger.

Dual sport is not competition. There are no prizes, trophies, or points for finishing first. It is always nice to feel competent—maybe that you are better than your riding buddies—but there are no first places or scores. Typically you will do well in some sections and worse in others. There is nothing to be gained by riding over your head or taking chances.

Skill, Not Guts

Skilled riders practice at least two or three times a week, every week, for many years. Don't make the mistake of thinking that you're an expert after 10 or 20 rides. This can be the most dangerous phase of learning to ride. You know how to twist the throttle, but you probably don't have the skills to save your butt when an unexpected log, dropoff, or pickup truck appears. Keep the speed down if you only ride occasionally.

Long ago, I belonged to a motorcycle club in Southern California. Once a month we went to Jawbone Canyon or Dove Springs in the desert, but I didn't have many other opportunities to ride in the dirt. We all tried to beat each other on club rides—the fastest speed, the biggest hill, and the gnarliest rocks.

On Mondays, I was often limping and occasionally on crutches. I was making the rookie mistake of riding over my head. Another clubmember joined a weekly motocross series and rode every week. His skills improved rapidly, while mine stayed about the same.

In my younger days, I would push myself and get angry about screwups—bear down, press on, and gut it out. Now, I see I that was foolish. Bearing down tightens muscles, making them rigid and unresponsive. Pressing on when you lack basic skills is the way to get hurt. Guts show well in movies, but in real life brains and skill win. Relax and think about the next section of trail, not the last mistake.

Note also that some heavyweight dual sports have 100 horsepower and a top speed of well over 100 miles per hour. Use this power off-highway with extreme caution. In the dirt, a fast moving 400-pound bike, loaded with accessories and gear takes a *very* long distance to stop.

Comfort Zone

Every rider has a comfort zone—speed and conditions that feel right. Skills, development drills, and frequent riding within your comfort zone are the best paths to improvement. Exceeding your comfort zone will actually slow your learning process.

Let's say you are having trouble riding smoothly down steep hills. You keep locking the front brake, sliding into ruts, and falling. Practicing on ever steeper hills will only lead to more spectacular falls. Instead, back off, find some level ground, and practice modulating the front and rear brakes independently and together.

Develop competence on smooth roads before moving to loose, rocky surfaces.

Then repeat the exercises in an area with ruts. Then go to small hills and practice some more. When you get back to the steep hill your troubles will be history.

Maybe you want to learn feet-up two-wheel slides in turns. Don't practice by blasting into corners at speeds you can't handle. Instead, take a long ride on smooth, curvy dirt roads at moderate speed. Feel the tires start to slide just a little. At the end of the day you will be much better at sliding and your skin will be intact. You will always make safer and better progress if you stay in your comfort zone and gain experience as opposed to forcing yourself to do things beyond your abilities.

Your comfort zone will move to higher speeds over more difficult terrain in proportion to the amount of riding you do. Spend part of each ride practicing specific skills and some time riding near the edge of the comfort zone. You will soon be riding better and safer.

Riding with Others

Riding with buddies is one of the best things about dual sporting. Eggs and pancakes at the Wigwam Restaurant, stories and jokes at rest stops, and a cold beer at Sparky's after the ride are the savory sauce that turns a great day into perfection.

At the same time, don't allow friends to change your attitude. Some will be faster, tempting you to ride out of your comfort zone. Resist the urge; keep within your skills and improve at your own pace. Some other riders will be slower; do not become bored and inattentive because of their snail pace. All will make dust; drop back and stay out of it as much as possible.

When I ride with my buddies we have a system. We let the faster guys go ahead and wait for dust to settle. If we are of equal ability we take turns leading and enjoying the clear air. At turns, each person is responsible for the rider behind, waiting for him to arrive before making the turn. This allows us to have a good social experience while reducing risks.

Finding a common comfort zone can be a real problem when new and experienced riders get together. The old hands are at ease with speeds and surfaces that newer riders simply can't

These riders are waiting at a turn for followers who have dropped back to let the dust settle.

handle. If you are new, find other newbies and ride with them.

Riding alone increases risk. Mechanical problems or injuries in a remote place are always possible. Do not ride alone until you are a seasoned rider. Even then, you will be safer with others.

Strong Body, Sound Mind

Use dual sport as a reason to exercise and stay in shape. Riding long distances over rough ground is mentally and physically demanding. Going fast on trails is strenuous aerobic activity. Dual sport riders don't need to be body builders, but they will have more fun when they are in decent physical condition.

Jog, play racquetball, ride a bicycle, or use a stair master, and keep your weight down. Abstain from alcohol and drugs when riding. Wait for a better day if you are hung over, haven't slept well, or are angry and upset.

CONCENTRATION

Concentration is simply paying attention. Highways are designed, maintained, and patrolled to create safe environments, but dirt trails are different. No maintenance crews patrol for rocks, no one marks danger points with signs or traffic cones. There are no lane markers, nor standards for width, curve radius, surface conditions, or sight lines. You are totally responsible for your own safety. On the highway you can daydream or fiddle with the radio, confident that the surface ahead will remain paved.

Riding with friends is fun, but don't let them tempt you from your comfort zone.

Almost anything could be waiting over the next rise on a backcountry road.

On the dirt anything is possible. Rocks, logs, ruts, holes, and washouts are the norm, not the exception. Seeing and avoiding danger takes total, unbroken concentration.

Picture yourself on an undulating desert two-track, riding at 45 mph and scanning ahead for danger. You crest a small rise and suddenly see a steeply cut washout strewn with boulders. You know that hitting it at 45 will be disastrous, but 15 mph in the standing position will be safe.

It takes about a quarter-second to react and hit the brakes, another half-second to stand, stabilize the bike, and get maximum efficiency from braking. It takes another half-second slow to 15 mph. The total elapsed time is about 1.25 seconds. You will have gone more than 100 feet, but slowed to a safe speed just before impact.

Now imagine what could happen if you look at pretty clouds and fail to see the washout until it is only 50 feet away. The bike will plow into it with brakes locked at 35 mph, and you'll go down.

Stop riding when you are looking at views or adjusting your GPS; concentrate on the road or trail when you are moving.

Never plunge into things you can't see. Dust could hide a ten foot drop; brush could hide an ATV, and trees could conceal an oncoming pickup. Slow down when you can't see.

FOCUS

Focus is what you see clearly. We seem to see everything at once, but this is only because our eyes focus very quickly. We really see only one thing at a time in sharp focus. Everything else—peripheral vision—is slightly blurred. When riding we must focus on objects which are potentially most dangerous, using peripheral vision for the rest.

Street Focus

City streets are filled with traffic and things that move. I used to ride in downtown San Francisco at rush hour. What a zoo! Streets changed directions, lights changed, lanes started and ended abruptly. People walked against the lights at intersections and darted from sidewalks in the middle of the block. Drivers changed lanes without caring who was in them, ran red lights, and drove as if beating the commute was more important than living another day. Busses pulled from stops with total disregard of anything in their path—move over or die. In the commute, focus meant tracking multiple moving targets and taking instant evasive action.

Dirt Focus

Off-road focus is very different. You must *not* track most potential hazards. Rocks, ruts, and washouts are stationary but you are moving. There is no point in tracking one rock that isn't going anywhere while you are speeding toward another. See, react, and focus quickly on the next threat. This takes practice and deliberate effort.

How much would this hurt on a dual sport?

Look where you want to go because you will go where you look.

The diagram below divides vision into three areas: focus, ground peripheral, and horizon peripheral. It is intended as an explanation, not a rigid rule of where to look. Keep your focus relaxed and let it flow with the terrain.

Focus is the area of greatest visual acuity. It has the best resolution and sees the smallest details. Focus should be directed at the lines you intend to ride—the places your wheels will actually travel. Use it to make sure the dirt is firm, the rocks are unlikely to roll from under your wheels, and the shadows are free of ruts.

Ground peripheral vision has less resolution and should be used to maintain awareness of objects you have chosen to avoid. For example, you focus on a rock, decide to avoid it and then focus on a clear path. As you change focus from rock to path, the rock remains in your peripheral vision and you are aware of its location.

Horizon peripheral vision keeps you aware of surroundings such as the horizon, a ridge, or peak. It can also alert you to possible changes in terrain such as a transition from sandy to rocky, and moving hazards such as other vehicles.

Know Before You Go

Have a clear picture of where you are going and what to do when you get there. You are always going to some point at the limit of your ability to focus on hazards. On a long straight road, the limit of your focus might be a half-mile away; on a tight twisty trail it might be only a few yards away. On the road, your next action might be to maintain speed and direction; on the trail, it might be to brake, plant the wheels on a bank, and turn.

Reserve your sharpest focus to identify hazards, but don't fix on one obstacle while speeding toward others.

You will go where you look, so look where you want to go. Don't fix your vision on things you want to avoid because you will be drawn to them as if they were magnets. All of your subconscious instincts work to keep you riding on the path that you can clearly see and work against riding into things you can't see. If you look at a big rock rather than clear ground to the side, you will most likely hit the rock even though your conscious mind is trying to avoid it. Look at the clear path you want to ride and that is where you will go.

The photo sequence on this page shows a blind corner from both approaches. Don't be tempted to ride on the wrong side; you never know what awaits around the bend.

If one rider is on the wrong side of the road, both of you will be startled and steer to the inside because it's the only clear path. Simultaneously, you will both hit the brakes and start to slide. A collision will be inevitable. Stay on your side of the road and slow down for blind corners.

I still remember the terror of coming around a curve, seeing a lifted jeep, sliding under the bumper and bouncing off a tire. It happened more than thirty years ago and the image remains vivid. Slow down whenever the next section of road or trail is hidden. You can't focus on hazards if they can't be seen.

ANTICIPATION

Dirt riding is a series of challenges—turns, rocks, ruts, holes, logs, hills, etc. In addition, turns on loose, slippery, and uneven surfaces are challenges because your tires could easily slip.

Anticipation is predicting how the motorcycle will react to these challenges and positioning the bike and your body to deal with them—before you reach them. Anticipation is the key to traveling safely at speed. If you are not mentally ahead, you will be physically behind. Your weight will be in the wrong place, and you will spend the day recovering from one mistake after another. Eventually, you will fall. Never ride behind the bike; never become its servant. Your job is to lead. Get mentally ahead and stay there.

You must train yourself to look beyond the ground below so that hazards can't surprise you. This may sound obvious, but isn't as easy as it sounds. Everyone has a tendency to focus on

Narrow, winding dirt roads are dual sport heaven—accelerate, brake, slide, and turn. They are also filled with blind curves. This picture shows a typical turn: blind and rocky on the inside. The proper technique is to slow down and ride the smoother dirt on the outside.

This picture shows the same curve from the other direction. You might be tempted to ride the outside line because it's smoother, faster, and you can see around the corner better, even though you will be on the wrong side of the road. Don't do it!

This curve is still blind—even on the wrong side of the road. This picture shows where you might first see someone coming toward you. The red lines show the paths the bikes will follow.

Rocks don't move; keep looking where you want to go.

specific, dangerous objects like rocks or ruts. While you are focused on one object, the motorcycle keeps moving and the next hazard rushes at you—unseen. It takes deliberate effort and practice to keep looking ahead.

The Steps of Anticipation

There are three steps to anticipation. They will be distinct if you are new to dirt riding. Later, as you gain experience and skill, they will blend into a continuous flow.

Recognition is becoming aware of something that could be a challenge. Every hour of experience you gain increases your ability to recognize hazards. Awareness usually comes from seeing things, but experienced riders use all possible clues. For example, a rocky slope above a road is a clue that rocks may have rolled into the way. A dip in the ridgeline is a clue that there may be a ravine or gully ahead.

Decision is choosing how you will deal with the challenge. The most common choice is simple avoidance. All manner of rocks, ruts, and slippery surfaces can be avoided simply by riding around them. Some obstacles completely block the trail and you must decide whether to ride over them or stop and look for a way around. If the challenge is a turn, you must decide which path will give the wheels maximum support and grip.

Preparation is getting the bike and your body positioned correctly to perform the action you have selected. In all cases, it is best to approach challenges in perfect control of the motorcycle. It is much better to reduce speed, get centered, balanced, positioned, and then accelerate smoothly away, than it is to approach out of shape. You will actually ride faster because you make fewer mistakes. You will also burn less energy and be much safer.

Note that it is critical to approach obstacles head on if you choose to ride over them. A motorcycle will roll right across big rocks and ledges if you hit them squarely. Glancing blows can easily throw you down. You must prepare by squaring the bike to the obstacle and slowing to a speed that can be handled by the suspension.

Banging into things, not properly anticipated, is a sure sign that you are riding beyond your abilities. If you have more than two surprises in a row, stop and think about what is happening and how to correct it. Are you looking in the wrong place, blinded by dust, or going too fast? The little scares you get are warnings. Do not ignore them; something bad is about to happen.

Anticipation at High Levels of Skill

You will not usually notice the steps of anticipation when you see professional racers on television or at live events. The overwhelming impression will be of blinding speed and incredible bravery, but it is anticipation that allows them to go so fast without crashing.

A few years ago, in late April, I was sitting on Union Street waiting for the first row of the Virginia City Grand Prix to appear. This race, which starts downtown in an historic Nevada mining city high on Mt. Davidson, has been popular with club racers for decades. It's not part of a national series and top professionals usually ignore it, but experts and amateurs from northern California and Nevada come like bees to honey. This year's spectators were in for a special treat because Shane Esposito, one of the top professional desert riders, was entered.

Shane, who eventually finished several minutes ahead of second place, was easy to spot in the pits. He was the one posing in front of the Kawasaki banner while his mechanics made final adjustments to a motorcycle that was already meticulously prepared. The rest of the entrants were removing well used gas cans, battered tool chests, and frayed lawn chairs from dented pickups.

The race started in rows of five on the main street and quickly turned down Union, a steep side street. With a roar of motors, the first row swept down the hill, jumped a cross street, and then jumped again at the next street. They looked pretty good going down the hill and jumping, but all hesitated about 100 yards away where the pavement ended with a jog onto dirt. I could hear them get off the throttle and see them slow.

I knew exactly what was happening, and if you have been reading attentively, so should you. The transition involved a huge change in traction, and they were slowing in anticipation.

Shane appeared with row five. He was already in front and jumped farther than his competitors, but his approach to the transition is what really set him apart. It would not have been so obvious against other pros; they all are fast. In this setting, the difference was startling. Shane knew exactly how his bike would react when it hit dirt. He maintained throttle and stayed centered. He was already past the transition as the following riders slowed and lost a bike length.

It's not simply that he was braver or willing to twist the throttle harder. The real difference was that his anticipation skills were highly developed. He recognized, decided, and prepared in one smooth, fast flow. He was already focused on the next challenging turn before he even started to execute the transition.

The local experts were also anticipating, but at a noticeably slower pace. They saw the transition, anticipated that it could be a problem, and slowed while deciding how to handle it. They got centered and balanced, and then hit the dirt in good control.

Shane was riding like a top professional, while the local experts were riding within their comfort zone—the way the rest of us should ride. Skills like Shane's will always be the ultimate goal, but most of us will be stuck at lower levels—taking things at our own speed and, hopefully, having safe fun.

These racers are hitting the brakes in anticipation of a transition from pavement to dirt.

FINAL THOUGHTS ON PUTTING YOUR MIND IN GEAR

Mental attitude, concentration, focus, and anticipation are your most important safety gear. Always remember that dual sport is not racing. There are no prizes for going fast, but there can be big penalties for crashing.

Your only objectives are to have fun and stay healthy. Ride within your comfort zone. Train yourself to focus on clear paths through obstacles, rather than the obstacles themselves. Concentrate on what you are doing. Always have a clear picture of where you are going—the next section of road, the next turn—and what to do when you get there. Stop and take a break when you get tired or frustrated. Don't try to go faster when you start making mistakes. Instead, stop and figure out what you are doing wrong.

Basic Riding Techniques

This chapter covers basic techniques to handle most dirt roads and easy trails. It includes:

- Basic Seated Position
- Controls
- Curves
- Riding Sections and Lines
- The Basic Standing Position

THE BLOODY SOCK

I am sitting in the garage at 5 p.m. studying a bloody sock and reflecting on the day. Don led a crisp fall ride to Yerrington, but the sock, and more specifically its foot, have been a concern since 9:30 this morning when I banged a rock on the railroad grade south of Virginia City. The bright flash of pain screamed injury; I should have gone home to suffer on the sofa, but why waste a day? Eight Advil and a big dose of optimism got me to Yerrington and back, but now it's time to face the consequences.

I look at the sock again; it's still bloody and I have stalled as long as possible. Careful tugging removes the sock as intended, and the nail of my long toe, which is an unpleasant surprise. An

Good riding techniques should keep you far away from here.

exploded pulp now occupies the space formerly home to the toe. My optimism has been excessive and it's clearly time to head for the emergency room. I slip a baggie on the end of my foot and beg my wife to drive.

She is thrilled. She would much rather spend Saturday night at Washoe Med than go out to dinner and a movie. I remind her of the "better or worse" clause in our marriage contract and she grumps me to medical aid.

Emergency rooms are not what they used to be. There was a time when you could go into one for a few stitches, flirt with a nurse, and be out in a couple of hours. Those days are gone forever. I spend nearly seven hours in a sea of injured, deranged, and seriously ill patients before the overworked duty physician arrives. He scans my X-rays and studies the ruined toe, then studies it some more.

The problem, he explains, is that there is very little tissue left to hold stitches. He will do his best, but it's not his fault if it turns out badly. I implore him to proceed and he sews intently. The toe eventually heals and I vow once again to keep my feet away from rocks.

Thus far, I have stressed the free and unstructured nature of dual sporting. Ride a heavy bike on fire roads or a lighter model on single-track. Dress in hunters' camouflage or the latest motocross livery. Ride a stocker or convert a racing bike. These choices are yours to make.

Basic riding techniques however, are absolute and non-negotiable. If I say, "Keep the balls of your feet on the footpegs whenever possible," believe it and do it. Learning and practicing these basics will add to your enjoyment and enable you to dodge your own bloody sock or a more serious injury.

Experienced riders should use this material as a basis for review.

Some of the methods described here and in Chapter 10 are inappropriate and possibly dangerous on heavy bikes with smooth tires. I will describe good technique for lightweight dual sports, but it is up to you to decide what feels comfortable on your bike, at your level of riding skill. Don't assume you can get away with everything in both chapters just because you bought a dual sport.

JUMP STARTING YOUR LEARNING

Here are three things that will speed your learning process:

Suspend skepticism. As we grow older, we develop a series of filters to avoid being cheated and apply them as we read, listen, or watch. Turn off the filters while you read this chapter. Everything here is as clear as I can make it; my only motive is to provide a basis for your riding safety. Focus on understanding the principles, not looking for hidden flaws. You are learning to ride, not signing a mortgage.

Do the exercises. Each basic technique includes a drill at the end that will speed your learning process. Practice the drills until you can perform the basic moves.

Practice regularly. You do not need to set aside practice days, but you should spend part of each ride perfecting your skills.

Imagine riding a twisty fire road, following a friend. Instead of doing it on autopilot, drop back a little before each curve, then speed up and practice braking and turning with good body position. You can even practice good body position while riding on the street. Use every opportunity to reinforce good habits and eliminate bad ones.

Riding skills and setup are intertwined. You can't ride well without a good setup and you can't perfect your setup without riding. Other chapters cover adjustments, tires, and suspension.

Practice the basics, improve your setup, and then practice some more.

DUAL SPORT IS UNIQUE

If you are good at tennis, skiing, or any other physical activity, your natural athletic abilities will serve you well; however, riding demands special techniques. Don't let friends tell you that it's like bicycling, or jet-skiing, or some other motorized sport. It may have superficial similarities, but it is a different discipline. Here are some of its unique characteristics:

High speed shortens available response time. You and the motorcycle will travel a significant distance while you recognize and react to potential dangers. You must focus your attention well in front of your position and match your speed to the conditions. Slow when you can't see; go faster when you can.

A 300-pound object has significant momentum. The motorcycle can cover rough ground at high speed when it is pointed straight ahead. However, its mass and the laws of physics resist turning. Plan your turns to take every advantage of smooth gripping surfaces or berms that can hold the wheels.

You can't use your feet and legs as a foundation. You can't interact directly with the ground; you must rely on the motorcycle. The bike is muscle. It has power, absorbs big hits, never tires, and never bleeds, but it has no sense and can't balance itself. You are brains and finesse. You make all of the decisions and communicate them to the machine with subtle changes in body position.

Small contact patches allow the wheels to be easily deflected (particularly the front). You are continuously balanced on two small contact patches with a traction budget determined by tires and ground. You must use this budget wisely or you will fall. Rocks can knock one or both wheels from under you, and ruts can hold them on an

Always assume that danger is lurking around the next curve and give yourself enough margin to avoid it.

unchosen line while your body goes in a different direction.

Riding surfaces change continually. In the space of a single minute you may be on hard pack, then sand, followed by loose rocks. You must always be alert to the upcoming surface and choose the best lines.

Anticipate the effects of tire angle, braking, and acceleration. Every input of balance, brake, and throttle is transmitted to the tires and changes their ability to hold your chosen line.

You will encounter many obstacles both visible and hidden. The number of potential hazards is unlimited. Rocks, branches, stumps, logs, other vehicles, old mine shafts, cliffs, and panicked deer are some of the main categories. They can occur in diabolical combinations.

I took up snowmobiling a few years ago and made the best progress after I stopped trying to relate it to motorcycling. About the only skill that transfers directly is the ability to master fear on steep slopes. Everything else is different. Learn motorcycling directly, not through the filter of some other sport.

Remember that safety is always your primary concern. The following exercises are easy enough, but you should not focus on them so completely that you become oblivious to possible dangers. Practice in places where there are few other riders and remain aware of your surroundings. The exercises are very basic and simple. Do them in order and master one before going on to another.

I am going to assume that you already know how to use the clutch, throttle, brakes, and shift lever, plus make easy turns. If not, get someone to show you. Practice starting and stopping until you can do it without thinking about each separate action.

BASIC SEATED POSITION

Cycle News reserves the front sections for coverage of top professional racers and puts local racers in the back. The top riders often have a "look" about them. They are centered on the bike, looking where they are going, and they are relaxed at speed. The local racers are not. No matter how much they spend on helmets, boots, and riding gear they still look like amateurs. Good body position is the key to good riding and it can make you look like a pro.

Dual sport riders spend most of their time sitting, so it is important to master a good seated position. The principles are the same for both racing and dual sport: you must be centered, focused, and relaxed. A good sitting position will let you handle all graded roads and even some rougher sections, so it is important to get it right.

Prop one handlebar against a wall and assume a good baseline seated position.

- Sit on your motorcycle with your butt forward on the seat. The exact position will

Sit forward on the seat, with hands relaxed, elbows slightly lifted, head up, and balls of your feet on the pegs.

depend on your body and the seat, but you should be forward on the saddle. This is the home position for your butt.

- Wrap your hands around the grips. It is not necessary to squeeze them. Overgrip the throttle so that it will be about one-eighth open when your wrist is straight.
- Bend your elbows and lift them up, as you lean forward until your head is over the steering stem. This is the home position for your head. Lift your head so you can see forward. Your back should be straight, but not rigid.
- Place the balls of your feet on the footpegs. You may need to readjust your butt to a comfortable forward position.
- Check yourself—butt forward, head over the stem, back straight, head and elbows lifted, balls of feet on pegs, with a body position that is firm but not tense.

Dabbing and Foot Slogging

Sooner or later you will have to put one or both feet down to save yourself from falling, or shuffle through a hard section. Try to sit forward in a centered, balanced position and keep your feet wide enough to miss the pegs. Look for, and avoid, rocks that could slam your ankles back against the swingarm.

▶ SITTING EXERCISES

On a road or flat, smooth field without traffic:

- ▸ Ride by a friend in what you believe to be a good sitting position.
- ▸ Ask the friend to compare your posture with the picture and offer suggestions. Having your friend take pictures of you would be even better.
- ▸ On a slightly choppy road or field without traffic:
- ▸ Lean forward when accelerating and to weight the front wheel in turns. Lean back to weight the rear wheel when braking. It is not necessary to move your butt; just lean.
- ▸ Relax to the point of being floppy and then tense just enough to have a firm posture. Note how it feels.
- ▸ Move back on the seat, squeeze the grips and ride with stiff arms. Note the difference. You will feel more jolts and have less control.

Go back to a good seated position. Lift your elbows, relax your wrists, straighten your back, and pull the bars slightly into your chest, noting how it feels. You will feel fewer jolts and have better control. ■

▶ SEATED TURNING EXERCISES

- ▸ While riding, relax your spine and push your left buttock gently down. Relax your arms as you push and the bike will turn left. Then push with your right buttock and the bike will turn right. Note that you are steering with body position rather than pushing and pulling on the handlebars.
- ▸ With constant throttle at low speed, use alternating pushes to create small, linked turns. Keep your head over the stem and look in the direction of the turn.
- ▸ Gradually increase the size of the turns and note how the bike feels. Let the bike fall into the turns as you push down with your buttocks and follow it with your body to remain centered.

Now go for a short ride using a good seated position. Practice good seated position on every ride until it becomes a habit. ■

Lean forward to accelerate— and back to brake.

CONTROLS

Most cars have automatic transmissions. Drivers steer with the wheel, brake with one pedal, and accelerate with the other. In contrast, motorcycles have handlebars and a twist throttle, plus levers for clutch, front brake, rear brake, and shifter. Riders can also control their bikes with body position and pressure applied to the seat, footpegs, and gas tank.

There are continuing efforts to simplify motorcycle controls. One manufacturer offers ABS brakes, another has linked the brakes so that pushing the rear lever operates the front brake. Yet another company offers an automatic clutch. These features may appeal to some riders, but most off-road racers have not adopted them. They live by precise lines in difficult terrain and prefer a full range of control options.

One control can be used for different purposes:

Clutch. Starting, stopping, and spinning the rear wheel.

Throttle. Controlling speed and steering. It is often safer to spin the rear wheel around a turn with the throttle than to steer around with the front wheel.

Front brake. Stopping and sliding. Sliding the front wheel without falling is tricky. In general if you feel the front wheel start to slide, even a little, you should release the lever.

Rear brake. Stopping and sliding. Sliding the rear wheel without falling is rather easy. It is often safer to slide the rear wheel around a turn with the brake than to steer around with the front wheel.

Leaning forward. Weights the front wheel in turns and increases grip. It also keeps the front wheel down when accelerating.

Leaning back. Lifts the front wheel over obstacles and increases traction when accelerating.

Shifting weight from side to side. Initiates turns.

All rider inputs are transmitted to the ground by the tires and wheels. The back wheel tends to take care of itself. It can slide and spin within a large range without causing you to crash. The front wheel does not like to slide at all. If you feel it start to go, take immediate action. Release the front brake and turn into the slide or you will go down.

Chapter 5 tells how to adjust the handlebars and controls. Read it and make adjustments before and during the exercises as required.

▶ CONTROL EXERCISES

On a soft, smooth field or road without traffic:

- Accelerate in first gear and return to a stop using both brakes. Experiment with throttle and brake control. Spin the rear wheel with the throttle then back off and spin again. Brake just to the point of sliding then back off and do it again. Try to develop a good feel for when the wheels start to slide.
- Repeat the exercise on a variety of surfaces—hard, gravel, sandy—noting how each feels.
- Accelerate in first gear and return to a stop using only the rear brake. Brake to sliding and back off, then brake to just barely sliding and back off.
- Accelerate in first gear and return to a stop using only the front brake. Brake to just barely sliding and back off. Be careful not to fall.
- Repeat the exercises on a variety of surfaces—hard, gravel, sandy—noting how each feels.
- Accelerate in first gear and slow using both brakes, then release the front brake and use only the rear brake to stop.

Coordinating brake, throttle and body position on linked turns is the best way to master basic seated skills.

- Add throttle and brake control to a series of linked turns. Accelerate out of one turn and brake into the next. Start slowly and get the moves coordinated. Then build a little speed as you become comfortable. It is not necessary to go very fast; concentrate instead on the rhythm. This works best on a section of smooth road with small sandy berms on each side to turn against. Your ultimate goal is to spin the rear wheel with the throttle, accelerate out of the turn, brake as you cross the road, release the front brake, and slide the rear into the next turn. This simple exercise contains most of the elements needed to master control of your dual sport. Practice it often.

Mastering the ability to apply just the right amount of pressure to each brake lever is very important. Practice until you can do it without thinking. ■

CURVES

Curves have three parts, an entrance, an apex, and an exit. The apex is actually the farthest point from a straight line connecting the start and end of a turn. I will use it to describe the middle part of the curve. Camber is the same as slope. Positive camber slopes uphill toward the outside of the turn and holds the wheels. Negative or "off camber" slopes down and causes tires to slip.

Everyone who has driven a mountain road has developed the technique of entering curves a little wide on the entrance, then going to the inside for the apex. This straightens the curve and you can go a little faster, but it is often the wrong technique for dirt riding.

Most trails, two-tracks, and dirt roads develop shallow grooves where there is lots of traffic. As a result, the outsides of dirt curves often have small berms that hold your wheels while the insides are off-camber. You can easily imagine a good line around the outside of the diagram if the shaded area is off camber.

It is usually better to stay on one side of a two-track and ride the berm around the turn than cross over for the turn.

Camber and Wheel Angle

Tires have their maximum traction and stability when they are perpendicular to the ground. They have less traction when the motorcycle is leaned over and when the ground is sloped. The wheels of a motorcycle traveling in a straight line are usually straight up. However, they are at an angle in turns and across slopes.

The wheels of a turning motorcycle are always leaned into the direction of the turn. This causes tires to ride on edge and have less traction. Always look for some feature to hold the wheels when you are turning. Even a graded road may have grooves that can be used.

Always look for something—a berm, rut, level spot, or bank—to hold the tires when crossing slopes. Maintain a slow steady speed and avoid abrupt braking and acceleration. It is often safer to ride down the rocky center of a ditch than the side of its bank.

In some locations there will be nothing to hold you. Even worse, the slope may be running in the

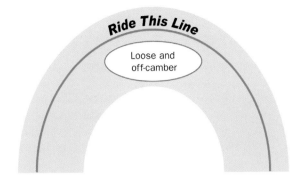

The good line in this diagram is around the outside of the curve since it uses a small berm to hold the wheels.

► CAMBER AND WHEEL ANGLE EXERCISES

Find some different types of turns: flat, banked, and negative slope

- ► Ride through them slowly, noting their feel.
- ► Gradually increase speed, but do not exceed your comfort level.
- ► Try different lines through the turns, noting any differences.

Long rides on smooth roads will not develop skills very rapidly. It is much better to practice specific skills in a small area until you master them. For example, if your objective is to master off-camber turns, find one and study it carefully. Then ride over it a few times at moderate speed and note what you feel. Stop and look at the turn again. Try to relate the ground to the feeling you have. Think about how you might improve, then try again and note whether you are better or worse. Keep repeating this process until you have a good feel for how the bike reacts and the best way to control it.

You can learn more about off-camber turns in twenty minutes of concentrated effort than in a summer of casual riding. Remember that your objective is learning, not speed. Learn the basics and speed will follow. ■

wrong direction. A very small negative slope can cause a fall. Sometimes it is possible to start your turn early or late to avoid the off-camber section. Slow down when the surface is slippery and there is nothing to turn against.

Another thing that affects traction is uneven ground. When you hit a bump or small rise you will have more traction up the face and less down the other side. Always seek smooth, bermed, or firm surfaces for turns.

Here the rider is using centrifugal force to turn on a bank. He has just ridden down a step and is using the bank to turn and set up for the next section to the left of the rocks.

This rider has chosen a bad, off-camber line with nothing to hold the wheels. His back end is already slipping into the rocks.

In this shot you can see the wheels bouncing off the ground. This is a very poor place to turn.

RIDING SECTIONS AND LINES

A section is a piece of road or trail that you ride as a unit. Its length is determined by what you can see and manage at one time. On a rocky trail this will depend on the number, size, and arrangement of rocks. A few small rocks can be handled easily and the section may be as far as you can see until the next turn in the trail. If the trail has many large rocks you may need to split the distance into smaller pieces. On a tight trail it will be as far as you can see before the next turn. Your objective is to see a section, anticipate how the bike will react, position the bike and your body properly, and then focus on the next section as it comes into view.

A line is the path you choose to ride. It is usually the straightest, smoothest route through a section. It should provide good traction and safely hold your wheels. It should avoid features that can knock or slide your wheels away from your line. A well-chosen line gives you confidence that the motorcycle can handle it and you can begin reading the next section.

On smooth, straight roads the concept of a section loses meaning. You can see everything and there is nothing to avoid. Attention flows continuously ahead looking for washouts or surprises.

We covered vision earlier, but it is so important that a few key ideas merit repetition here. Our center of vision has the sharpest focus. It should usually be directed to the next area you are trying to read and understand. Peripheral vision is not as sharp, but covers a much bigger area. It provides clues about surrounding terrain and potential distant hazards.

Sometimes a small part of the section will be hidden or particularly difficult. You will then need to make quick glances to make sure you can safely handle it. For example, suppose you can see a smooth line 30 feet to the next turn, but there are three rocks halfway that you must avoid. Focus your attention on reading the turn and give the rocks a quick glance as you approach. Do not focus on the rocks and risk an unseen hazard in the turn. Keep your vision as relaxed as your body. Fixing on a rock or obstacle will draw you to it. Look at the safe path, not the danger.

► SEEING EXERCISE

Your goal is to scan ahead, choose a line, set the motorcycle on that path, and then scan ahead again. You will practice this later, but for now do the following exercise.

On a road or flat, smooth field without traffic:

► Ride at about 20 mph looking at the ground just in front of your front wheel.

► Ride at about 20 mph looking a comfortable distance in front of you.

Looking just ahead of the wheel makes it very difficult to ride because you can not see what is ahead and choose a smooth line. You would never do it on purpose, but will be doing it inadvertently, if you allow yourself to fix on specific objects. Rocks and ruts aren't going anywhere. You must see them, change direction to avoid them, and scan for the next obstacle. ■

At this point the rider is entering a rocky turn and has already chosen a line to avoid the rocks. Now he is starting to focus on the next section.

► SECTION EXERCISE

On a short, easy length of trail with many turns:

► Ride through in both directions, seeing sections and lines. Start slow and work up into your comfort zone.

► Stop and think about what is happening. Are you choosing good lines? Are you prepared for the turns? Are you smooth and relaxed? Where are you having trouble? Why?

Repeat the exercise on a new section of trail. ■

Your mental capacity is also limited. With experience you will react better to multiple features, but always focus on where you want to go. Let subconscious reactions handle the rest.

The motorcycle is always most vulnerable when it is changing direction and most stable when it is going straight. Use most of your vision and mental focus to plan the turns.

THE BASIC STANDING POSITION

A good standing position has many benefits. It uncouples your body from the motorcycle and splits the work between you and the bike. If you hit a rock, the springs compress and your knees flex at the same time. Now, you and the bike work as a team to absorb the force. Your head barely moves and your vision remains sharp.

You can also move around on the bike and see over brush to choose better lines. Placing your weight on the footpegs lowers the combined effective center of gravity and increases stability. Quickly weighting one peg or another allows you to recover from rocks that deflect the wheels.

The standing position can also be very tiring. Most dual sport riders can only stand over rough ground for a few minutes—maybe ten or twenty at most—before their thighs start to ache. They tend to sit most of the time and stand for more difficult sections. Regardless of how long you can stand, the position is highly valuable and should be learned by everyone.

At first it will be difficult to balance on your legs. Acceleration and uphills will throw you back and

Keep knees slightly bent in the standing position with no weight on your arms.

pull your arms. Deceleration and downhills will throw you forward. Simply riding on smooth roads in a good standing position will improve your balance. You are doing it right when there is virtually no weight or pull on your arms.

Prop one handlebar against a wall and assume a good baseline standing position:

- Stand on the motorcycle with the balls of your feet on the pegs. Knees should be bent slightly and at the narrow juncture of tank and seat. The exact position will depend on your body. This is your home standing position.
- Wrap your hands around the grips. It is not necessary to squeeze them. Overgrip the throttle so that it will be about one-eighth on when your wrist is straight.
- Flex your elbows and lean forward until your head is over the steering stem. Lift it so you can see comfortably ahead. This is the home position for your head.
- Your back should be straight, but not rigid. Move your butt back to counter the effect of leaning forward. You should be slightly flexed but not hunched over.
- Check yourself—butt slightly back, head over the stem, back straight, head lifted, elbows flexed, wrists relaxed, balls of feet on pegs, and your grip firm but not tense.

Chapter 5 tells how to adjust the bars and controls. Read it and make adjustments before and during the exercises as required.

Spring on Top of Spring

Think of the suspension and your legs as two sets of springs. The suspension is a big spring at the bottom and your legs are a small spring on top. The objective is to isolate your head and upper body from the movements of the motorcycle. The suspension takes big hits and absorbs most of them, but the remaining energy is transmitted toward your body. Then, your legs absorb this remaining energy. When done properly, your head barely moves and vision stays sharp. Your weight is uncoupled from the bike, which is free to react to the ground. The motorcycle takes care of itself and you concentrate on keeping yourself centered and balanced.

Stay balanced and relaxed in the standing position, and be ready for anything.

With experience, you will anticipate where the bike is going and place your body in position to deal with it. For example, you see a rock that will deflect the bike to the left and start moving your weight to the left before the motorcycle starts moving. Then, you will be perfectly positioned to absorb the jolt and stay centered when it actually deflects.

Remember that keeping your head still and body centered will maximize vision, balance, and control.

Controls in the Standing Position

You must be able to use the controls in the standing position and move smoothly between sitting and standing. Do the seated control exercises in the standing position and as you move between standing and sitting positions. Then go for a short ride using a good standing position.

Finally, ride over rougher ground at gradually increasing speed, relaxing your knees to absorb the hits. Look as far ahead as possible and let the motorcycle work under you.

The riding techniques described in this chapter will get you safely through many situations. Practice them every time you ride until they become good habits. Chapter 10 covers more advanced methods.

▶ *STANDING EXERCISES*

On a road or flat, smooth field without traffic:

- ▸ Ride by a friend in what you believe to be a good standing position.
- ▸ Ask the friend to compare your posture with the picture and offer suggestions. Having your friend take pictures of you would be even better.
- ▸ On a slightly choppy road or riding area without traffic:
- ▸ Lean forward when accelerating. Move your butt back to maintain balance when braking. This is important; maintain balance by moving your butt, pushing or pulling the bars as little as possible.
- ▸ Relax to the point of being floppy and then tense just enough to have a firm posture. Note how it feels.
- ▸ Squeeze the grips and ride with stiff arms. Note the difference. You will feel more jolts and have less control.
- ▸ While riding, relax your spine and push your left peg gently down. The bike will turn left. Then push with the right peg and the bike will turn right.
- ▸ With constant throttle at low speed, use alternating pushes to create linked small turns. Keep your head over the stem and look in the direction of the turn.

Gradually increase the size of the turns and note how the bike feels. Let the bike fall into the turns as you push down and follow it with your body to remain centered. ■

This rider is leaning forward to maintain balance as he climbs a step.

This rider has his butt back to compensate for going downhill through some powdery ruts. The front suspension supports minimum body weight and is free to react to the ground.

FINAL THOUGHTS ON BASIC TECHNIQUE

Magazines like *Dirt Bike* and *Dirt Rider* are filled with pictures of top professional racers and test riders, but they do not always illustrate good riding techniques. They are colorful, exciting, and amazing, but are chosen to sell magazines rather than teach. Most often they show extreme or even awkward positions. The photographer and test rider go to a track and the rider performs increasingly radical turns and jumps. A great magazine picture might actually be taken seconds before a bobble or crash.

The pictures are wonderful fun, but look at them with a critical eye if you are learning to ride. Occasionally they show a top professional in complete balanced and relaxed control. These are the techniques to emulate. Others show riders who are way off center, fighting for control, doing a stunt, or desperately unbalanced. Learn to recognize those flaws and avoid them.

Everybody gets out of shape and needs to recover, but those moments should be the exceptions. Remember, good basic riding techniques are focused, relaxed, smooth, and balanced.

10

Advanced Riding Techniques

This chapter contains information and riding exercises that will make you comfortable in a wide range of situations. It does not address starts and jumps, which are the essence of motocross, but it does cover mud, sand, rocks, snow, and ice, which are part of the dual sport experience—and which you are likely to encounter on many rides. We will cover:

- Types of dirt
- Sliding Turns
- Loose surfaces
- Whoops
- Slippery surfaces
- Rocky surfaces
- Hills
- Greasy surfaces
- Cross grain
- Obstacles
- Trees and brush
- Water crossings
- Snow and ice
- Vertical exposure

The chapter contains a number of exercises. Use them to develop your skills.

Riding a wide range of terrain and conditions can be deeply satisfying.

CAUGHT IN CHANGING CONDITIONS

A pale November sun sinks into haze over Verdi Peak and it's getting harder to see the ruts on Garson Road. Larry, Phil, and I spent the day higher in the mountains looking at potential OHV routes. Now my friends are far behind in their Jeep Rubicons and I am on the Suzuki at 8000 feet, heading for home.

Conditions were good in the morning when we climbed this same road. Low overnight temperatures, light rain, and snow had created a partially frozen surface with good traction, but it's different now. ATV-mounted hunters, scanning the slopes for mule deer, have been going up and down all day, churning the melting water into the clay. The result is ten miles of sloppy mud.

Puddles, thawed by the afternoon sun, are freezing again but the bike's hand warmers keep my fingers from stiffening. The Suzuki squirms and slips at every input of brake, throttle, and steering. I stand on the pegs in the straights, and look well ahead, chugging along in third gear as smoothly as possible. Mud clings to the tires so I maintain speed to throw off the sticky goo and keep the knobbies from turning into slicks. Stretches of snow separate one mud section from the next and passing wheels have smashed the morning's flakes into icy ribbons.

I sit to negotiate switchbacks while the front wheel slips, then slips again. The Suzuki is talking. It seems to be saying, "I think you are OK, but stay focused and don't go any faster." It sounds good to me.

A brake light flashes ahead and soon the backs of two other dual sports appear in the gloomy shadows. They are going slowly and sliding all over the road. Following them will break my rhythm and cause the tires to load up with mud. The slower I go, the worse it gets.

I quickly squeeze by and accelerate away as they wobble and skid. The sun has set, it's getting darker, and it's time to get off the mountain. The road improves near Boomtown and soon I am on the freeway heading for home.

Learning all the variations of riding surfaces is one of the great challenges and adventures of dual sporting. Different terrain, changes in weather, and passing seasons can either be enjoyable opportunities to ride, or miserable experiences, depending on your skills and attitude.

TYPES OF DIRT

Let's start with the basic mechanics of dirt before covering riding techniques. Scientists classify dirt by particle size and chemical composition, but particle size has the biggest impact on riding. No one expects you to measure dirt grains, but knowing how they work will help you understand the various riding techniques and how to match them to the surface. Clay, sand, gravel, and rocks are common names for particles of different sizes.

Clay

Clay is composed of very small particles and forms a variety of surfaces. Water does not drain through the small spaces between particles. Rain or melted snow stands in puddles or mixes with clay to make greasy, sticky goo. Motorcycles can churn through shallow mud, but deep bogs can stop Russian army tanks.

Clay becomes very hard when it dries and bakes in the sun. The resulting surface depends on what happens as it dries. Passing traffic often smooths shallow mud into smooth surfaces almost like pavement. Wheels passing through deep mud create big ruts. The clay preserves them as it dries, producing a hard, jolty ride with many edges that can deflect or trap your wheels.

*This **KLR650** is buried to its axle in mud on the Black Rock Playa. This surface looks dry, but the clay below is still saturated with water from winter rain. It took two people more than an hour to free this bike. Note that the rider is sunk to the top of his boots. Every time he tries to lift the bike, he sinks while the bike stays down in the muck.*

Late in summer, the clay on this downhill has dried into fine dust—like flour. It's extremely slippery and hides rocks and ruts below.

Heavy traffic pounds dry clay into powder. It lies in piles on top of harder ground, hiding whatever rocks and ruts are below. Wheels push completely through to the underlying surface while the fine, clay dust billows into choking clouds and sprays around wheels like streams of water.

127

Surfaces like this mixture of damp sand and gravel offer superb traction.

Gravel and Sand

Gravel and sand are bigger particles with significant air spaces between them. They don't turn into mud when it rains because water flows between the particles and drains away. Gravel and sand may be coarse or fine, wet or dry.

The weight of a motorcycle on its tires causes dry particles to slide past each other. Tires sink into the loose surface, and must push particles aside to move forward. This causes tires to wander and wobble and it is hard to steer. However, sand is not slippery and rarely throws you down.

Sand is looser in some places than others and may also bear the tracks of other riders. Wheels tend to follow these tracks, making it hard to hold good lines. It also quickly forms endless dips, known as whoops, which can be very tiring to ride.

Wet sand particles stick together and provide a firmer surface. Damp sand is a lot of fun and a good place to master some riding techniques. There are few things better than a twisty sand road after it rains.

Slippery Surfaces

Improved dirt roads are often created by spreading gravel over clay and the result is a harder, better-drained surface. However, dual sport riders often encounter gravel that is lying on top of the soil rather than mixed into it. Loose gravel on hard ground acts like thousands of tiny ball bearings. The resulting surface is very slippery and can easily throw you down.

A straight line over big, anchored rocks is often safer than one over smaller, looser rocks.

Rocks

Rocks are really big particles ranging from small stones that can be ridden almost like gravel, to big boulders. Some rocks are buried in the earth and provide excellent traction. Others can easily roll a wheel from under you. The ability to distinguish safe lines of fixed versus loose rocks is crucial.

All of the particle sizes can be mixed together to create an endless variety of surfaces. Most dry, graded roads offer firm support and allow knobs to sink slightly into the dirt. You can sit on the bike and it goes where you steer it. The techniques in Chapter 9 work well. However, more advanced techniques are required for loose and slippery surfaces.

SLIDING TURNS

Racers use aggressive turning techniques to get through corners as fast as possible. Competitors must always brake hard, maintain speed through the apex, and accelerate at maximum speed. If they fail, someone will pass. Dual sport riders can use the same techniques, but are less interested in pure speed. They want to maximize traction, safety, and stability while minimizing energy drain.

▶ EXERCISE - SLIDING TURN ONE

This is a basic sliding turn that has many uses. It is also the foundation for more aggressive turns. The initial objective is to feel the rear wheel slide and learn to modulate the amount of slide with brake and throttle. Strive for smoothness and control.

Find a firm, damp, sandy area; avoid deep, loose sand or slippery sand over hard pack. Look for some turns with small berms. Repeat the control exercises described in Chapter 9 and spend some time doing linked turns. When you are warmed up and comfortable, do this exercise.

- Enter a turn at medium speed.
- Brake hard enough to barely slide the rear wheel, but not hard enough to slide the front.
- Slide forward on the seat toward the gas tank and lean back slightly to maintain balance while braking.
- Tip the bike into a smooth, sweeping turn, keeping both feet on the pegs.
- Lift your outside elbow and push the tank with your outside knee.
- Keep your body squared with, and parallel to, the bike. Look where you want to go.
- As the bike slows pull in the clutch.
- Gradually decrease pressure on the brakes, but continue sliding the rear wheel.
- As you near the apex, lean forward to weight the front wheel and begin to apply throttle.
- Use the clutch to feed just enough power to keep the rear sliding.
- Continue lifting your elbow and pushing with your outside knee.
- Continue releasing the brake and applying throttle.
- Steer away from the turn to straighten the bike and accelerate away.
- Return to your normal seated position.

This simple turn involves many separate steps and you must coordinate all of them. It might be good to focus on the slowing, turning part and get it right, before tackling the accelerating part. Make sure that you have a clear grasp of what you are supposed to do and when.

Practice getting everything in the right order even if you need to begin by riding slowly without sliding. Pay particular attention to the lifted elbow, body position, and outside knee pushing the tank. Get the moves right and speed will come with practice.

This rider is sliding the rear wheel into a turn with the brake and spinning it out with throttle.

This technique does several things. Moving forward weights the front and increases its traction. The elbow and knee stabilize your riding position and apply leverage to the bike. The rear wheel is doing part of the turning and relieving pressure on the front. You do not need to slide the rear very much. Strive for smoothness and control.

Things to think about: Keep the ball of your inside foot on the footpeg. Do not slide forward onto your arch and allow your toe to drop into harm's way. Lift your foot from the peg and brake with your toe. Push your knee against the tank to stabilize it and modulate the brake by flexing your ankle.

Note whether any part of the turn seems awkward and try to isolate the problem. It will take many sessions to get this right, but it is well worth the effort. This technique will allow you to ride curvy roads, at speed, for hours on end with good stability and very little energy drain. ■

▶ EXERCISE - SLIDING TURN TWO

This turn is much the same as Sliding Turn One, but it rolls the tires on edge and extends your inside leg near the apex. It can be used on sharper looser turns, but requires more energy. Practice on smooth bermed corners until you are coordinated and confident.

- ▸ Start the turn as in the previous exercise.
- ▸ When you tip into the turn, push the inside bar down and lift the outside elbow.
- ▸ Roll the bike under your butt so that you sit toward the outside edge of the seat. Do not lean your body over with the bike. Keep it more upright.
- ▸ Slide the rear wheel outward with the brake.
- ▸ At the same time remove your inside foot from the footpeg and swing your leg forward with your knee flexed and toes pointed up.
- ▸ Weight the outside peg.
- ▸ Remain square on the bike and look where you want to go.
- ▸ Apply throttle and release the brake to keep sliding the rear. Experiment with using the clutch to feed just the right amount of power to the rear wheel.
- ▸ Finish the turn as described in the previous exercise.

The effect of these moves is to tip the tires on edge where they have less traction, making it easier to slide the rear with brake and spin it with the throttle. The bike will come around smartly. The forward leg puts even more weight on the front and is ready to catch you if you start to fall. Keep your knee flexed and toes up in case your foot hits the ground. Use the brake and throttle as in Sliding Turn One, but with more emphasis. Once again the goal is smooth, controlled turns.

Things to think about: On right turns it is not possible to use the brake and extend your leg at the same time. Brake hard and early then use the throttle to spin the wheel through the turn as you extend your leg. ■

This rider has his outside elbow lifted, inside leg off the peg, and is using the brake to initiate an aggressive sliding turn.

Momentum resists slowing and turning; it always acts to maintain speed and direction. The wheels must generate sufficient turning force to counteract momentum. Dirt surfaces don't allow them to grip the ground well and the bike can fall quickly once its front wheel starts to slide.

The sliding turns transfer some of the turning chores to the more stable rear wheel by causing it to slide around the corners. It does not take much of a slide to stabilize the bike and carve smooth stable turns. Sliding Turn One uses a very gentle slide; Sliding Turn Two is more aggressive.

Practicing in a Ditch

The photo shows a short section of a little sand wash. It is about 6 feet deep with smooth sides and a sharp turn every 20 or 30 feet. This one is almost a mile long. It is a terrific place to develop seeing, line selection, and turning techniques. Try to find something like this in your area.

Practice riding up and down the ditch. Stay in the bottom without cutting corners so that you have the maximum opportunity to react and turn. Start slowly and work on smoothness, then gradually pick up the pace. The constant demands of seeing new turns and reacting to them will lead to rapid improvement.

A ditch or tight sand wash with many turns is a great place to practice.

Rocky outcroppings on the sides of sand washes can indicate big steps or drop-offs ahead. This one plunges about 15 feet.

Keep your vision up and look ahead in whoops. Do not ride them one at a time, focusing only on the one directly in front of you.

TECHNIQUES FOR LOOSE SURFACES

Sand is the ultimate loose surface and you must compress it with speed and pressure to support your wheels. Get up to speed quickly and skim across the top. Maintain speed through turns, striving for large smooth arcs. The bike will wander, but going slower will only make it worse. Stay centered on the bike, and maintain a good grip—without becoming rigid.

Sand dunes have a packed, rounded side facing the wind and a downwind side that is soft and steep. Do not blast up the hard side without knowing what's over the top. Very fine, deep sand is especially hard to ride. I once sank a front wheel to the axle on completely dry, fine sand. Beach sand contains a lot of salt. Riding on the beach or splashing through the surf can accelerate corrosion and rust.

Pay attention to your surroundings when riding in sand washes. Rocky sides bordering washes can indicate boulders in the wash, a step, or drop-off. I know several washes that have twenty-foot vertical drops.

TECHNIQUES FOR WHOOPS

Under the pounding of numerous dirt bikes, soft surfaces quickly develop little dips called whoops. They can be deep, spaced very close together, and go on for miles; they can be quite exhausting to ride.

In whoops, stand centered and relaxed with knees slightly flexed. Keep the front end light, but do not try to pull it up for each whoop with the bars. Don't fight yourself by pulling up with your arms and pushing down with your legs at the same time.

Lift your head and look well forward, rather than fixing on the next whoop. Make sure your knees and back are flexed, but not excessively bent. It is very important to have the bars high enough to straighten your back. Riding whoops in a hunched position is extremely tiring.

Racers learn to skim across the tops of whoops and clear several at once with the front wheel. You can try to master these techniques, but the faster you ride, the more energy it takes. It is often better to stand in the center, strive for a pace you can maintain, and let the motorcycle work beneath you.

 WHOOP EXERCISE

Ride a section of whoops at moderate speed focusing on the next whoop. Note how it feels. The whoop will look large and you will continually plow into the next one. Now ride the same section looking five or six whoops in front. Note the difference. The whoops will magically seem smaller and easier to ride. ■

▶ *SLIPPERY SURFACE EXERCISE*

Find a slippery turn with a rut or berm that will hold your wheels. Practice turning against it; start slowly and gradually increase your speed. Practice sliding turns against the berm. Very small ruts will often support the wheels so look for them, and use them, as you ride. ■

A rocky, twisting road can be ridden safely at speed by turning on patches of firm ground and riding straight through the rocky sections.

TECHNIQUES FOR SLIPPERY SURFACES

Hard underlying surfaces, lightly covered by sand, loose dirt, and rocks are slippery. The loose material acts like ball bearings beneath the wheels and knobs skate on top rather than biting into them. Traction is usually better when there is some moisture in the ground. Be especially cautious in the spring as the ground dries and changes from grippy to slippery.

It is very important to seek lines that support the wheels when turning on slippery surfaces. Take advantage of berms and camber (slope), look for firm patches and use them for turns. Slow down for turns that do not offer support. Be judicious with the brakes and modulate them when you start to slide. Be especially alert to the possibility of oncoming traffic because you will have difficulty stopping.

TECHNIQUES FOR ROCKY SURFACES

Large rocks can be very hard on motorcycles, flattening frame tubes, bending wheels, and pushing levers through cases. They can also be very hard on bodies if you fall. Rocks deserve respect, but there is no reason to avoid them. Rocks also have many virtues. They provide excellent traction, do not form whoops, are not dusty, and don't stick like mud.

▶ *ROCK EXERCISE*

Find a short section of trail with a mixture of rocks, bare ground, and turns. Try various lines at slow speed, connecting the bare spots with straight lines in the rocks. Turn on bare spots or firmly anchored small rocks. Try different lines and note the effect. Start slowly and gradually increase speed. ■

The first key to successful rock riding is having a compliant suspension. Wheels must move up and down and stay in contact rather than deflecting. The second key is to carefully choose lines, and in particular, turning points. The motorcycle always wants to go straight. It can travel over fairly big rocks if it hits them straight on, but it does not turn well in rocks. Even a small rock can knock you down while turning.

Most rocks are encountered on two-tracks and trails. The sections usually have rocks of different sizes and small areas of dirt. The basic technique is to connect the dirt areas with straight lines through the smallest, most stable, rocks. The dirt areas are then used for turns.

A relaxed, neutral standing position is good for the rocky parts, but you may prefer to sit in the turns. A skilled rider can travel at speed, in complete control, using this approach.

Occasionally, there will be longer stretches of different size rocks with no dirt. Here, the basic technique is to turn on the smaller, more stable rocks or even a large flat one. The straightest line between turning points may include some larger rocks, and it may be safer to ride over them than try to weave through. With practice you can even hit them at angles if you anticipate how the bike will deflect and move your body to stay centered. The standing position works best.

Be especially mindful of your feet. Move them well back on the pegs. Scan for rocks that could bang them from the side. You may need to slow down and lift them occasionally, but try to keep them on the pegs whenever possible.

You may also need to dismount and "bulldog" over rocky steps and ledges. To do this stand close to the left side of the motorcycle and use the clutch plus your body strength to move forward.

Be careful not to slam the skid plate really hard into rocks or they will flatten the frame tubes. Be careful not to bang the cases or levers and break them. Turn back if the rocks become more than you can handle. As always, develop your skills on terrain within your comfort level.

TECHNIQUES FOR GREASY SURFACES

Mud is a "greasy" surface. It is slippery, sticks to everything, flies up onto your goggles, and does not compact under the wheels. It is possible, and fun, to negotiate relatively thin layers of mud, but impossible to travel through really deep bogs.

Be aware that seemingly dry surfaces can conceal bottomless mud below. Dry lakes are especially treacherous, and a parched, cracked surface can hide disaster.

Do not go for a mud run with street tires or worn knobbies. New tires with long sharp knobs can make the difference between riding and getting stuck.

The first thing to do with mud is evaluate whether there is any chance of getting through. You must decide how deep it is likely to get. An inch or two over a harder surface is fun, but anything more could trap you. Turning back may be the best option.

Note whether you are throwing mud from the spinning tires. If not, you can ride mud almost like wet sand and have a blast. Throwing mud off the front tire is a sign that it is sticking to the tires—and everything else. Keep the wheels turning fast enough to clean mud from the knobs. As a minimum, you should see it flying from your front tire. If you slow down, it will build up, destroying traction and eventually stop the wheels from turning. The slower you go the worse it will get.

Maintain speed and let momentum work for you with smooth lines. Look for lines that support your wheels and ride the straights in a balanced standing position using the smoothest lines possible.

Maintaining speed through corners is difficult because the bike doesn't want to steer. Again, strive for lines that support the wheels and try to be smooth.

Mud also sticks to you. It flies onto goggles and covers boots. If you fall, it sticks to gloves and then transfers to the controls. Stay well away from other vehicles that can shower you with mud. Keep your feet on the pegs and your body on the bike.

A front fender extension may keep most of the goo off your goggles. Carry a towel or rag and use it to clean your lenses when they are dirty. Thoroughly rinse the lenses with water before wiping, or scratches will soon ruin them.

Stop and investigate before plunging into deep mud.

This mud has a lot of sand in it and offers excellent traction even though it is thoroughly wet.

133

▶ *MUD EXERCISE*

Find a short stretch of surface mud with curves that you can charge through. Try different lines that will support your wheels, and different speeds both standing and sitting. Note how they feel. ■

A muddy bike is hard to clean and I don't spend much time trying. At home, I scrape the thickest deposits from the skid plate and swing arm into a bucket. Then, I hose off the easy mud, and put the bike into the garage. The mud sticks like crazy when it's still wet, but falls off easily after it dries. The rest of the mud falls off early on my next ride. Of course, I have to clean thoroughly before any maintenance, but usually wait until most of the mud has fallen off by itself.

It's fun to ride mud occasionally, but it's also hard on the bike. It will ruin chains, brake pads, and rotors very quickly.

TECHNIQUES FOR GETTING UNSTUCK

When you are upside down on a hill, or down to the cases in mud, it is time to stop and assess the situation. Do not struggle without a plan. It will just burn all your energy and you may still be stuck.

It is very hard to lift a bike when the handlebars are lower than the wheels. If at all possible, try to fall uphill so that you have less distance to the ground and the bike lands in a position to be righted easily.

If you can't climb a hill, turn sideways just before you stop. If the bike falls, lift it from the uphill side.

This bike was freed by stomping a firm surface to the side and then lifting and dragging the bike onto it.

If it does fall with the handlebars downhill, drag the bike by one of the wheels. It will pivot around the footpeg which is probably stuck in the ground. Keep dragging until both wheels are downhill. This is not good for the plastic, but it works. If your buddies can get to you, they may be able to help lift and save the plastic.

Focus on regaining the trail if you fall from one and don't know what's below. Do not go deeper into an unknown canyon from which you may never escape.

If you stop going forward in mud or snow, try not to bury the rear wheel. It's okay to stay on the throttle while you are still inching forward and have some hope of reaching firm ground, but stop as soon as it becomes hopeless. Turn off the motor and evaluate the situation if it looks like you are getting in deeper.

Getting unstuck when you are case deep requires two things. First, free the wheels by rocking the bike from side to side; then get them on a firm surface. Sometimes, you may be able to roll the wheels after they are free, but more often you will need to lift.

Prepare a good surface before lifting. You may need to stomp a firm place in the snow or cut branches to cover mud. Also, plan where to go after the bike is free. It is hard to turn a stuck motorcycle, but the best option is usually to head straight for the nearest firm ground. You may need a path of stomped snow or branches to get there. When you are prepared, lift, start the engine, and walk the bike out.

Do not risk getting stuck without confidence that you can get unstuck. Two or three people should be able to get out of most anything, but freeing a heavy motorcycle on your own may be impossible. You may want to practice getting out of some easy situations to gauge your abilities.

TECHNIQUES FOR HILLS

Climbing hills is thrilling. The roaring exhaust, throbbing motor, and spinning wheel are a big rush. Some play riders are hill specialists and spend hours going up and down the same hill.

In general, the same principles that apply to level ground also apply to hills. Stay centered, relaxed, and balanced; use the controls just as you would anywhere else. Lean forward when going up and lean back when going down. Stay seated on smooth ground and stand for rough ground. Look for lines, places to make turns, and ride rocks, the same as usual.

The worst thing you can do is go straight to a big, steep hill without practicing and warming up on lesser challenges. You get tense when you exceed your comfort zone and it really ruins your style. Develop skills on easy hills and gradually move to more challenging runs.

Very steep, rocky, or rutted hills present special challenges. Keep your weight well forward when climbing. Avoid a sloppy, butt-back, straight-arm position.

It is always better to climb with speed and momentum. Climbing after you have slowed to walking speed and started to shuffle with your feet is very difficult. The rear wheel may dig into soft ground and sink. The bike will start to wander and fall and you will be unable to stay centered. Turn sideways if it becomes obvious that you can't make it. Then go down and try again.

If you simply must keep going and still have traction it may be best to plan and execute small sections. For example, climb to the next level spot, rest, and plan the next ascent. Be aware that spinning a rear tire in rocks will rip all the sharp edges off knobs in a very short time.

Bouncing Over Ledges

Hitting a ledge at full power when climbing will kick the rear end up. This may cause loss of traction and failure to make it to the top. Try to gain speed before the ledge, then hit it with the front wheel while still under power. Ease off the throttle just before the back wheel hits and reapply power immediately after.

Try to absorb the hit with your legs so that your body does not fly up. Be ready to shift your weight forward and slip the clutch if the bike starts to wheelie. This takes coordination and should be practiced on small hills and ledges until it feels right.

This rider is leaning forward and using good seated position to ride easily up this rocky hill. Practice on small hills first.

▶ HILL EXERCISE

Find a small, smooth hill. Practice going up and down, starting slowly and working up to speed. Try sitting and standing, braking and accelerating. Gradually move to bigger and rougher hills.

Caution about going downhills and getting trapped: At one of the Cowbell Enduros in the '70s, hundreds of riders descended a muddy trail to the Eel River and were unable to climb out. Old timers still talk about a night in the rainy woods and how helicopters were needed to recover the bikes. I missed that one, but have spent most of several different days pushing uphill through nearly impassible mud or snow. Do not go down a slippery slope unless you are sure that you can get out the bottom or climb back up. ■

Shifting on Hills

Ideally you should not shift while climbing because it interrupts delivery of power to the rear wheel. In actual practice, shifts are often necessary. The most common situation is to start in a high gear, then shift down as the hill gets steeper or the trail turns.

Shift soon enough to maintain speed. Strive for smooth delivery of power to the ground. Shift quickly to maintain speed, but use the clutch to feed power smoothly to the rear wheel and avoid spinning it unnecessarily. Adjust the clutch and shift levers so that you can easily reach them.

Downhills and Side Hills

Lean back when going downhill. Try the standing position with your butt well back. Use a small application of throttle to turn the rear wheel while braking. A sliding rear wheel is almost useless.

Ruts or rocks that can't be avoided are a problem on steep downhills. Nothing is worse than picking up speed and losing control while headed for something that is going to crash you.

▶ OBSTACLE EXERCISE

Weaving from side to side on a medium rutted road is a good way to practice. Cross the rut with each weave and make wide turns to hit the rut squarely. Apply a little throttle just before each hit. This will give you a feel for the way the bike reacts. ■

Weight the downhill peg and use careful throttle control to negotiate side hills.

Often, there is a better line to the side. You can also kill the engine, but keep it in gear, and use the clutch as a rear brake, while paddling with your feet. You may need to bulldog the worst part on really gnarly terrain.

Motorcycles do not like side hills and the rear wheel will try to slide down. Weight the downhill peg and ride as smoothly as possible. Try to get to a ridge if possible.

Some roads contour around hills. Without maintenance, they revert to the native slope. Dirt washes from the hill and creates off-camber slopes on the uphill side. Sometimes it is better to ride the downhill side, but other times it will accumulate rocks or wash out. Pay attention and change sides as necessary.

OBSTACLES

Obstacles are things like ruts, logs, and big rocks. The best thing is to try and avoid them. However sometimes they block the entire way and you must ride over them. The most important techniques for obstacles are always to hit them in perfect control of the motorcycle—centered and balanced, head on, and at a speed that will allow the suspension to deal with them.

It is always best to hit obstacles head-on and with a light front wheel. Hitting them at an angle will cause the wheel to deflect and could put you down. Hitting them with the forks compressed will make things much worse. There is no need to wheelie over things; a small application of throttle will extend the forks and unweight the wheel, allowing it to move freely over the obstacle. Slow down to a reasonable speed if necessary and then apply some throttle just before contact.

Cross-Grain

When you follow ridges and washes you are going with the grain. When you are traveling across the ridges and washes you are going cross-grain. When you are traveling cross-grain, remain aware of the terrain above you. Water flows down-slope, cutting washes and ditches. You may be able to anticipate them by watching the ridges or hills above. Slow down when you expect something and avoid plunging over a bank, or into a rocky ravine.

The worst thing you can do with an unexpected dip is crash into it, with the front brake locked, and forks compressed. Practice riding across small dips, gradually increasing speed to see how the bike reacts. Stand and get centered on the pegs. Move your butt back and keep the front light. If you are surprised by a big dip, brake hard, then release and lift the front end with the throttle just before going in.

Trees and Brush

Tight, twisting trails through trees and brush are great fun, but keep your feet and knees in, so you don't bang or catch them. Scan continuously for stumps and stout branches that could attack from the side. If you really want to go fast, make a scouting ride before you open it up.

Hit all logs straight on. Even a small log can throw you down, particularly if it is wet. The proper technique for crossing larger logs is to lift the front wheel with the throttle just high enough to roll over the log, slide across with the skid plate, and unweight the rear so that it does not throw you forward as it strikes the log. Obviously, this requires coordination and practice.

It is easy to ride over logs up to about eight inches in diameter. On larger ones, I bounce the front over, hang the skid plate on the log, and then lift the rear over. It isn't pretty, but I don't cross enough logs to get good at it and I often fall with the other technique. I would rather build a small ramp of logs and branches than risk injury.

Sometimes it is possible to bypass a log. Always go uphill unless you are absolutely sure you can climb back onto the trail. In the spring, carry a small saw to cut detours in the brush. Logs are a sign that the trail has not been cleared. It is not uncommon to cross one or two and then be turned back by logs too big and numerous to pass.

Water Crossings

Most roads and trails cross streams in places with good, hard bottoms. Riding across a few inches of water on a good bottom is no big deal. Slow down so you don't get wet, and motor across. You can even lift your feet to keep your boots dry.

With a good bottom and slow current, it is possible to ride water about 20 inches deep. Scout on foot if necessary.

Rocky crossings, hidden bottoms, and deep or fast water are different. It is imperative to judge the depth before starting across. I once saw a bike completely disappear in muddy water when it dropped into an invisible hole. Even if you don't disappear, water could enter your engine requiring a lengthy drying out process, or causing serious damage. If you don't know, don't go.

Nobody likes wet boots, but a walking reconnaissance may be prudent. Pouring water from boots and wringing out socks on the other side will only take a couple of minutes. Trying to get all the water out of an engine and air cleaner could take an hour—if your battery lasts long enough to do it. It is also hard to estimate the depth of clear water all the way across a wide stream and it may be best to push across slippery bottoms with big rocks.

Fast water has tremendous force. Even a foot of it can move you downstream when you are bouncing over a rocky bottom. Stay out of deep, fast-moving streams. Big mud holes with invisible bottoms could hide slippery logs and rocks. Try to avoid them or skirt the sides.

SPECIAL SITUATIONS

Here are a couple of situations that can easily be avoided if they are not your idea of fun. Other riders thrive on them.

Snow and Ice

There are almost as many types of snow as dirt and it changes constantly. The main variables are depth, temperature, water content, age, and prior use. A light fall snow is an absolute blast to ride. Wheels sink through it to the ground below giving excellent traction and the scenery is very pretty. Long fresh knobs are mandatory for this kind of riding.

At 5000 feet in Reno we often get several light snows with melting between—perfect winter riding. However, at higher elevations snow depths of 10 to 15 feet are common, and then it's snowmobiles only.

Hard frozen snow supports motorcycles on level ground or going downhill. By late spring you can chug through most mountain drifts that have repeatedly thawed and refrozen. Climbing is almost always impossible because the rear wheel spins and soon buries itself. Even a small slope can be impassable.

A thin frozen crust over soft snow is a problem. Wheels fall through and it's very difficult to steer because the hard layer holds the front wheel and keeps it from steering in response to your input. It is also hard to steer in someone else's track for the same reason. The tracks of jeeps and trucks freeze and become very slippery. It is often possible to find a line of fresh snow on the side.

Days with light snow cover offer gorgeous scenery and challenging conditions.

The snow is hard enough, but it's going to get deeper as the road climbs. It looks like time to turn back.

These club members are trying to recover a bike that fell from the trail thirty feet above. Luckily, the rider was not injured.

It is possible to ride ice with studded tires, but ice is a disaster without studs. It can throw you down before you can react, and really ring your bell. Once down, it can be difficult to lift the bike. You may not even be able to stand—boots slide, tires slide, and you and the bike slip downhill. This can be a serious problem if you are sliding into something that can trap you. You may need to cut brush and stand on it, just to get upright.

Vertical Exposure

Some roads and trails border river canyons with steep vertical drops. A narrow rocky trail next to a 40- or 50-foot drop exposes you to serious injury.

The incident pictured above occurred on a club ride. The trail above is very narrow and washed out. The rider made a little mistake and fell off the trail. He landed in a bush near the top, but the bike slid about 30 feet into a creek below. Fortunately, there were no injuries and we were able to get the motorcycle out.

You may encounter trails that are way beyond your comfort level. They may not have been maintained in decades, may be barely wider than the wheels, have no place to turn around, and border dizzying drops. Avoid narrow trails in river canyons unless you are skilled and have a good idea of what you are doing.

FINAL THOUGHTS ON ADVANCED TECHNIQUES

You can have great fun on graded roads and easy trails, but unless you reach for greater challenges, you will be missing the best part of the dual sport experience. Difficult terrain is endlessly fascinating. The satisfaction of conquering hills, logs, bogs, and obstacles can keep you smiling for half a week.

Falls are fairly common, but speeds are usually low so damage is minimal. It is usually safer to spend a few hours at low speed on technical trails than it is to blast around at high speed on roads. You will come back dirty, tired, and grinning, even if you tip over a few times.

Each of the various surfaces and obstacles you may encounter require specialized techniques. Practice the exercises in this chapter, gain proficiency, and go for it.

Maintenance and Trailside Repairs

Dual sports take a terrific beating on rough roads and trails. They pound over countless thousands of rocks, whoops, ruts, and washouts, slog through oceans of mud, ford swift streams, gulp huge quantities of dusty air, and occasionally crash. Modern dual sports are amazingly durable and able to survive these insults for long periods of time—if they get proper maintenance.

Some riders try to minimize mechanical work by riding newer bikes and taking them to the dealer for repairs, but sooner or later they will have a trailside emergency, and need to deal with it. This chapter covers routine inspection, basic maintenance, tire repair, and common trailside fixes.

SAVING THE DAY

We are riding to Pah Rah Peak and its stunning views of Pyramid Lake. Warm morning sun has

Sooner or later you will be faced with a trailside repair. The right tools and some basic knowledge will get you going again.

melted the early frost, leaving beautiful, damp earth with perfect traction. I am waiting at a turn for Don who is about 200 feet away, and not moving. After a few minutes I ride back to see what's up. Don's motor will start, but dies as soon as he opens the throttle. He and Jon are discussing probable causes as I arrive.

Clearly it's time for a trailside repair, but what should we fix? Jon thinks it might be electrical because his bike acted the same way and had a loose connection. Dean thinks it's a stuck float valve. I think that the needle clip has fallen off. We start the bike again and it idles perfectly, but dies immediately when Don opens the throttle. The problem is most likely in the fuel system.

We verify that gas flows from the tank by removing the hose, and then remove the seat and tank to access the carb. Don has worked on this KTM many times and his well-organized fanny pack has all the tools he needs. We loosen and rotate the carb, then remove the slide. Don spreads his jacket on the ground to make a clean, safe place for all of the removed parts and to make sure that everything is accounted for.

The needle should be held in place by a clip and rise with the slide, but it doesn't. Don's motor dies as he opens the throttle because it's getting more air, without any more gas. The needle clip is still sitting in the slide and Don removes it, then crimps it back onto the needle. Within about 15 minutes, we are back in business.

The day turns out beautifully as we carve perfect turns through gorgeous, wet sand, climb rocky two-tracks, and enjoy some of Nevada's finest scenery. However, it could have ended with us towing Don back to Bordertown. Some mechanical knowledge, the right tools, and good trailside work habits have saved our day.

A trailside repair can save a beautiful day. It sure beats towing the bike home.

PREVENTING TRAILSIDE EMERGENCIES

It's essential to deal with emergencies, but the best place to fix anything is in the garage, not on the trail. Rain, mosquitoes, dust, or finger-numbing cold are not conducive to making good repairs. Regular inspections and maintenance help keep trailside repairs to a minimum.

Inspections are a good way to spot problems before they become serious. And they are easy. Let's start with routine inspections before moving on to maintenance and repairs.

Regular Inspections

Give your bike the "onceover" before every ride. Check gas, oil, coolant, tire wear, and tire pressure; look at everything on the bike as you do it. Methodically check all nuts and bolts for tightness every few rides while the bike is new. After everything settles in, you can check less frequently. If you are planning an important ride, perform the "once over" several days in advance so that you have time to fix any problem you find.

Give the machine a thorough inspection about once every thousand miles. The frequency should vary with your riding style; inspect more frequently if you ride hard.

Manuals, Tools, and Parts

Make sure you have an owner's manual, parts manual, and shop manual. Some shop manuals are terrific, with pictures and detailed proce-

dures for every possible repair. Some are barely adequate, but all are better than guessing what to do. Parts manuals contain exploded views of every major assembly. Clymer and Haynes are two other sources of repair manuals for many popular models. They are well-written, filled with pictures, and cover most every type of repair.

Develop good work practices. Your objective is to prevent trailside repairs, not cause them. Work on one thing at a time and don't rush. Make digital photos of anything complicated as you disassemble it (to remind yourself how it goes together) and check the work when finished. Always coat bolts that thread into aluminum with a high temperature grease to prevent them from seizing and ruining the threads. Be careful not to overtighten

Does anyone have spare clutch plates in their fanny pack?.

► ONCEOVER CHECKLIST

- ► Try to wiggle the front wheel, fork tubes, and steering stem— there should be zero play.
- ► Note the condition of the front tire and brake pads.
- ► Tap each spoke with a wrench and listen. Any spokes that have a dull sound are loose and must be tightened with a spoke wrench.
- ► Lift the front wheel and spin it, looking for wheel and brake disk wobble.
- ► Place a straightedge on the brake rotor and look for wear.
- ► Check the condition of the brake pads and replace them when they are about two-thirds worn.
- ► Look for leaks of fork or brake fluid.
- ► Perform the same checks on the rear wheel, brake, shock absorber, and swing arm.
- ► Note the condition of all cables and hydraulic lines.
- ► Check all fluid levels.
- ► Note the condition of the chain and sprockets. Both chain and sprockets will need to be replaced if the chain is loose on the rear sprocket or the sprocket teeth are worn.

Check the brake rotor with a straightedge. Rotors usually wear more in the center of the shiny area where they are gripped by the pads.

The chain and sprocket are worn if you can pull the chain away from the sprocket.

- ► Adjust the chain free-play to factory specifications.
- ► Methodically check all nuts and bolts for tightness.
- ► Inspect the handlebars, levers, and switches.
- ► Look at the bottom of the engine and frame for dings.
- ► Look at the teeth of the footpegs; how worn are they? The teeth can be re-sharpened with a file.
- ► Wiggle the kick starter pivot to check for wear.
- ► Check the pipe and muffler for damage and leaks.
- ► Note the condition of the plastic and seat.

Start the engine and let it warm up.
- ► Make sure it starts quickly and idles smoothly.
- ► Listen to the motor—clicks and whirs are normal, but clanks, grinds, and whines are not.
- ► Check the headlight, tail light, brake light, turn signals, and horn.
- ► Clutch operation should be smooth.
- ► The brakes should work well enough to lock the wheels—always check them immediately after any repairs or adjustments.
- ► The transmission should shift smoothly into each gear. Check to make sure the shift lever is tight on its shaft.
- ► The motor should accelerate smoothly and briskly.
- ► After the motor is hot, look at it carefully for any sign of leaks.
- ► Check the oil level and its condition.
- ► Sniff the radiators—leaking anti-freeze smells like alcohol.
- ► Rev it up and look for excessive exhaust smoke.

Decide whether you will repair anything you discover, or take it to a shop.

bolts. Use a torque wrench when in doubt (so you can apply exactly the correct amount of torque).

Most experienced riders keep a log of maintenance and repairs. They record suspension settings, oil changes, and overhauls. These logs enhance the value of a used bike and help prevent trailside catastrophes.

You don't need a roll-away stocked with every Snap-On tool in the catalog. You do need a volt/ohm meter, sockets, combination wrenches, screwdrivers, and Allen wrenches that fit your nuts, screws, and bolts. Companies such as Harbor Freight have some nifty, cheap tools and gadgets, but I advise you to buy good quality wrenches that fit the nuts and bolts precisely. Sears Craftsman tools are good, and are often on sale.

Most motorcycle dealers stock very few parts. In the old days you went to the shop and waited for an overworked parts person to order whatever was needed. Then you went back in a week to discover that, often as not, the wrong part had arrived. Now you can go online, find the part, and order it yourself. A Google search under "motorcycle parts fiche" should turn up several suppliers.

It is good to keep a few high-wear spares on hand. Brakes wear quickly and bearings and seals often fail without warning, so keep some backups of those parts on hand.

Periodic Maintenance

Owner's manuals have recommended schedules of periodic maintenance. Read yours and understand what is necessary to keep your bike in top condition.

There are big differences in recommended maintenance between some models. For example, the Honda XR 400 was designed for casual, low-stress use. Its manual only lists a few service requirements and the intervals between servicing are long. The KTM 450EXC was designed for professional racing at the highest levels. Its manual lists many service requirements and the intervals are short.

Dual sport activities place fewer demands on engines than racing, and service intervals can be longer. The KTM manual suggests rebuilding the engine every 90 hours for hobby use, but most

Service manuals and a maintenance log will save time in the garage and leave you more time for fun on the trail.

Keep a few high-wear items—bearings, brake pads, seals—on hand so that you don't have to wait for parts when you need them.

RECOMMENDED INSPECTION OF THE 250/450/525 EXC ENGINE USED FOR HOBBY - ENDURO COMPETITIONS BY YOUR KTM WORKSHOP (ADDITIONAL ORDER FOR THE KTM WORKSHOP)						
a 100 liter fuel consumption is equivalent to approx. 15 operating hours	60 hours 400 liter	90 hours 600 liter	120 hours 800 liter	180 hours 1200 liter	240 hours 1600 liter	270 hours 1800 liter
Check the clutch disks for wear	●	●	●	●	●	●
Check the length of the clutch springs	●	●	●	●	●	●
Check the cylinder and piston for wear		●		●		●
Check the groove on the piston pin retainer for wear (visual check)		●		●		●
Check the camshaft for wear (visual check)		●		●		●
Replace the camshaft bearings		●		●		●
Check the length of the valve springs		●		●		●
Check the spring cap for wear		●		●		●
Check the eccentricity of the valve disk		●		●		●
Check the valve guides for wear		●		●		●
Check the radial clearance of the rocker arm rollers		●		●		●
Check the elongation of the timing chain		●		●		●
Check the chain tensioner tooting for damage (visual check)	●	●	●	●	●	●
Check the eccentricity of the crankshaft journal		●		●		●
Replace the conrod bearings		●		●		●
Check piston pin bearing		●		●		●
Replace the balancer shaft bearings		●		●		●
Replace the crankshaft main bearings		●		●		●
Check the entire transmission including the roller and bearings for wear		●		●		●
Check the length of the bypass valve spring		●		●		●

NOTE: IF THE INSPECTION ESTABLISHES THAT PERMISSIBLE TOLERANCES ARE EXCEEDED, THE RESPECTIVE COMPONENTS MUST BE REPLACED.

ENGLISH 23

This KTM maintenance schedule lists many service items which require regular attention.

dual sport riders change the oil, adjust the valves, and wait for something to need obvious attention before fixing anything. You need to decide which approach to use, depending on your style of riding.

Common Maintenance Tasks

Most riders do their own simple maintenance. Here is a list of maintenance items usually performed by users.

Air filter. Look at the air filter after every dusty ride. Clean it when dirty, being very careful not to drop crud into the air tract where it will be sucked into the engine.

Most dual sports are equipped with oiled foam air filters and cleaning them is a messy job. Manufacturers recommend that the filter be cleaned with a low flash-point solvent, allowed to dry, and then oiled. Low flash-point means something like mineral spirits or kerosene. Gasoline is highly flammable and dangerous.

Disposing of the solvent can be a problem. You can't put it in the trash and running it down the drain pollutes the ground water. Small quantities of solvent will evaporate in a shallow pan if left in the sun for a couple of days.

No-Toil makes biodegradable filter oil and solvent which they claim is environmentally friendly. You can read about their product at notoil.com. Other manufacturers offer a wide range of filter oils which claim to be "super tacky." Regular motor oil works just fine.

Check the air filter after every dusty ride.

Oil and filter change. Change the oil regularly. Some dual sports hold several quarts and the oil and filters can be replaced when the oil starts to look dirty. Others hold only one quart and need fresh oil and filters every 500 miles.

It is normal for a bike to need some oil after a few hundred miles of hard riding. High rates of oil consumption indicate that something is wrong. Lots of blue exhaust smoke when accelerating indicates worn rings, worn valve seals, or both.

Brakes. Brakes wear quickly on dual sports that are ridden hard, especially in muddy conditions. Heat travels through the brake pads to the calipers and can overheat brake fluid. Replacing the pads when they are about two-thirds worn will reduce heat transfer to the calipers.

Check the brake pad pins and replace them if worn. Brake calipers slide on another set of pins. Pull the calipers and inspect those pins. Give them a very light application of high temperature grease before reassembly.

From left to right the parts shown are the brake caliper holder, the caliper, and a set of EBC brake pads packaged with new pins.

You must push one brake pad back toward the caliper to get the new pads in place. After installation, pump the lever until the pads seat against the disk. *Do not pump before the disk is in place*, but always do it immediately afterward. Then go for a test ride and make sure you can stop.

Brake disks. Manufacturers specify a minimum thickness for disks, but they usually wear unevenly. The straightedge test (shown previously) will show whether you have a problem. Replace the disk when you see a gap between the shiny part where the pads wear against the disk, and the straightedge. Otherwise, the new brake pads will not make proper contact with the rotor and your braking power can be dangerously reduced.

Brake fluid. Replace the fluid every year. Always use the specified type from a tightly sealed container. Carefully clean the outside of the fluid reservoir and remove the top. Then attach a hose to the bleeder valve on the caliper so that old fluid will flow into a waste container. Make a loop in the hose so that fluid, not air, will flow back into the caliper. Barely loosen the bleeder valve on the brake caliper and pump the old fluid out with the lever. Work slowly and keep replacing the fluid as you go. Be careful not to let the fluid level fall too far or air will get into the brake line.

Brake bleeding. Air in brake lines gives a spongy feel at the lever. Air usually accumulates near the highest point of the line. Make sure the master cylinder (the one at the lever) is the highest point in the line. In front, turn the forks and lean the bike. Remove the master cylinder from the handlebars and hang it from something if necessary. Then compress the brake pad back into the caliper. This will push fluid and air out of the line.

The loop in this waste line ensures that brake fluid, not air, will drain back into the caliper when you replace the fluid.

You may also need to bleed at the caliper using the screw-in bleed valve located there. Pump the brake lever, barely crack the bleed valve, and then retighten it. You can wrap a loop of old inner tube around the handlebar and brake lever to apply pressure to the front lever while you bleed. Repeat this until no more bubbles appear and the lever feels firm. Make sure to replace the fluid in the reservoir as you bleed. Test the brakes immediately after bleeding.

Chain and sprockets. An O-ring chain is lubricated at the factory and has rubber rings on both sides of each link pin to keep the lube in and dirt out. Steel sprockets and O-ring chains last for many thousands of miles. Aluminum sprockets wear quickly and are not recommended for dual sport use.

Replace the sprockets and chain together when the rear sprocket becomes visibly worn. Running a new chain on worn sprockets will quickly ruin the chain. Running a worn chain on a new sprocket will quickly ruin the sprocket.

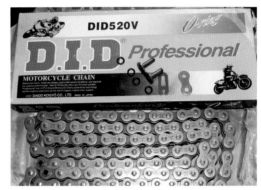

This O-ring chain is packed with factory grease. Grease on the pins inside the O-rings lasts many thousands of miles.

Some riders rarely lube an off-road, O-ring chain because they think it attracts dirt and accelerates wear. Other riders lube frequently with a product designed specifically for O-rings. Running O-ring chains in snow and water will soon wash away the grease behind the O-rings causing the chain to wear rapidly. Even if you spray lube on the outside, it will not penetrate the O-rings to lube the inside of the chain.

Battery. Use a battery tender if you ride infrequently. The small batteries on dual sports don't last very long. Ask your dealer about expected life and replace the battery before it leaves you stranded.

Wheels. Check for loose or broken spokes after every ride while the bike is new, then look at them every time you check the tire pressure. Tighten any loose spokes you find. Broken spokes can usually be replaced without removing

Use a long drift to drive out worn wheel bearings from the opposite side. Tap in new ones, being careful to keep them square to the hole.

These screw adjusters set valve clearance. This assembly is from an engine that was ruined when a rock broke an oil line.

the tire. It's a good idea to keep a few spare spokes on hand if your riding style is aggressive and likely to break them.

Inspect the wheels every time you replace tires. Try to wiggle the wheels on the axle before removal and replace the wheel bearings if you feel any play. Spin the wheels and look for side to side wobble. Correct wobble by tightening the spokes on one side and loosening on the other.

Axles. Remove any mud and corrosion from the axle with rust-inhibiting oil and fine steel wool. Do not use sandpaper, which will remove the plating and make things worse. Some of the newer axles are coated with teflon. Clean them with a wet cloth.

Valve adjustment. Your manual will give intervals and specifications for setting valve clearance. Some bikes have screw adjusters. Remove the adjuster covers and look at the rocker arms. Bring the engine to top dead center after the intake valves close. Both intake and exhaust rockers should now be slightly loose. Measure and set the clearance per instructions in the service manual.

Other bikes have bucket and shim adjusters. To adjust these valves, you must remove the valve cover, timing chain, and sprocket plus the cam. This work is beyond the scope of simple maintenance and you may want a mechanic to do the job.

Too much valve clearance can cause accelerated wear. Too little clearance can destroy the valves. They need to close firmly on their seats to

transfer heat and operate within an acceptable temperature range.

Forks. Replace the fork oil and seals at least every 10,000 miles. Measure the oil level before you drain it. The proper way to measure the oil level is to remove the fork tube from the motorcycle, remove the spring, fully compress the fork tube, and measure from the top of the oil to the top of the tube. Make sure you use the recommended weight of new oil and set it at the right level. Each fork tube has a dust cover and seal. Dirt will eventually work its way past the cover and destroy the seals. Lift the covers and clean them every thousand miles. Do not ride with dried mud on the fork tubes. Clean them first.

Shock. Have a qualified technician replace the shock fluid and seals every 10,000 miles.

FLATS AND TIRE CHANGES

The most frequent trailside repair is fixing a flat tire. Repairing a flat can be a ten-minute job or a time-consuming pain in the butt. The result depends on your choice of tire, preparation, tools, and technique. Most dual sports are equipped with tube type tires so I will cover them here in detail. Following that are some notes about tubeless tires.

Avoiding Flats

Many flats are the result of rim cuts caused by pinching the tube between the rim and a rock or hard surface. Medium weight tubes, tire pressure of 18 psi, and reasonable speed will prevent most rim cuts.

Nails are the other big cause of flats. Nails are particularly common around old mines, abandoned buildings, and dump sites. Park away from those areas and walk in.

Check tire pressure before every ride. Also, big hits from unanticipated rocks may force air past the valve. Stop and check air pressure after such a hit. Be aware that air pressure will increase because of hot weather and high speed. Do not reduce tire pressure back to 18 psi if the tire is hot.

Tires and Tubes

There are huge differences in tires and tubes. Some are very easy to change and others are frustratingly difficult, even in the garage with good tools and an air compressor. In general, tires with a soft carcass and rim protector design are easy to change. An example is the Dunlop 739 motocross tire. It has very flexible sidewalls with grooves on the outside that fit the rim. The soft sidewall is easy to mount and the grooves naturally center a tire on the rim. This tire is a good all-around performer in the dirt and not at all scary on the pavement, although it does wear very quickly.

Some people think stiff sidewalls and thick tubes are the key to avoiding flats, but most dual sport flats are caused by nails, which can puncture any type of rubber. Stiff sidewalls and overly thick tubes are difficult to change. Also, some tires are very difficult to center on the rim. It may seem silly to choose tires based on ease of changing, but it can be the key to rapid repairs.

The street tube on the left is too thin; the motocross tube in the center works well; the heavy tube on the right may be overkill for dual sport.

> ### ▶ *NOTE ON TUBELESS TIRES*
>
> It is virtually impossible to install a tubeless tire onto a rim without an air compressor. In case of a flat, stop immediately and remove any nails. Be aware that tire manufacturers recommend against plugging tubeless tires from the outside. Here is a quote from the Dunlop website:
>
> "Only small, straight-through 3/16-inch diameter or less punctures in the tread area may be repairable, if no secondary damage has occurred. A tire repair can be properly made only if the tire is removed from the rim; a thorough internal inspection is carried out; and the repair is made from the inside out. A repair must fill and seal the injury, i.e. vulcanized plug and patch. Only specially trained Technicians are qualified to repair a tire. Do not attempt to repair it yourself."
>
> However, in a remote area you may have no alternative other than using a plug inserted from the outside. Almost any auto parts store will have a selection of tubeless tire repair kits that should work in an emergency. Do not consider your repair to be a permanent solution. Have the tire replaced or properly patched at the first opportunity. ■

There are three grades of tubes: street, motocross, and motocross heavy. Street tubes are very thin and useless on dual sport bikes. Malcolm Smith, Kings, and Bridgestone make motocross tubes that are medium heavy. These are easy to mount and work well. Motocross heavy tubes are *very* heavy and harder to change.

Be Prepared

Take a good look at your bike. It usually takes as long to remove and replace the wheel as it does to replace a tube. Bevel sharp edges that might interfere with the wheel spacers. Practice in the garage and develop an efficient sequence of operations.

Make sure you have the right tire repair equipment and that it is in good condition. As a minimum you need wrenches to fit the wheel nut, valve stem nut, rim locks, valve core, and anything else that must be removed and replaced. Medium length tire irons (about 8 inches long) work well. Examine the tire irons and smooth any sharp edges. Carry a spare 21-inch tube which can be used on both front and temporarily on the back. Make sure it is a new one; not some suspicious relic found in the garage.

Push the tire to the center of the rim, hold it with your knee, and take very small bites with the irons to start the tire off the rim.

► REMOVING A PUNCTURED TUBE

When you have a flat, immediately stop and look for nails. Remove any that can be seen.

Then, you can carefully ride a few miles while looking for a good spot to change the tube. This riding may also break the tire bead. Find a rock, log, or berm to support the bike. A shady spot without mosquitoes is a bonus in the summer. Establish a place for parts where you won't kick them into the dirt and lose them forever.

Here is a step by step procedure to remove a tube from its wheel:

- ► Remove the valve stem nut. Remove the valve core and let all of the air out. Back off the nut from the rim lock to the end of the screw but do not remove it.

- ► Remove the wheel and place it on the ground with the brake disk facing up. Support the rim against a small piece of wood if you can find one and stomp on the tire to break the bead if it is not already broken. Then, turn the wheel over and break the opposite bead, being careful not to bend the brake disk with your stomping. It is possible to replace a tube while one bead is still seated, but the time saved is usually lost later because it is harder work. You can experiment in the garage to see which works best.

- ► Push one side of the tire down into the center of the rim—its smallest diameter—with your knees. Take the hooked end of your tire iron and pry the tire over the rim. Work from the valve stem, being careful not to pinch the tube between the iron and the rim. Place the other tire iron close to the first one where the tire is rolled over the rim, and pry the tire over the rim. Take small steps at first while the tire is tight and larger steps later when the tire is loose.

- ► Reach into the tire and pull out the tube, starting opposite the valve core. Then, hold the wheel with your knee, pull up on the tire, reach in, and remove the valve stem from the wheel.

Carefully inspect the outside and inside of the tire. Find out what caused the flat and fix it before working with a new tube. I once saw two people try to pump up a new tube while the nail that caused the flat was still sticking out of the tire. Don't let this happen to you. ■

Always carry a complete set of tire repair supplies when traveling off-highway.

Cans of air with flat fixer are virtually useless. There may be some type of slow leak that can be fixed with these bombs, but it is much better to swap the tube and get going, than waste time on something that is not likely to work.

Most riders carry small CO_2 cartridges and an adaptor that screws to the valve stem. It takes two cartridges to inflate a rear tire. I carry a tire pressure gauge and a good (small) bicycle air pump. You never know how many flats you will get and a pump does not run out of air.

Also carry a patching kit in case you ruin the spare tube. It is difficult to patch tubes in the field because they are coated with a slippery chemical left from manufacturing. It is always better to replace a tube on the trail than to attempt a patch, but sometimes you have no choice. Carry solvent and sandpaper to clean the tube before patching, and a roller tool to press the patch onto the tube. Make sure the glue is dry to the touch before applying the patch. Check the spare tube, patching kit, air bottles, and pump at least once a season.

If you have the right tires, tools, and a spare tube, the battle is more than half won and the actual changing should be easy.

TRAILSIDE REPAIRS

It is possible for almost anything to happen to off-highway vehicles. (I once managed to get my snowmobile stuck, upside down in the branches of a tree six feet above the snow, but that's another story.) However, most trailside repairs fall into

▶ *REPLACING A TUBE*

Now that the old tube is out, the next task is to mount a new one. Here is the procedure:

- Get a new tube. Make sure the valve core is tight and not leaking. Most people like to put a small amount of air into the tube before going further. This gives the tube some shape and makes it easier to put in place. Line up the valve stem with the hole in the rim. Push the tube into the rim for a few inches on either side of the valve stem.

- Switch to the other side of the wheel, temporarily pry the tire away from the rim with a tire iron, and use the ground to hold the tire iron in place. Switch back to the side with the tube hanging out. Hold the wheel with your knee, reach in, and push the stem into the hole.

- Put the stem nut on the end of the stem and give it a couple of turns. Do not screw it all the way on. Release the tire iron on the other side and make sure the tube is not pinched between the wheel and tire. Then go around the wheel, pushing the tube into the center of the rim. Make sure the rim lock is not pinching the tube. A crooked stem can be corrected by moving the tire on the wheel.

- Now you have the new tube on the wheel in the correct location. Push the valve stem down into the rim and start the bead back onto the wheel with a tire iron. Make sure the valve stem can

It is very important to push the tube away from the rim. Otherwise, you are likely to pinch it with the tire iron and ruin it.

move freely after you have started the bead on the rim.

- Hold the tire down into the center of the rim with your knees and keep working around.

- Be very careful not to pinch the tube between the rim and tire iron. It will cut the tube and you will be stuck with two ruined tubes instead of one. Work slowly and carefully.

- When you get to the rim lock, push it toward the center of the wheel. Then, lever the tire in between the rim lock and the rim. Make sure the lock moves freely and is not pinching the tube. Work around the wheel taking small steps at the end when the tire is tight.

- The last couple of inches will be hard because there is no room to slide the iron between rim and tire. You can usually stomp the tire into place.

- Replace the valve and tighten the valve stem nut. Inflate the tire and check its pressure. If you are changing tubes in the garage and have a compressor, it is good practice to let the air out of the tube and then re-inflate it.

- Tighten the rim lock. Inspect your work for leaks and replace the wheel.

Keep the old tube. If you are on a several-day trip, you can patch it that night. Check it overnight for leaks and it will be ready to use again. ■

Hold one side of the tire with an iron resting on the ground, then pull the other side up, reach in, and insert the valve stem.

► CHANGING A TIRE

When your tires become worn, they will need to be replaced. Changing tires is easier when they are hot and soft. Put them in the sun for 15 minutes or bring them into a heated room. Soapy water, applied from a spray bottle between tire and rim, also helps. After removing the tube as described above, reach across the tire with an automotive tire bar, about two feet long, and lever it off the wheel. Lean on the tire as it is coming off the rim and get your weight on it.

Use an automotive tire iron to start removing a tire from the wheel. Sit on the tire and then use a motorcycle tire iron to finish the job.

Push the brake side of the wheel into a new tire and lever it on. Start in the vertical position so you can get your weight on the wheel to hold it into the tire, then shift to the floor to finish. An air compressor is just about mandatory if you plan to change many tires in your garage. ■

well defined categories. Here are some of the more common problems and how to fix them.

Lost bolts. Carry spares. A few carefully selected diameters and lengths will cure most problems. Also carry some tape and soft, easily twisted wire. You can find soft wire in the section of a building supply that sells steel reinforcing bar for concrete.

Electrical problems. Electrical components take a real beating on rough trails. Filaments in bulbs break, connections corrode, and switches vibrate to death. Isolating a problem often requires a trial and error approach. Suspect the fuses or battery if a problem affects several components. Isolate the cause if only one component fails. For example, remove the bulb and verify that it is in good condition. If the bulb is good, trace the wire back to the switch and make sure that the wire is not broken or shorted. Then examine the switch if necessary.

Broken control cable. It is often possible to fashion an emergency repair with soft wire on the end of a cable. I once saw a friend grab the end of his broken throttle cable with a vise grip. He then taped the vise grip to the throttle and rode on.

Holes in cases and radiators. Clean the area as well as possible and use quick-setting epoxy such as J-B Stick Weld to repair the leak. It may be necessary to whittle a wooden plug from a stick. It is possible to run on one radiator if you can devise a way of blocking the leaking side.

Motors do not run very long without oil. You can use oil from the forks to replace lost engine oil in case of dire emergency.

Boiled brake fluid. Prolonged, hard use of the brakes will get them hot enough to boil the fluid. Cool them with water or release bubbles in the line by loosening the bleed valve while you push the lever.

Setting the rear pedal too high and continuously dragging the brake is the most common cause of boiling so make sure your pedal is properly adjusted before you start riding again.

WHAT TO DO WHEN THE ENGINE DIES OR WON'T START

Nothing is scarier than having the engine die when you are 70 miles from services. Calm yourself and proceed methodically; it is usually possible to get it running again. Engines need a mixture of gas and air, plus compression and spark to start. You must identify what is missing and restore it. Start by thinking about what happened before the motor stopped.

Did you fall? It is often hard to start after a fall because gas flows into the intake tract and creates

To bleed a boiled rear brake, push on the lever while cracking the bleeder valve. You should see a few bubbles appear.

an overly rich mixture. Turn off the gas, open the throttle, and spin the engine with the starter. About 20 revolutions will usually cure the problem. Then, turn on the gas and go through the usual starting drill.

Have you recently fixed anything? Go back and check any work that could affect starting.

Were you riding in water? Check your air cleaner. If it is wet, you need to wring out the water. Drain the carburetor to make sure there is no water in the float bowl and remove the spark plug. Be very careful not to drop dirt into the cylinder. Wipe, blow, wash with water, and do everything possible to clean the plug and surrounding area before removal. Then, dry the plug and spin the motor to expel water from the cylinder. Make sure to ground the plug against the cylinder before you spin the engine, otherwise, you might damage the coil.

Did it quit suddenly? This is usually caused by no spark or no gas. If your electric starter doesn't work you probably blew a fuse. If the starter works, but won't start the engine, check to see

whether gas is flowing from the hose into the carb. Tipping the bike on its side should cause gas to drip from the vent hoses, indicating that the float bowl was full.

If there is gas, check for spark. Clean the area around the plug and remove it. Test for spark by grounding the threads against the motor and spinning the engine. Remember not to spin the engine with an ungrounded plug or you may damage the coil. It is difficult to see spark in bright sunlight so shade it with the bike or your body. If there is no spark, look for loose or damaged wires.

Did you turn it off, and now it won't start? If the problem is not gas or spark and the hard starting has been gradually getting worse it might be due to improperly adjusted valves. When was the last time you checked them?

As valves wear into the cylinder head, they get tighter against the cam or rocker arms. Eventually they will fail to close completely and the engine won't have enough compression to start.

If the bike stops running, the first thing to do is think.

It is possible to set screw-type adjusters in the field with a bare minimum of tools. Remove the spark plug and valve covers. With the transmission in low gear, use the rear wheel to turn the engine through top dead center after the intake valves close. Watch the rocker arms above the intake valves (at the rear of the cylinder). You will see them push down to open the intake valves. After they return to their original position, the piston will be rising on the compression stroke. Bring the engine to top dead center on the compression stroke. You can use a screwdriver in the spark plug hole to feel the piston rise and determine top dead center.

Now try to move the intake and exhaust rocker arms. They should have a small amount of freeplay. If not, loosen the adjusters and retighten them until they barely touch the rocker arms. Then open the adjusters one half turn to get some clearance. This isn't precise, but should be good enough to get you home.

Starts but won't accelerate. This is possibly a loose wire or faulty ignition coil, but more likely something is loose in the carburetor. Check the wires in the ignition circuit first. Then, disassemble the carb looking for loose or clogged jets.

Were there unusual noises or smoke? This type of failure is rare, but strange noises may indicate that something inside the engine is broken. Serious internal damage is usually impossible to fix on the trail. You must plan on towing to a road.

A nylon web about one inch wide and 20 feet long makes an effective tow strap. It can be wound into a compact shape and is strong enough for the job.

Towing a disabled motorcycle is not as easy as it used to be. In the old days, dual sports had exposed frame loops supporting the rear fender and handlebars with cross braces. You simply attached one end of a tow strap to the frame of the towing bike. The other end was looped around the handlebar cross brace of the bike being towed and you were ready to go.

However, many modern bikes lack fender loops and cross braces. Steering dampers and headlights also interfere with attaching a strap to the towed bike. It is usually possible to loop the strap around the frame of the towing bike. It may be necessary to remove the headlight of the towed bike to get a good attachment point.

The towed rider should loop the strap around the handlebars and keep the end in one hand. The strap will pull and jerk as the motorcycles go over bumps and the towing rider will not be able to see what is happening behind him. The looped strap gives the towed rider the ability to break the connection if necessary to avoid a fall.

FINAL THOUGHTS ON MAINTENANCE

One of the best parts of dual sporting is the wonderful feeling of satisfaction that comes from competence—the ability to handle everything that nature throws at you. Mechanical preparation and repairs are an important part of the experience. Spend the time to learn how your bike works and perform the recommended maintenance. The skills you learn in the garage will serve you well when something happens on the trail.

Section 4
INCREASING YOUR ENJOYMENT

Near the end of his career, Ricky Carmichael, who earned 21 major motocross and supercross titles, said he was still learning more about riding. Motorcycling is that kind of sport. You can delve ever deeper into its physical, mechanical, and mental aspects.

Dual sport in particular is a broad, deep well of potential enjoyment. You can splash on the surface with a few rides each year, or dive deeply into its many physical and mental levels.

Not everyone has the time or inclination to become a dual sport zealot, but you may want to get further into it. If so, this section is for you. It covers organized activities, exploration, and dual sport touring.

A motorcycle, some gear, and basic skills are just the beginning. Dual sport can offer a lifetime of pleasure.

12

Organized Activities

Dual sport offers much more than just riding. It also presents many opportunities for making new friends, sharing adventures, and developing trails. This chapter introduces some of the possibilities.

NATIONAL ORGANIZATIONS

National organizations protect your right to ride through legal action and lobbying. Some riders become active in their national organizations and serve as officers and on committees. Becoming involved will expand your horizons and multiply your potential.

American Motorcyclist Association

The AMA, founded in 1924, focuses on rights, riding, and racing through its government relations work, by sanctioning riding activities, and by overseeing professional and amateur racing events. In addition, the AMA is the sole American affiliate of the Federation Internationale de Motocyclisme (FIM), the international governing body for motorcycle sport and touring activity. Their website is at ama-cycle.org

Improving local riding trails can be enjoyable and rewarding.

The AMA establishes types and classes of racing and sanctions promoters to hold events. Participants are eligible to earn points in regional and national championships. The AMA also charters clubs which can then hold sanctioned events. Their website, amadirectlink.com, has a list of chartered clubs.

Off-Road Business Association

ORBA is a trade association composed of off-road related businesses united to promote common goals that support prosperity and growth of the off-road industry. Although ORBA is a non-profit corporation, its officers and directors make decisions and take actions aimed at keeping off-road related businesses operating and profitable.

Membership in this organization is open only to businesses, but they are actively working to preserve riding opportunities. They have a very informative website at orba.biz.

Off-road volunteer organizations that are working at the grass-roots level on specific land use issues can apply to ORBA for financial and political support. ORBA Directors decide which issues to support, based on potential impacts to the off-road industry.

Blue Ribbon Coalition

The Blue Ribbon Coalition champions responsible use of public lands for the benefit of all recreationists. Their website is at sharetrails.org.

DUAL SPORT CLUBS

A motorcycle club can greatly expand your dual sport activities and enjoyment. Clubs provide many benefits. They offer an exceptional way to meet new people, participate in memorable

These club members are enjoying a wonderful May ride in the high desert.

rides, and make long-lasting friends. Your spouse and children can also make new acquaintances. Clubs are particularly attractive to people who move to new areas and want to connect with others who share their love of motorcycling.

Club members provide a deep well of knowledge about riding technique, setup, riding areas, and routes. They offer endless opportunities to swap trail stories and lie about your riding abilities. Members are there to help if you fall or break down. They cheer when you make it to the top of an impossible hill and jeer when you land on your butt in the mud.

Clubs offer the opportunity to participate in organized events and trail building. They provide a forum to protect your riding rights and push back against those who want to close every trail, everywhere.

Clubs aren't usually listed in the yellow pages so you may have to do some digging to find one. Go to the AMA website, ask at the local dealer, or talk to people at local races.

You will have more fun if you join with riders who share your interests and have similar riding abilities. Clubs come in different flavors ranging from loosely organized, social riding groups to exclusive cliques of serious racers. Here are some examples:

Different Types of Clubs

I was a founding member of my first club. Someone placed a notice on the company bulletin board. It said something like, "Meet in room 102 on Monday at 5:30 pm if you want to start a dirt riding club." About ten people showed up and we founded the TRW Dirt Riders. We had no charter or bylaws. We met once a month for beer and pizza, and scheduled one ride a month during good weather. The rides were almost always at Jawbone Canyon or Dove Springs and they were family campouts. The kids rode mini bikes and the wives gossiped while the men, and some women, rode. We had a president to conduct meetings, but didn't need a secretary because we never took minutes. It was loose, disorganized, and fun.

My next club was the Richmond Ramblers and they were more structured. They had an AMA charter and promoted an annual, for profit event. They owned their clubhouse, had a beer and wine license, and conducted well organized but hilarious meetings, complete with awards for unusual clumsiness.

Some Ramblers had professional racing licenses, most everyone raced at some level, and the general degree of riding skill was quite high.

We held monthly rides, occasional campouts, and many trips to local races, either to compete or to watch.

My current club, the Dust Devils, is somewhere between the other two. We are AMA chartered and sponsor the annual Ride Reno 200—a two-day dual sport event, complete with a banquet at a local casino. We hold a monthly meeting and schedule rides and campouts during months with good weather. Our rides are for street-licensed motorcycles. Member abilities range from beginners to former racers. Nurturing new riders is important to our club and everyone is welcome.

Most clubs are very candid about the type of members they are seeking, so describe yourself and see whether you have a good fit. It is not necessary to find a dual sport club. Most riding clubs have members who love all types of riding, and you may find dual sport riders among them.

You Get What You Give

Your club experience will be pretty much what you make of it. If you join and never go on any rides you will receive nothing. If you join and get involved you will enjoy a full measure of benefits. Don't wait for the club to come to you; take some initiative.

At first, make an extra effort to become part of the group. Clubs are usually composed of sub groups with different backgrounds and interests. Some members are likely to be lifelong friends, while others are recent arrivals. Long time members already have riding buddies. Take a pencil and paper to the first few meetings. Talk to people and try to find others whose interests and skills match yours. Don't wait for them to invite you; call and suggest something. Appear on time with a well prepared motorcycle. Call again after the ride to say that you enjoyed it.

Another sure fire way to meet people and earn respect is to volunteer and get involved in club activities. The Dust Devils have officers—president, vice president, secretary, and treasurer. We have a legislative officer, event coordinator, web master, ride calendar coordinator, and loop captains for our two-day event. There are also ride leaders and people who contact sponsors, handle signups, and attend AMA meetings. All of these positions offer opportunities to interact with others, do something for the club, and have a good time.

DUAL SPORT EVENTS

Clubs and promoters organize rides of one or two days which are popular ways to see new areas. The courses usually have 100 to 300 miles of good roads and trails in scenic areas and may include an overnight stay and banquet. Barstow to Vegas is the most famous event, but there are many other good rides.

Seeing the views from this pass at 8000 feet is even better on a club ride.

Soon this area will be crowded with riders arriving for sign-in.

A list of rides may be found at the website dualsportmagazine.com. This site has links to about 60 ride promoters in the U.S. and other countries. Many rides are also listed in the AMA calendar or on AMA district sites.

Dual sport events are sanctioned by the AMA if the club or promoter is chartered. Events are non-competitive and there are no championships or points. The rider experience is basically the same whether or not the event is sanctioned.

Organized rides have many advantages:

- The organizer selects a sampling of the best roads and trails in the area.
- Talking to the other riders and seeing the bikes and setups is a good way to learn and improve.
- You will be traveling with a large group that can help if you get into trouble.
- The organizer usually provides sweep riders to make sure everyone is safely off the course.
- You often get a cap or T-shirt.
- Some clubs provide great door prizes or raffle prizes.
- The ride may include lunch or a banquet.

A Typical Event

Every ride covers different terrain, but the basic features are similar. Let's follow two hypothetical riders, Ron and Sharon, as they ride one day of the Dust Devils Ride Reno 200. Ron is a new rider and Sharon is an old hand who rode the event last year.

Event promoters use mailing lists of prior entrants and electronic web flyers to promote their events. They also post notices in surrounding shops. Sharon gets a flyer in the mail about three months prior to the event and invites Ron to ride with her.

Promoters charge between $50 and $100 depending on the length of the ride and whether it includes a banquet. The entrance fee pays for permits, insurance, banquets, T-shirts, and food, if any. The rest goes to the promoter. All of the Dust Devil's labor to organize and stage the event is voluntary. We give part of our profit to charity and spend the rest on a club Christmas party and to promote next year's event.

Unloading at dawn and anticipating the day's adventure is a special moment.

These riders are heading for the sign-in table. They will start when they are ready and ride at their own speed.

Sharon fills out the entry form and mails it along with a check and self-addressed, stamped envelope to the Dust Devils. The club responds, telling her that she has been accepted, and provides a description of the ride. Descriptions vary depending on the ride, but they all cover the same basic points. Shown on the following pages is a Ride Reno 200 example that covers a lot of good riding information.

Sharon and Ron drive in from Sacramento on Friday night, try a few hands of blackjack in the casino, and turn in early. They wake at 6 a.m., eat in the coffee shop, unload their bikes, gear up, and ride to the start. Ron is nervous because it's his first ride, but nervous in a good way. Sharon is looking forward to the day because she had a good time last year and enjoys the role of old pro.

▶ INSTRUCTIONS FOR DUST DEVILS MOTORCYCLE CLUB – RIDE RENO 200

OCTOBER 8TH AND 9TH, 2005

GENERAL INFORMATION

Thanks for entering this year's ride. The courses offer a broad look at northern Nevada, including spectacular scenery, ridge running, historic sites, single-track, two-track, sand, and pavement. Riders will be going into the Tahoe National Forest on Saturday and into the Peavine Mountain area on Sunday. See the Dust Devils MC website (dustdevilsmc.com) for in-depth general information about the ride and courses. Click on the "Ride Reno 200" link in the left margin, then click on "General Event Info."

LOCATION AND SIGN-IN

Both days of the ride will start and end at the Boomtown Casino/Hotel plaza, below the BIG lighted sign. Boomtown is located adjacent to Interstate 80, approximately ten miles west of Reno.

Sign-in and start will be below the BIG lighted sign, to your left as you enter the plaza from the freeway exit, in front of the Truck Stop and Restaurant. Report there first thing Saturday morning to get your rider pack that includes the roll chart(s) and other event items.

If you have any last-minute riding buddies, we do accept walk-up entries on Friday and before 8 a.m. on Saturday. Although we usually don't run out of roll charts and other event items, we can't guarantee availability for walk-up entries.

BANQUET AND DRAWING

Saturday evening we will hold the banquet in the Boomtown Casino/Hotel ballroom. It will be a full buffet dinner. The no-host bar will open at about 6 p.m. and the buffet will open at 7 p.m. Pre-paid dinner reservations and additional sales are handled at the door. Dinner will be followed by a raffle drawing with several thousand dollars worth of prizes. A raffle ticket is included with your entry fee, but additional tickets may be purchased at the door.

Boomtown has been highly receptive to hosting our event. Please respect their facilities. Avoid excessive noise and speed. Remember, the sign-in area is a TRUCK STOP. Watch for trucks and be courteous to them.

THE RIDE

Saturday: About 150 miles. Gas is available about 70 miles into the ride at Sierraville. The lunch stop is also in Sierraville and is noted on the roll chart. If you're in Sierraville later than 3 p.m., we recommend you come back via the highway. Use the course map to find the way (the course map is enclosed in the rider pack provided at sign-in). Otherwise, if you are running late after lunch, several "bail-outs" are noted in the latter half of the chart.

Sunday: About 80 miles. It will be a short day; figure five hours at a reasonable pace, including a stop for gas and refreshments at about 50 miles out. The loop will run in and around Peavine Mountain, in the Humboldt-Toiyabe National Forest. As always, any bail-outs and food/gas will be noted on the chart.

This is not a race! You will have an enjoyable and challenging ride running an average speed of 25 mph. Stop and enjoy the views. Often they are noted on the roll chart. You may want to bring a camera.

Riding with a buddy is mandatory! If you don't have a riding partner, we'll assign you one.

LIST OF DOs

- Carry your driver's license, vehicle registration, and insurance info (both health and vehicle) with you.
- Pack your camera and cell phone—you never know when you'll really be glad you did!
- Use an odometer adjustable up and down by tenths. It's possible (but problematic) to use a street style spin-to-reset or push-to-reset odometer.
- Bring the right motorcycle. The courses are designed for lighter dual sport bikes. Heavy bikes (over 350 lbs.) such as those classified as "adventure" dual sport bikes are not recommended. However, if you feel confident in using a heavy bike, it's really up to you.
- Run a spark arrestor and a good muffler. Some, or all, of the course will run on USFS land where a spark arrestor is mandatory and a 96 dB exhaust noise limit may be enforced by USFS officials.
- Jet for higher elevation: The courses vary between 5000 and 9000 feet above sea level.
- Run the right tires. Full knobby tires are strongly recommended.
- Thoroughly inspect your bike and make sure everything is in good repair before loading it. Check your registration and lighting equipment. Your bike needs to be street legal for this ride.
- Be prepared for rocky sections. Tire pressures of 18 psi (front) and 16 psi (rear) are recommended. This affords a good tradeoff between rock protection and traction. Be equipped to do a trailside flat repair and bring tools for other minor trailside repairs.
- Be prepared for a range of weather during your ride. Fall in Reno brings a wide variety with temperatures ranging from 40º to 100º F, but it's usually our nicest time of year.
- Wear riding gear that will protect you in the event of a mishap.
- Carry at least a liter of water or hydrating sport drink—two if it looks like hot weather.
- Carry enough fuel. Plan for at least 100 miles in case you get lost. The longest course distance between gas stops is 70 miles.
- Ride single. Skilled riders who have experience riding double off-road could probably handle it, but most would not have a good time.
- Start your ride before 8:30 a.m. We provide an early and late sweep to assist you in the event of a problem. The late sweep leaves at 8:30; if you leave after that, there will be no sweepers behind you.
- Pay attention to your roll chart. We may hang ribbon in a few key spots (a ribbon sample will be on display at sign-in), but most turns are indicated only on the chart. If actual mileage between turns does not reasonably match, you are off-course. Go back to the last place you were on-course, reset to the indicated mileage, and try again. Look for trail markers like the brown USFS strip signs. They are noted on the chart and provide confirmation you are on course.
- Anticipate hazards. The courses use public roads and trails, most of which receive little or no maintenance. There are no danger markers. There could be obstacles, washouts, or vehicles anywhere on the course. Slow down for corners and when dust obscures the ground in front of you.
- Stay on the course. Cross country travel is strictly forbidden by our permits and public land usage rules. In the event of a problem, don't go off the course looking for assistance. Our sweepers carry cell phones and a contact sheet is provided at sign-in. Take it with you. If you need assistance and carry a phone, call in a request. Reception is possible in most areas. Otherwise, ask the next rider to report your location.
- Be considerate of residents and non-motorized recreational area users. Noise, excessive speed, and dust are our worst enemies. ■

Start Day 1
Saturday, October 8, 2005

Go to I-80 side of truck stop

RESET ┼ Reset Odometer at Stop Sign

Section 1-1, All
Dog Valley Road

0.00	⬆	Stop sign at truck stop
0.10	⬅┼	Stop sign
0.50	⬅	Stop sign
1.80	➡	Bridge Street
2.50	➡	Dog Valley Road
3.50	⬆	Pavement Ends
5.80	Y	Reset at Intersection

Riders will follow this roll chart over peaks and valleys, on roads and trails, for most of the day.

The sun is just rising as they reach the sign-up and other riders are gathered in small clusters surrounded by their motorcycles. Ron and Sharon sign some forms and get roll charts and maps of the ride.

Craig loads a GPS while Jeff explains the fine points of navigation.

Talking with other riders is half the fun. This event started from a casino and the sign has the odds inside at the tables, not on the ride.

A roll chart is an adding machine tape with printed instructions for the day's course. A small segment of a roll chart is shown on this page.

Sharon shows Ron how to roll the tape onto his chart holder. Ron brought his GPS and goes to a table where some Dust Devils with laptops are downloading tracks and waypoints.

Now they are ready to ride, but in no hurry to leave. One of the best parts of the day is seeing other peoples' setups and talking about motorcycles. They meet some guys from Oregon and Sharon falls in love with a beautifully prepared Husqvarna.

They finally start at about 8 a.m. By this time, most of the mad dogs, straining at their leashes to ride, are long gone, and there are big gaps between departing riders. They zero their odometers at the start and begin following the instructions on their roll charts.

They ride slowly through the small town of Verdi and up the Dog Valley Road where pavement ends. The last rain was weeks ago and it is very dusty. Ron drops back and lets most of it settle as the road climbs to a small saddle, then drops steeply into a beautiful meadow, ringed by aspens in fall colors. The course has a nice rhythm and sections of easy road follow more difficult stretches.

There is a downhill and rocky, rooty section that gets Ron's full attention, but nothing he can't handle. About 20 miles out, they come to the first/hard easy split. At this point the roll chart has options for those who want to ride on roads and those who want challenging trails. Things are going well and they choose the hard way. It's not too hard and they are rewarded with a wonderful view from a ridge top.

Spectacular scenery is a big part of the ride.

The route descends and climbs as it snakes past meadows and streams. Willows and aspens in bright fall colors highlight a backdrop of pine, manzanita, and sage. The sky is deep blue, punctuated with fleecy clouds, the air is cool and fragrant, and it's a great day to be riding.

At Bear Valley, about 40 miles out, they come to another hard/easy split and again opt for the hard way. This one is tougher. A rocky two-track descends into a steeply cut canyon, then rises back to the ridge and descends again. Ron's abilities are tested to the limit as he negotiates steep pitches of big rocks and dodges fallen trees. They make it to the bottom without mishap and head into Sierraville for lunch at the Country Store.

The tiny store, adjoining lawn, and parking lot have been transformed into motorcycle heaven. Its all big smiles and dusty faces as 200 riders eat hamburgers and wait for a turn at the gas pumps. Ron and Sharon see the guys from Oregon and swap riding stories until they notice that the crowd is much smaller. A Dust Devil reminds them that it is 2 p.m. and they still have 70 miles ahead.

The next section following an overgrown railroad grade is the best yet. The trail twists and turns through overhanging branches as it crosses small streams in deep shadows. Sharon opens it up and is rewarded with a huge rush of speed-induced adrenalin.

This event is not a speed contest. It's okay to take a break whenever you want to.

After gas and burgers in Sierraville they will be back out on the trail. It's another great chance to kick back and tell lies.

At the banquet, the creek crossing gets deeper with each retelling of the story.

The event coordinator checks raffle tickets for a ton of cool stuff donated by local shops.

Starting a trail maintenance day is a chance to see old friends and meet new ones.

The day and course flow pleasantly onward. It is getting near 5 p.m. and most of the other riders are long gone. Ron is getting tired and starting to ride slower. On another rocky downhill, two riders fly past and wait at the bottom. They introduce themselves as the Dust Devils sweep and suggest a shortcut that will get our riders back to Boomtown by six, in good time for the banquet.

The banquet is almost as much fun as the ride. There are close to 300 people in the room talking happily about their day—"When I hit that rock...," "The deer ran right in front of me," "It took us an hour to change the tire," "My bike beat me to death in the rocks," "Mine was smooth as silk," "I took a wrong turn after lunch." Memories are always best when you have others with whom to share them.

The talk is followed by an elaborate buffet, introduction of loop captains, and the raffle. Ron wins a new set of riding gloves, donated by a local shop. Then, it's early to bed and another day of riding tomorrow.

Organized dual sport rides are a tremendous value. You get most of the benefits of a professionally organized tour, at a fraction of the cost. If you later decide to return to an area on your own, you will have a good feeling for the terrain, and a sound basis for planning some more great rides. The adventures of Ron and Sharon are imaginary and every ride is different. Sign up for some dual sport events and make your own good memories.

ADOPT A TRAIL

All good roads and trails need maintenance. Heavy use destroys switchbacks and exposes huge rocks and ledges. A big downed tree or washout can completely close a popular route. Adopting a trail can be rewarding and fun.

The Dust Devils have adopted about 10 miles of single-track on Peavine Mountain. Follow us through a June work day as we repair and reroute some sections.

We meet at the Keystone Trail Head. The Dust Devils worked with other local groups to shape the Peavine Travel Management Plan and this access point is one of the results. Some roads were closed, but we got this new motorized staging area so, on balance, the plan was a good deal.

Members begin arriving a good half-hour before the 9 a.m. departure. This is a social day as much as a work day so the volunteers stand around talking, and looking at motorcycles. Bud has new boots, Steve has a good story, and Ralph, the new guy, is introducing himself and listening.

At 9 a.m. we start riding up the mountain to meet Larry, our USFS OHV Manager, at the work site. He is law enforcement and does hand out citations, but he does it with a light touch. He makes sure that people understand the problem and know how to correct it.

I saw him stop some people for a spark arrestor check. It turned out that he had cited them several months earlier and now they were all legal. They showed no signs of hard feelings and chatted with Larry for about 15 minutes before riding on.

After a short, pleasant ride we meet Larry in the pines. His Forest Service truck is filled with tools and equipment—rakes, hoes, Pulaskis (similar to a pick axe), hard hats, and a chain saw. He gives us some basic instruction on safety and tools, and leads us to the first section.

ATVs have been widening the trail, which is designated as single-track. This is a big problem everywhere around Reno. First, small ATVs use the trail, then wider ones follow, and Jeeps follow them. Soon there is a new road instead of a trail. We already have 100 miles of road on Peavine and don't need more.

We drag branches and tree trunks from the surrounding area and create a narrower twisting trail. Next we test it with our motorcycles to make sure it flows.

Now we move to a different location where the trail runs down a creek. Larry wants to move it up the bank so that the creek will drain well. We form a line and move through the area with surprising speed. Larry leads with the chain saw cutting an occasional bush to open a new route.

Three people with Pulaskis follow Larry to define the trail. Three with hoes follow them to smooth it, and another three use rakes to finish the surface. We move right along the bank at a slow walking pace and create a hundred yards of nicely curved new trail. Then we go back and throw brush in the old trail to close it.

This trail is in national forest and the rangers must approve all projects. These two rangers are great people to work with.

Larry is showing the club how to reroute a section to make it more interesting.

To get things done, you must establish good working relationships with local officials. It takes patience.

This is work, but fun work. It's really cool to be creating new trail instead of looking at "Area Closed" signs. We break for lunch and it's a great time to talk to Larry and learn about things the Forest Service is planning.

We reroute some more sections in the afternoon and then ride back to Keystone. Everyone agrees that this has been a most enjoyable and productive day. Eventually we will route and sign all 10 miles of the single-track.

PRESERVING RIDING OPPORTUNITIES

Many dual sport riders work actively to protect their riding opportunities on public land. National forests have hundreds of thousands of miles of dirt roads and trails. Land administered by the BLM has a similar number. However, riding opportunities are shrinking even as population growth generates additional demand for recreation opportunities. Environmentalists have portrayed motorized recreation as a threat to resource preservation. They are well-organized, well-funded, and tireless in their efforts to create more wilderness and close existing roads and trails.

The Forest Service and BLM have intense budgetary pressures. More and more people are using public land, but there isn't enough money to maintain old roads and trails, much less build new ones.

Many of the traditional routes on public land cross private parcels at some point. The legal status of roads crossing private parcels is often cloudy and can only be settled by going to court.

Washington sets the policy on motorized recreation, but local officials make decisions about specific roads and trails. They are continually updating management plans, which specify which routes are available for motorized recreation, and must seek public comment on every proposed action.

Each Forest Service District has a website filled with valuable information including maps and conditions. They also have descriptions of proposed actions, such as the following:

NOTICE OF PROPOSED ACTION

Description: Update the travel management plan for the Martis area to designate roads, access, and motorized trailheads. The project may also include rerouting roads for habitat improvement, designating an OHV loop, and closing roads.

Concerned people can have a significant impact on the results, but merely writing a letter or attending a meeting is not likely to be effective. The best approach is to establish a working relationship with local officials. Here is an example of an effective approach.

The mountains to the west of Reno are in the Toyiabe National Forest. Most of the land is wilderness, but three roads offer access to the 8000-foot level where there are 50 miles of routes open to motorized recreation.

Phil is a member of the Hills Angels Four Wheel Drive club. He is particularly interested in preserving the Hunter Lake Road, which crosses some private parcels in Reno and then climbs 3500 feet to Big Meadow.

Phil learned the history of the road and how it was preserved for public access when the wilderness was created in the 1960s. He attended council meetings and encouraged the city to recognize the historic status of the road. He wrote letters about the condition of the road and invited the District Ranger and OHV Manager to tour it with his four wheel drive club. The club adopted the road, placed signs, and made minor repairs.

This probably sounds like a lot of work, and it is. However, saving 12 miles of road is a big project with a big reward. Phil enjoys the work and his results are a source of tremendous personal satisfaction.

Now, Phil has a working relation with the Forest Service. They recognize that he has knowledge of local conditions and makes well considered comments. Phil and I recently cooperated on a response to a proposed action. All citizens are equal before the Forest Service, but you can bet that our 15 pages of detailed analysis, suggestions, and alternatives carried more weight than a three-line E-mail.

ETHICS

You will get more from your riding experience if you adopt and follow a set of ethical guidelines. This is a personal matter, but I highly recommend it. Most of this is common sense. Be courteous to other people on the trail—slow down or stop for hikers, horses, and bicyclists. Stop and chat if there is an opportunity. Treat public land as if you own it yourself; you do.

 ### SUGGESTIONS FROM TREADLIGHTLY.COM

- Stay on designated routes.
- Travel only in areas open to off-highway motorcycle (OHM) use.
- Be considerate of others on the road or trail.
- Leave gates as you find them. Respect private land.
- Yield the right-of-way to those passing you or traveling uphill. Yield to mountain bikers, hikers, and horses.
- Keep the noise and dust down.

Respect the environment and trail users. By using common sense and common courtesy, what is available today will be here to enjoy tomorrow. ■

Tread Lightly! Inc. is a national nonprofit organization with a mission to proactively protect recreation access and opportunities in the outdoors through education and stewardship initiatives. They also offer training and restoration programs strategically designed to instill an ethic of responsibility in a wide variety of outdoor enthusiasts and the industries that serve them.

The organization's goal is to balance the needs of people who enjoy outdoor recreation with our need to maintain a healthy environment; it's leading the way to help remedy current recreation issues. Tread Trainer™ is a training course designed to train participants in practical methods of spreading outdoor ethics to the public with a curriculum specifically focused on motorized and mechanized recreation. Their website is treadlightly.org.

FINAL THOUGHTS ON ORGANIZED ACTIVITIES

This chapter has covered some of the dual sport activities that appeal to me and my riding buddies, but the possibilities are endless. Use the unique combination of a license plate and dirtworthiness to pursue your own interests. Meet new friends on the trail, join a club or organize your own, help stage an event, adopt a trail, teach a class, ride to good fishing spots, take pictures of scenery few others see—and reap the full rewards of dual sporting.

13

Exploring and Navigation

We are following the Pony Express route, looking at remains of old stations. This trip started in Reno and will follow the route 450 miles to Ibapah, Utah. Some of the stations are ruins and others are just places on our map. Now, we are stopped to view decaying buildings near Grubb's Well.

Mick turns south on an alkaline track in the direction of Eureka, our day's destination, then stops and turns north. We are tired and eager to find a motel and shower, but follow without question. He has been leading for nearly two days, through a hundred dusty intersections, and hasn't made a wrong turn yet. Two hours and three stations later, we see Eureka.

The next afternoon, we reach Wells on the Nevada/Utah border, having traveled 600 miles, over nine snow-capped ranges and as many desolate valleys of low brush and dry lakes. Mick's trip planning and navigation skills are awesome. We never get lost, always find gas when we need it, and have a marvelous time reviving the spirit of brave riders galloping between stations in 1860, delivering letters from Missouri to California.

Any vacationing motorist can get directions from Reno to Wells from Yahoo Maps, but some of the Pony Express stations we visited aren't even in the database of places. The old roads do not appear on most maps; some look like they haven't seen travelers for years. No guide book tells whether there is food in Cherry Creek, or if the battered pump in Ibapah actually has gas.

Mick's success is based on research more than skill at reading a GPS. He has gathered maps, visited websites, read books, and made phone calls to get the all the necessary information. After that it's relatively easy to enter waypoints and follow the needle across Nevada.

LOST OR CONFUSED?

Dual sports really shine at exploring new areas and taking long trips. You can connect dirt roads and trails with brief stretches of pavement, and then go into town for gas or a motel. You can find every trail within 200 miles of home, explore the Baja Peninsula, retrace the Lincoln Highway, or ride the Rockies. Seeing different landscapes and finding new routes can be exhilarating.

However, getting lost is an unavoidable consequence of exploration. Some people have good directional sense while others seem to be perpetually confused. Everyone will eventually make a

The old station at Grubbs Well is not easy to find without some map work and a GPS.

With much experience in this matter, I have concluded that being lost occurs in varying degrees. I submit for your amusement these definitions.

Clueless. There is no specific destination, but everyone gets home before dark.

Confused. The leader knows the route to the next destination, but turns at the wrong intersection or in the wrong direction.

Seriously confused. The leader recognizes his mistake, makes another mistake, then repeats the first mistake, thinking he missed something.

Disoriented. The leader believes that the destination is in the wrong direction.

Seriously disoriented. The leader's mistake is obvious to others and he argues with them, insisting that he knows the direction. This usually results in appointment of a new leader.

Lost. The new leader begins riding aimlessly, looking for something that looks familiar.

Seriously lost. The leader admits he is lost and the whole group begins riding aimlessly looking for something that looks familiar. Everyone starts to worry.

The purpose of this chapter is to make sure that you are never more than temporarily confused. Everyone can develop good navigating skills and the exercises in this chapter will make you a confident explorer. ■

These riders are not lost. The are merely confused.

wrong turn—or several. My friends and I spend many days bumbling around in the woods, never quite sure of where we are.

Any day on a dual sport is a good day so a little confusion is acceptable. As the late Jesse Goldberg said, "You aren't really lost until you are out of gas and out of daylight." However, it's always more satisfying to actually reach your destination than spend the day following one dead-end road after another.

TERRAIN FEATURES

These days, everyone assumes that navigation means Global Positioning System (GPS), but that is only one of the tools available to us, and sometimes the least useful. Navigation is a combined process involving terrain features, maps (both paper and digital), the compass, dead reckoning, and even clues like sun position, slope, or water noise.

There seems to be an endless variety of terrain, but there are actually only a few patterns that repeat themselves on different scales—ridges, drainages, peaks, and valleys. Recognizing these patterns can make you a better navigator.

Memorizing the appearance and names of local peaks and water bodies makes it easy to navigate in your area.

Almost every place worth riding has elevation changes. The high ground may be mighty ranges like the Sierras or smaller ones like the Pine Nuts. It may be low hills or even river banks in otherwise flat plains. Specific peaks and hills make excellent landmarks. Learn the names of all peaks in your riding area, and how to recognize them from the ground.

Rivers, lakes, and streams are excellent landmarks. Learn the names of these features in your area and understand the areas they drain. Learn to recognize them on the ground.

Be mindful when crossing from one drainage basin into the next. Water starts flowing in a different direction at the divide, following the slope downward will lead to a new set of destinations. Pause at the divide and look at the terrain. Keep track of how many drainages you have traveled and how to retrace your route.

Dry washes and ridges are excellent routes in deserts where cross country travel is permitted. It is often possible to follow a wash, then climb to a ridge and continue. On the other hand, year-round creeks are usually choked with brush and are often impassible.

When you arrive in a new area, stop and see how it is made. Note the peaks, ridges, and drainages. Learn to recognize and use the available landmarks.

It is much more difficult to navigate in mountains with heavy forests because trees block most views of terrain features. In that setting, maps are absolutely necessary and it may be necessary to make repeated trips into the area to learn major landmarks.

Always carry a compass for emergencies. Heavy fog or low clouds can hide landmarks and cause total disorientation. The compass can be a life saver if the weather changes. The website geocities.com/Yosemite/Falls/9200/navigation_map_compass.html has a good discussion of navigating with map and compass.

NAVIGATING WITH MAPS

The next step beyond recognizing terrain features is to use maps. They are the key to understanding and enjoying new riding opportunities.

Sources of Maps

The U.S. Geological Survey (USGS) is the primary source of mapping information in the United States. Their website www.usgs.gov contains a lot of valuable information.

In the past, surveyors went into the field and recorded all of the roads and structures in rural areas. Now, maps are updated from aerial photographs. The results are published as Quadrangle maps in various scales. They are available from the USGS and at locations catering to hikers and hunters.

This rider has stopped at a divide in a desert range to note his position. Seven miles ahead, past a dry lake, is a paved road leading to a gas station. Behind him are 40 miles of open desert, where the nearest pavement and gasoline are two mountain ranges and three valleys away. This person can ride all day using these mountains as a reference. However, he may become seriously disoriented if he crosses into the next range without being aware of what he is doing.

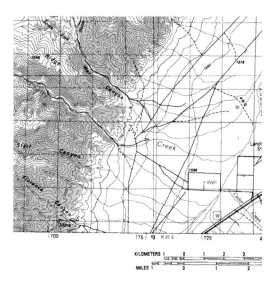

USGS Topographic maps show all of the major features—mountains, valleys, streams, and roads.

The USGS website has a clunky map viewer. They also have digital photos of most places. Terraserverusa.com also has a map viewer. Be aware that many USGS maps haven't been updated for many years. Some show old roads that no longer exist, without showing newer ones.

According to the USGS website, "The mission of the Cooperative Topographic Mapping Program is to provide the nation with access to current topographic maps. The 5-Year Plan calls for a dramatic realignment of USGS roles to deemphasize data production in order to focus on partnerships for data sharing." At the risk of cynicism, it sounds like they are going to attend more meetings and produce fewer maps, but still the USGS is currently an invaluable resource for dual sport navigators.

USGS sells its data to a variety of companies that modify and repackage it into paper and digital maps. For example, *DeLorme* publishes good state maps based on USGS data and bound in 11 by 15 ½-inch format. These State Atlas & Gazetteers show many dirt roads. I used them to plan our first trips to Nevada 20 years ago and still use them to plan long trips.

The U.S. Forest Service publishes maps of each forest, but they often lack grids and many show only the main roads. Each forest is making an inventory of OHV routes and some have posted the results on-line. Bureau of Land Management maps are based on the USGS quadrangle maps.

Dirt roads and trails are transient. Every year, loggers, ranchers, and visitors create new routes. At the same time, slides, washouts, and trees eradicate old ones. No single map has every road and trail. Try to get several different maps and compare them.

TOPOGRAPHIC MAPS

Virtually everyone has used highway maps to navigate from one town to another, but there is more to back-country navigation than simply following major roads to selected designations. You may be in an area with a spider-web of unmarked roads and trails most of which dead end in nearby mountains. Successful navigation depends on your ability to determine where you are and to choose a route which will get you to your destination. Most GPS receivers have mapping

DeLorme offers complete topographic maps for each state, bound into convenient books.

capability, but when you zoom out to see the big picture all of the secondary roads disappear. It is often easier to plan your routes on maps, even if you have a GPS.

Topographic maps are an indispensable resource, so let's cover the basics. For dual sport navigation the most important parts of a topo map are the legend, contour lines, grids, and roads.

The Legend

This is printed material, usually at the bottom and it contains several important items:

The *scale* is a ratio of map distance to the corresponding distance on the earth's surface. For example, a scale of 1:50,000 indicates that one foot on the map equals 50,000 feet on the ground. *Bar scales* are printed rulers used to convert map distance to ground distance.

The *declination diagram* indicates the angular relationships of true north, grid north, and magnetic (compass) north.

The map *date* indicates when it was printed.

The meaning of various *symbols* is explained. For example, two lines are a paved road; two dotted lines are a dirt road.

The *contour interval* shows the vertical distance between adjacent contour lines of the map.

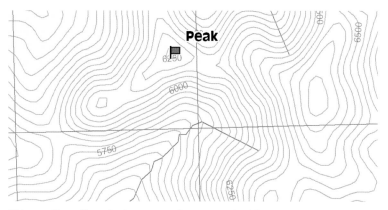

This small section of a topo map shows a peak, ridges, and water courses. Steep slopes are indicated by many closely spaced contours.

Contour Lines

Topographic maps use contour lines to show features like mountains and valleys. Contour lines represent constant elevation. For example, every point on the 5,000 foot contour is 5000 feet above sea level. Contours depict the size and shape of terrain features.

Patterns of contours pointing away from the peak are ridges. Patterns pointing toward the peak are canyons. The wavy blue lines are creeks. By looking at contour lines you can see which areas are flat and easily traveled or mountainous and more difficult to traverse.

Grid Systems

Grids are reference systems that relate maps to corresponding points on the earth. Perhaps the best known grid system is latitude/longitude. Each position on the earth is designated in numbers which correspond to positions on circles drawn around the globe. Circles of latitude are parallel to the equator and any two circles will always be the same distance apart all the way around the earth. Circles of longitude are not parallel and converge at the poles. Thus the distance between any two logitudinal circles becomes smaller near the poles. This makes it difficult to relate coordinates to actual positions on the ground.

The Universal Transverse Mercator (UTM) system is less known, but more useful for ground navigation. It divides the surface of the earth into one meter squares and gives each of them a unique address. Thus the UTM grid is always

square and can be 1000 meters on a side or any other convenient size. This makes it easy to plot positions on the ground and calculate distances between them.

The UTM address or reference always contains a zone number and two other numbers which are north and south positions in meters within the zone. The explanation which follows explains how it works. If it contains more than you ever wanted to know about UTM, just remember the basics: UTM divides the surface of the earth into one meter squares and gives each a unique reference number.

The UTM Grid

The UTM system divides the surface of the earth between 80° S latitude and 84° N latitude into 60 rectangular zones. Each zone is 6° of longitude in width and centered over a meridian of longitude. Each zone is 1,000,000 meters from north to south. The zones are designated by a number and letter. The numbers are west to east and the letters are south to north.

The UTM Grid system divides the surface of the earth into 60 rectangles.

UTM solves the problem of fitting square areas to a curved earth in three ways. First, it excludes the polar areas, second, it uses rectangles that are narrower than they are tall, and third, it tapers the boundaries of the zones, making them narrower as they get farther from the equator. This can be seen clearly in the picture of zone boundaries below.

Once the surface of the earth has been divided into rectangular zones, it is possible to establish new grids which divide the rectangles into smaller squares right down to one meter. The purple grid on the grid boundary illustration represents 2000 meter squares.

This map which spans two UTM zones shows how the grids at zone borders are tapered to fit flat map squares to a round earth.

Locations within the grids are given in meters from reference lines. The north/south reference is always the equator. The center of the rectangle from west to east is always designated as 500,000 meters, but the edges start and finish at values chosen to make the rectangles fit.

Here is an example. The center of Reno is at UTM 11S 0258300, 4379100. 11S is the Zone and it covers most of Nevada. 0258300 is the easting and all distances east to the Utah border will simply be bigger numbers. The northing is 4379100 and this is the actual distance, in meters, from the equator. It is seldom necessary to navigate with accuracy greater than 100 meters and it is easy to estimate where you are on a map that has 1000 meter or 2000 meter grids.

Within a zone you can add and subtract the co-ordinates to calculate distances. For example, Fernley at 11S 0306700, 4386600 is 306700 - 258300 = 48400 meters east of Reno and 4386600 - 4379100 = 7500 meters north of Reno. It is also easy to count grid squares and make a rough esti-mate of the distance.

The UTM grid is printed on some maps. Oth-ers have reference numbers on the margins and you can use them to draw your own grid. UTM is particularly useful with digital maps which allow you to print grids and with GPS which allows you to find your exact position on the map. These topics will be covered later in this chapter. See dmap.co.uk/utmworld.htm for more informa-tion about the grid.

Exploring a New Area with Maps

Here's a good way to explore a new area for day rides. Start by picking an area about 50 miles square (as much as you can explore in a day) and get topographic maps for it.

Study the maps, noting major terrain features such as mountains, ridges, canyons, valleys, rivers, and lakes. Test your knowledge by making a pencil sketch of the most important features. Note main and secondary roads and highlight a loop through the area. Roughly calculate the dis-tance and note any obstacles or points of interest. Include some mountains, if possible, so you can observe the area from high ground.

As noted above, deserts that have some moun-tains for landmarks are easy to navigate because you can usually see where you are. Before going to the area identify the key peaks and roads con-necting them. You can start from a known place, then orient yourself on the map and navigate from one mountain to the next. The landmarks make it easy to explore side roads, trails, and sand washes.

Areas that are heavily wooded and cut by deep canyons are difficult to navigate. It is hard to see landmarks and usually impossible to cross the canyons without bridges or good fording places. In those conditions, you must plan a route, navi-gate the roads from one intersection to the next, and keep track of your location at all times. It may be best to stay on major roads the first time in an area, noting minor roads and trails that look interesting for subsequent trips.

When you get to the area, orient yourself on the map and then proceed to follow the route.

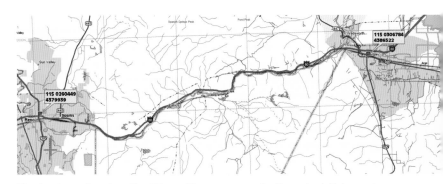

Fernley is east and north of Reno. You can compute the actual distance by subtracting the UTM coordinates for each city.

▶ MAP NAVIGATION EXERCISES

Here are some map navigation exercises that you can use to develop skills and build confidence.

- ▸ Make a pile of dirt or sand with a peak, one ridge, and one canyon. Assume it is 1000 feet tall and draw a simple contour map (with 200-foot contour intervals) showing the features.

This instructor is showing how the pile of sand would look if it were drawn as contours.

- ▸ Choose a nearby area and study its maps. Go to the area and orient yourself on the map. Note key landmarks. Pick a landmark and estimate the distance by looking at the map.
- ▸ Ride to it and reorient. Read the UTM coordinates from your map.
- ▸ Use the map to pick a spot between landmarks. Estimate the distance using the coordinates and the grid. Ride to it using your odometer and the appearance of the terrain to judge your position.
- ▸ Ride to several intersections and mark each on the map as you reach it.

Terrain features and topo maps are cheap and easy to use. Digital maps and GPS require a substantial investment of money and time. They are fine if you like technology, but do not get sucked unwittingly into spending your riding days at the computer or fiddling with electronics. Dual sport is primarily about riding. ■

Estimate distances between intersections and use the odometer to keep track of how far you have gone toward the next intersection. Stop as often as needed to reorient and note your position. At home, establish a filing system for the maps and keep them for future use.

DIGITAL MAPS AND AERIAL PHOTOS

The USGS maps and aerial photos are available to companies who package them so they can be stored and viewed on personal computers.

Sources of Digital Maps and Photos

Microsoft and the USGS have a partnership, TerraServer-USA, which stores and displays digital maps and photos. The TerraServer-USA website is one of the world's largest online databases, providing free public access to a vast data store of maps and aerial photographs of the United States. TerraServer-USA is operated by the Microsoft Corporation as a research project for developing advanced database technology. Check it out at terraserver-usa.com.

Several companies package the USGS data on CDs or DVDs and bundle it with a viewer/printer. For example, DeLorme's *Topo USA* offers detailed maps of the entire USA, including Alaska & Hawaii on a single DVD. Their website is at www.delorme.com. Other products like TopoGrafix's *ExpertGPS* allow you to download maps and photos as needed. Their website is at topografix.com. A Google search for "topo maps" will find many digital mapping programs.

Features of Digital Navigation Programs

With a good digital mapping program you may never need to buy another map. The state, region, or even the entire country will be instantly available for viewing and printing. The best digital mapping programs have several modules.

Viewer searches for and displays all of the information from the USGS database at various scales.

Navigator allows you to define routes and estimate distances.

GPS interface sends to, and receives from, GPS receivers.

Drawing allows you to draw lines and shapes, and make notes.

Printing allows you to make your own paper maps.

Gee whiz features—3D displays, slope calculation, simulated flyover.

The most important consideration in choosing a program is how well the modules work. Some scroll across a very large area, allowing you to see the north and south of a state or region without needing to load different maps. Others require you to load a new map for each small area. This can become a real pain when planning a trip in the boundary between two maps. Some allow you to see exactly what you are printing and others don't. Some hide and reveal information at different scales in ways that can be annoying. Some work well with a variety of GPS models while others display cryptic error messages.

Unfortunately, there is no easy way to test functionality prior to purchase. I have had acceptable results with *Topo USA* and Garmin *Map Source* but products are continually changing. My best advice is to ask your friends for current recommendations and buy from a retailer who will accept returns.

The ability to plan a route on your computer screen, draw it on a map, and estimate the mileage is invaluable for planning trips into new areas. You can print maps with a 1000-meter UTM grid and carry them clipped behind your number plate. Once you have the maps printed and clipped, use them just like any other topo maps.

Uses of Aerial Photos

Aerial photos don't show slopes as clearly as contour maps, nor can they show roads that are hidden by trees. However, they can reveal important details. The National Aerial Photography Program (NAPP) of the USGS provides a standardized set of cloud-free aerial photographs covering the U.S. over five-to-seven year cycles. Several software companies offer programs which download both USGS maps and aerial photos on demand, plus send and receive GPS waypoints and tracks. *ExpertGPS* works well for this purpose.

Different digital mapping and photo programs may show different roads, bridges, mines, and other features, depending on when they were updated and how the mapping companies decide to

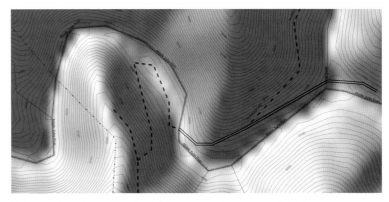

This section of an older digital topo map shows a road which crosses many contours to descend steeply into a deep canyon. It then crosses the Yuba River and climbs the other side. The important question is whether there is a bridge over the river at this point or whether the Yuba must be forded.

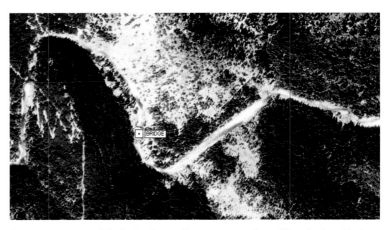

A more recent aerial photo shows the same crossing with a feature that looks like a bridge, but the photo resolution is only fair and the photo is likely to be several years old. Regardless, the photo provides an important clue that there is a bridge and that crossing will be possible.

Google Earth has stunningly detailed images of urban areas—like this shot of San Francisco's Market Street, with cars clearly visible on the street. Google also has very good quality images for many remote areas. It is well worth investigating. Download it free at google-earth.com.

These riders are using a Garmin GPS 76Cx to navigate this empty country. The GPS 76Cx has a color display and gives turn-by-turn instructions.

This Garmin navigation screen shows a directional arrow and distance to the next waypoint.

display features. It is wise to check several sources when planning trips.

GPS

GPS offers several useful benefits to dual sport navigators: finding your exact current position, pointing toward a chosen location, and displaying routes and maps.

Basically, a GPS receiver computes your current position and stores it in memory. A single position is called a *waypoint.* A series of waypoints, in consecutive order, is a *route.* The collection of all the positions you have traveled is a *track,* an electronic record of the trip.

Most GPS devices also store and display maps. You can see exactly where you are on the map and which roads will take you to the destination. Most units allow you to select a destination and then compute a route that will take you there. If you will be riding mostly on highways and major dirt roads the GPS mapping features may be all that you need.

However, you need to spend some time learning the features of your GPS if you want to successfully explore secondary roads and trails that may not even be on the map. The following section will help you master GPS navigation.

GPS Features

GPS receivers calculate your position on earth relative to satellites in space. The satellites are like beacons with known positions, and the distance to them determines your position. A good description of the technology may be found on the web: colorado.edu/geography/gcraft/notes/gps/gps_f.html. However, you don't need to understand the technology to use GPS.

A GPS receiver must have an unobstructed path to at least three of the GPS satellites to compute your position. Heavy tree coverage and deep canyons block reception and the GPS will stop working properly until you move to a better location. Also, be aware that most GPS models do not orient themselves to north and show proper directions to waypoints unless they are moving.

A GPS has an LCD display screen displaying several "pages" of information including: satellite status, mapping and tracking, navigation screen with a directional arrow, trip computer with various statistics, pages for waypoints, routes, and setup menus.

A good user interface is very important. My first GPS had a most confusing set of menus and submenus, and it was nearly impossible to do anything without the manual. Most shops will open the box and let you stand at the counter and read the manual. Don't buy if it looks complicated. You may be using it under difficult conditions when you are tired, frustrated, and seriously disoriented.

Several different manufacturers offer a wide selection of models ranging in price from about $100 to over $1,000. Vibration and crashes are

The Garmin Etrex Legend, shown with its User Guide and computer cable, is inexpensive and adequate for most backcountry navigation.

hard on GPS. You may want to buy a cheaper one so you can replace it without regret.

Many riders like the Garmin Etrex Legend, priced around $160, for trails and rough two-tracks. It has a simple user interface and enough memory to store long tracks, and hundreds of waypoints. Most digital mapping programs can transfer routes to it.

Read the owner's manual at home and learn the functions. Do not go into the field without mastering the basics. You will only become frustrated as you fumble and your buddies comment about your impaired mental capacity.

Loading Maps into GPS

Maps can also be loaded to GPS. For example, the Garmin *Map Source* program downloads detailed area maps to their units. Basic models have black and white screens measuring about one inch by two inches. More expensive models have larger color screens. However, it is hard to use

A RAM Mount GPS holder provides a secure, vibration-absorbing mount.

maps on the GPS screens, even units with larger screens. They show a tiny area when you zoom in to see detail and lose detail when you zoom out to see a larger area. You may prefer to bring paper maps even if your GPS has mapping capability. Never concentrate on the GPS when you should be scanning ahead for danger.

GPS Mounting

RAM Mount (at ram-mount.com) has a complete line of GPS mounting hardware. RAM stands for Round-A-Mount. Most of the product line is based on a patented design using a rubber ball and socket.

Some riders power their GPS unit from the motorcycle electrical system. You can wire it directly to the battery on a fused circuit. It is also possible to just use batteries in the GPS. *Always* bring a few extra batteries for backup in either case.

Exploring a New Area with GPS

Here are some pointers about using your GPS and mapping program to explore a new area. Start by reviewing digital topo maps of the area, noting the nature of the terrain and key landmarks. On a digital map, place a few waypoints at key intersections to define a rough loop.

▶ GPS NAVIGATION EXERCISE

Some people are fascinated with creating and following tracks. However, understanding and using waypoints is the real key to exploring new areas and creating your own routes.

Note that this exercise is designed to build proficiency with GPS plus digital maps, but it is also possible to establish waypoints using only the GPS. Your user manual will have instructions. The exercise assumes that you have a GPS and digital mapping program and know how to use them.

Begin the exercise at home.

- Set the GPS and mapping program to display UTM coordinates. Select the correct datum for the map. For example, Topo USA uses NAD 27 for UTM coordinates. Set the GPS to the same datum as the map. Select the same options for both GPS and map—metric scale, true north, grids, and contours on.

- Display on your computer screen a digital map for an area of a few square miles. Select an area close to home that is open, rather than heavily wooded. It should also have a few landmarks and roads.

- Enter three waypoints a few miles apart at turns on roads, and number them 0001 to 0003. Print a paper map.

- Power up your GPS and if possible select an option to use it without satellite reception. This is "GPS off" on mine. It is actually running, but not recording my current position data.

- Clear the GPS trip computer and all tracks, waypoints, and routes.

- Send the waypoints from your mapping program to the GPS and verify that they have been received.

- If you have a mapping GPS, load a map of the same area so you can compare the GPS and paper maps and note their relative ease of use.

- Turn off the GPS.

- Manually place a mark on the paper map between waypoints 0001 and 0002 and write its coordinates on the map. Use the grid to determine the coordinates.

Now go to the field with your paper map and GPS mounted on the handlebars. Bring the user's manual if you are still shaky on any points.

- Turn on the GPS and acquire the satellites.

- Tell the GPS to "GoTo" waypoint 0001. Ride a bit until the needle stabilizes in the right direction and follow it to waypoint 0001.

- Now tell the GPS to "GoTo" waypoint 0002. The needle should now point to the next waypoint and display the straight line distance. Pay attention to your surroundings. Do not focus on the GPS and crash into something that you should have seen.

- Use terrain features to navigate to your manually placed mark. Stop and compare the GPS coordinates

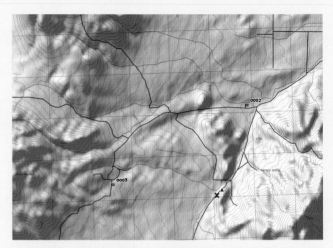

Here are three waypoints that will be used in a navigation exercise. This rider will master the basics before starting a long trip.

Here, a rider is marking his current location in the GPS. If needed, the GPS can point him back to it.

to the ones you wrote on the map. How close did you get?

- At the waypoint, look at the map, orient yourself on the map and ground, and note any relevant landmarks.

- Mark this position as a waypoint using the appropriate buttons on the GPS.

- Continue following your route to 0002 and 0003. Then turn off the GPS. Otherwise, it will record your track all the way home.

At home upload the GPS track into your mapping program. Compare your track with the waypoints. How did you do?

This exercise covers the basic steps needed to plan routes on digital maps, transfer them to GPS, and follow the route on the ground. Practice until you feel comfortable and then try some more difficult routes. ■

This is the only place for many miles where this river canyon can be crossed. It was easy to find with a GPS waypoint.

Next, add waypoints for the intersections between the key waypoints. Pay particular attention to unusual intersections like five-ways which may need extra waypoints. Add some confirmation waypoints at important landmarks like summits and stream crossings.

You should zoom in on the map and place the waypoints about two-tenths of a mile past the intersection. On the ride your GPS will recognize that it is approaching a waypoint and the navigation needle will swing toward it, showing you the correct direction to turn.

Number the waypoints as 0001, 0002, etc. leaving some unused numbers between intersections for possible revisions. When you finish, review your work and convert waypoints to a route. A route is a collection of waypoints in sequential order. Your GPS will automatically advance to the next waypoint as you pass the current one.

Some of the programs don't talk to each other because they store position data in different formats, but they usually talk to the GPS. It is sometimes easier to use the GPS as an intermediary than fight the formats. I use an old version of *Topo USA* to establish the waypoints, upload them to my GPS, download them to *Map Source,* convert them to a route, then load the route back to the GPS. Your software may provide an easier way. Check your work and print some paper maps with UTM grids, showing the waypoints.

When you get to the area, turn on the GPS and use the navigation screen to go to the first waypoint. Remember, the navigation arrow does not point in the right direction unless you are moving, so ride a short distance until the arrow stabilizes. The screen will then display a proper arrow and distance to the first waypoint. When you get there orient yourself on the paper map and note any landmarks. Then proceed to follow the route to the next waypoint.

As you go around curves in the road, the needle will continue to point, as the crow flies, to the next waypoint. It may sometimes appear that you are headed away from where you want to go. Just follow the road because the waypoint should be found at the next possible intersection.

If you have placed waypoints two-tenths of a mile past intersections, the arrow will swing to the correct direction as you approach them.

Follow the arrow through the waypoint. The GPS will then advance to the next waypoint and display the distance and direction.

A few waypoints at major landmarks may be all that is needed in the desert, but you will need waypoints at every intersection in heavily wooded mountains. In those areas, establish lots of waypoints and confirm your position frequently.

In heavy tree cover, the GPS loses contact with satellites and its navigation needle may swing to the wrong direction for a few minutes before the screen goes blank. This can happen just before an important turn. If it does, try to get to a clear area and confirm your location before heading off in the wrong direction. If you do get off the route use the GPS coordinates and map to plot your location and get back on course.

A loop with outgoing and returning roads that are close together can cause problems. The GPS may direct you to the next *nearest* waypoint, even though it is on the incoming route, when you actually want to follow the outgoing route. In this situation you may need to consult the map, find the proper waypoint number, and give the GPS a manual "GoTo" command. Your instruction book will explain how to do this.

Navigating is especially difficult in areas with a mixture of public and private land because roads on the map may not be open for public use. You may ride many miles, only to be stopped by a locked gate. Allow extra time and gasoline for navigating near private land.

FINAL THOUGHTS ON EXPLORING

The great thing about dual sport navigating is that you can have fun even if you are slightly confused. It feels great to be outside on a good day seeing new country. No matter which approach you use—terrain features, map, GPS, or even determined bumbling—get out and explore your area.

14

Trips and Touring

This chapter contains information to help you plan and execute overnight and longer trips on a dual sport. It does not cover topics such as visas, vaccinations, and getting your bike through customs. Those topics are covered very well in books such as *Adventure Motorcycling Handbook* by Chris Scott, Trailblazer Publications, or *The Essential Guide to Motorcycle Travel* by Dale Coyner, Whitehorse Press.

TWO DAYS ARE BETTER

It's the summer of 1980 and my friend Gary is talking me into a three-week, 7000-mile trip to British Columbia and Alaska. "If one day on a motorcycle is good, two must be twice as good," he says. I nod. "If two days are twice as good, three days must be three times as good." I nod again. The plan is to truck the bikes to Quadra Island, BC, and then complete the tour by motorcycle and coastal ferry.

It's an easy sell. I am between jobs and wives, and looking for adventure. Gary is my hero. He introduced me to enduro riding and has been a test rider for Honda. As he describes the trip, I forget that he once talked me into riding a moonlight enduro in the desert on a moonless night.

"Be sure to bring rain gear," he says. "You can stay warm, if you can stay dry." I should have paid more attention. Gary has been testing the new Honda Gold Wing for months in every state and season, and knows a lot about riding in foul weather. The emphasis on rain gear should have raised a flag.

Now it is five weeks later and I am shivering in a muddy motel room, surrounded by muddy gear, with a muddy bike parked in front, waiting for my turn in a hot shower.

The day started well as we disembarked from the ferry in Prince Rupert and scrounged the local laundromat for bleach bottles in which to carry extra gas. We rode east on Highway 16 following the Skeena River in a beautiful canyon graced by numerous waterfalls. At Highway 37 we turned north onto dirt, and rode through forest, sharing the road with a logging truck that made incredible dust and was impossible to pass.

After stopping for a bread and cheese lunch, we poured extra gas into our tanks just as the first rain drops began to fall. At first, we welcomed the dust reduction, but then it started to pour. The road turned to snot, the tires flung it in our faces, and we struggled to stay upright and moving. No problem; we're tough.

Three hours later the tiny outpost of Tattoga Lake, near Iskut, showed in our fogged and spattered goggles. It was a typical backcountry affair—general store, restaurant, gas, and a few rooms under one roof, fronted by rusty vehicles

A dual sport trip can be one perfect day after another.

Gary tapes a headlight broken by a big, rock-spitting mining truck—note the rubber rain suits and clamp-on windshield.

Here, the intrepid travelers enter the Yukon—they're not exactly the first to visit, but it's a first for them.

of various ages. In our situation, it looked like paradise. All thoughts of camping on the first night of our camping trip had long since passed, and we grabbed a room with eagerness that mocked our "rough it" aspirations. We spread damp riding clothes around the room, ate dinner, and turned in early to the smell of drying wool underwear.

In the morning, the room looked like a mud-wrestling pit—mud in the shower, mud on the linens, mud on the carpet, and mud on the walls. But outside, things were looking good. The rain was gone, the road was drying, and the sun was shining. Yesterday's troubles were history and we set forth eager for more adventure, grateful that the manager wouldn't see the condition of our room until we were miles away.

Over the next two weeks there were some more muddy days, but mainly we had incredible scenery, good companionship, and terrific fun. That trip was more than 25 years ago and I still remember our days. Gary was right. "If one day on a motorcycle is good, two are twice as good."

While dual sport touring can produce the stuff of wonderful life-long memories, you need not approach every dual sport trip as a major event.

Don't let all of the possibilities and considerations spoil the fun. Plan a local route with a mixture of paved and dirt roads, pick a weekend with good weather, throw some after-ride clothes in a backpack, stay in a motel, and enjoy yourself.

ONE OR TWO NIGHTS

Short trips allow you to get away without taking vacation days from work or neglecting your family. Short trips also let you gauge your riding endurance and test your packing list with little risk. Here is a good way to start your adventures.

Planning an Overnight

Pick a destination within 150 miles of your home, looking for places that are off the main tourist paths. Then get a DeLorme state *Atlas and Gazetteer* and look for interesting back roads. The fine red lines are usually open to the public; dotted red lines may or may not be open.

Plan a route to your destination using some highways and fine red lines. Note the dotted lines for possible exploration and estimate the total mileage for your trip. About 150 to 180 miles is usually a full day, but leaves plenty of time to

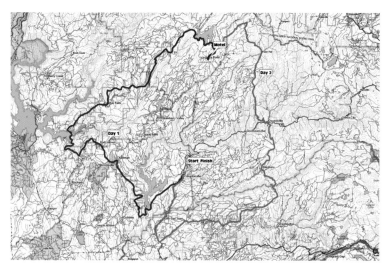

Start sketching your trip on the map. Short, easy trips can be great fun.

Motorcycle trips are more fun with friends along.

dismount, stretch, eat, and take pictures. If you live deep in some endless metropolitan maze of freeways, malls, and cul-de-sacs, you may want to truck or trailer the bike to a starting place.

Invite a riding buddy or two. It should be relatively easy to find someone to go with you on an overnight. Short trips are more fun with friends.

Make a copy or sketch of the maps you will be using and highlight the route. Put them in a plastic bag. Clip them behind the front number plate or keep them in a tank bag where they are easy to reach.

Search the internet for your destination. It will usually turn up some motels and points of interest. I make reservations when traveling to small towns on weekends.

Check the weather forecast a few days before the ride and then again the day before. Good forecasts can be found at wrh.noaa.gov. Note the high and low temperatures plus the probability of rain. Try to ride on warm days with little possibility of rain. Stay home on cold rainy days. Be aware of local conditions. It can be 50 degrees and foggy on the Northern California coast, but 90 degrees a few miles inland.

Solo or double? A basic consideration of all trips is whether to ride single or carry a passenger. The race-derived lightweight bikes don't have passenger pegs and their frames may not be strong enough to support the weight of two riders. The heavier dual sports can generally carry the load plus enough baggage for two.

If you intend to carry an inexperienced passenger, it may be wise to ease into it. Start with short trips and frequent rest stops to see whether he or she really enjoys the experience. Listen to feedback and look for clues. There is little to be gained by equipping an unenthusiastic partner for long distance touring; shorter trips might be a better option.

If you find a willing partner, remember that dual sports usually have small seats and poor wind protection. You will both become very uncomfortable if you attempt marathon days in the saddle. Plan trips in areas with interesting things to see and do off the bike. Ride a while, stop and walk a while, and pause for snacks and soft drinks. Days like this can be very enjoyable for couples.

If you plan to ride off-highway make sure that your passenger has boots, knee guards, and elbow protection. Rough dirt roads and trails are hard on both rider and passenger. Neither of you will be able to stand for bumps so you must ride slowly over them. Even at slow speed you will get pounded and use a lot of energy, so don't attempt long stretches of rough stuff unless your passenger really likes this type of adventure.

Steep hills and rocky sections are especially challenging with a passenger. In these situations it may be better for your partner to walk short distances than to risk a crash. You may get into a situation where forward motion stops and it looks like you are going to drop the bike. Show the passenger how to step off on the uphill side when you yell "get off" and practice this maneuver a couple of times.

Backpacks

Backpacks have become very complicated, but more is not always better. One of my recent acquisitions has four zippered pouches, two mesh pouches, three inside pouches, bungee cords, and a padded back. However, there isn't room to pack the regular overnight stuff plus a gallon container for extra gas.

My old faithful pack has padded straps, one big compartment with a draw string, and one zippered flap. It holds all the gear for an overnight plus a gallon of gas. It will hold a compact chain saw, or a takedown rifle, or a ten-pound block of ice. The new bag has been demoted to photo gadget bag and the old one is back in service on trips. Make sure that whatever you buy will hold all of your stuff.

Safety

Remember that your objective is always to return home alive and uninjured. Trips, especially long ones, are not the venue for risk-taking. Waiting for hours with excruciating injuries for a care flight, if one is available at all, is not on your agenda. Ride with extra care when you are far from home.

Security is an issue when you leave your bike and riding gear somewhere. I have never had a problem, but here are some simple things you can do to make sure cycle and helmet stay where you left them. Your choice will depend on local conditions.

The simplest solution is to carry a padlock and place the shackle through your helmet strap and front brake disk.

With a cable lock that fits easily into a backpack, you can lock bike and helmet to a tree.

Dual sports can cover rough ground at substantial speed allowing you to reach remote areas in short time. All types of photography, hunting, fishing, and trail maintenance equipment can fit into a backpack to enhance your recreation experience.

▶ PACKING FOR AN OVERNIGHT

Since you will only be gone for a couple of days there is no need to bring a lot of stuff. The easiest luggage solution is to pack some clothes and toiletries in a backpack.

Here is a suggested packing list:

- On your body:
  - Wallet with money, driver's license, registration, proof of vehicle insurance, medical insurance card, and credit card
  - Riding clothes including fanny pack, riding jacket, and camera (on fanny pack belt)
- In a backpack:
  - A lock or cable to secure the bike
  - Pants or shorts
  - Shirt
  - Socks
  - T-shirt
  - Underwear
  - Handkerchiefs
  - Light shoes or sandals for walking
  - Cap
- In a toiletry kit inside the backpack:
  - Sun block stick, insect repellant
  - Tooth brush and small size paste
  - Razor is optional for one night
  - Needle and thread
  - Small container of Vaseline (which can be used for dry chapped skin, lips, etc.)
  - Bag with your medications and some band aids
  - Trail snack
  - Ear plugs
  - Batteries for electronic gear
  - Maps
  - Swim trunks (optional)

Bring your fanny pack with the regular tools and spares.

For cold weather, add wool underwear, sweater, ski mask, and vest. For quick trips across a nearby border, add passport, visa, and proof of "in country" insurance.

If there is a possibility of rain, wear rainproof riding gear and put everything into plastic bags inside the pack; bags are also a good idea for dusty conditions. This same basic approach will also work for three- or four-night trips. You can wash undershorts and T-shirts at night or take extras.

Lay everything out and check it against your packing list before you start stuffing it into the bag. Then, put all of your gear and bags into one place in the garage so you won't forget anything at the last minute. ■

▶ CONSIDERATIONS FOR LONG TRIPS

Start out by defining your personal resources and goals:

- ▸ Do you have a specific destination in mind?
- ▸ How many days do you want to ride?
- ▸ Do you want layover days?
- ▸ What is your budget?
- ▸ What do you know about the proposed destination?
- ▸ How will you learn more?
- ▸ What level of comfort do you want?
- ▸ Do you want to include photography, historical exploration, or other activities?
- ▸ Are you going to stick to roads or throw in some single-track?
- ▸ Will you do the entire trip by motorcycle or will you truck the motorcycle to some starting place?
- ▸ How experienced are you?
- ▸ Are you in shape?
- ▸ What is the condition of your bike?
- ▸ What does your bike need to become trip-worthy?
- ▸ What clothing and touring accessories do you have?
- ▸ What will you need to buy?
- ▸ Who will ride with you?
- ▸ Have you ridden together before?
- ▸ How well do you get along?
- ▸ How experienced are they?
- ▸ If you are planning a non-English-speaking destination, what languages do you/they speak?
- ▸ What is your backup plan in case of bad weather, breakdown, or injury?

Answers to some of these questions may be obvious, but others may require you to gather additional information. Make notes as necessary to summarize what you know and what you need to determine. Planning longer trips is rarely something you can do in one session. More often, you will define some preliminary goals, gather information, and modify your objectives until destination, mileage, and route match your interests, abilities, resources, and time available. ■

Bike security is no problem here. Dual sports are welcome at this hotel in Mexico.

These adventurers are on a five-day tour at the bottom of Copper Canyon, in Mexico.

LONGER TRIPS

Trips of a week or more require a substantial commitment of time and money. Planning is the key to getting a good return on your investment.

Trip Planning

Start planning your trip by choosing a tentative destination, season, way stops, and budget. Most trips are loops—going to some destination by one route and returning by another. However, cloverleafs or figure eights may be better routes in some areas. It really depends on where the interesting terrain is located. There is little point in droning on to some distant goal if the surrounding country is filled with terrific scenery and riding opportunities. It's quite all right to stash your clothes in the same motel for two or three nights and ride to the north, south, east, and west. You may also want time to beachcomb, swim, or do other things in an area.

Start talking to your friends and determine who is available and interested. Maybe you can share the planning activities.

Next, begin accumulating information. Gather maps and study them. The DeLorme *Gazetters* are an excellent source of detailed maps about many areas. AAA produces good maps and tour guides. The official travel website of British Columbia has good information. The internet is a terrific travel resource, as most travel destinations around the globe now have websites. Most states and Canadian provinces also have websites to help tourists.

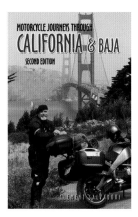

The Motorcycle Journeys series of Whitehorse Press is a great source of information.

Check for books about the area. It's always more fun when you know a bit about the history and geology. Whitehorse Gear at whitehorse-gear.com has a terrific selection of touring books and accessories. Make sure you know where gas can be found, how far it is between gas, and where you can find accommodations.

Pay special attention to the climate. You will be exposed to it constantly, and a trip in the wrong season, with the wrong gear, can be unpleasant. Good climate information can be found at worldclimate.com. This site has average rainfall and average high and low temperatures by month.

AVERAGE TEMPERATURES FOR RENO

	MARCH	MAY	JULY
AVERAGE	41.2	55.2	70.7
HIGH	51.6	72.9	91.8
LOW	24.3	40.1	51.3
DIFFERENCE	27.3	32.8	40.5

Some areas have huge swings in temperature by month and by day. Here are some temperatures for Reno:

The average daily temperature for July is 70, which sounds quite pleasant. However, the average high is about 92 and the average low is 51. Temperatures for individual days could easily be 10 degrees hotter or colder. This means that riding temperatures in Reno could be 40 early in the morning or 100 in the afternoon. Look at March. It is usually unpleasant to ride early in the morning, but quite nice in the afternoon.

▶ BIKE CHECKLIST

A fairly new bike should be in good shape, but check it anyway. Old faithful requires closer scrutiny. Here is a checklist:

Tires. Make sure they will go the distance. Mount long-lasting tires for long trips. For example, Dunlop 739s last about 800 miles, but 606s last about 3000. You may need to stage tires on really long trips by shipping them in advance to places on the route.

Wheels. Check the spokes and true and balance the wheels. Tires wear more rapidly on unbalanced, untrue wheels, and they are less comfortable to ride.

Brakes. Replace the pads before any long ride. Bring spares if you expect lots of mud.

Battery. Start with a new battery if the old one has been in service for more than a year.

Chains and sprockets. Replace them if you see any signs of wear.

Radiator and hoses. Check for leaks and cracked hoses.

Damage. Repair any leaks and replace any bent or cracked parts. Pay close attention to the fork and shock seals, looking for signs of fluid. If they have seen long service, replace them.

Tight and right. Go all over the bike checking for tightness. Use the tools from your fanny pack to make sure that you have one to fit every nut, bolt, and screw.

Air filter. Inspect, clean, and oil it. You can carry a pre-oiled spare in a plastic bag for dusty trips. Another approach is to clean a dirty filter on the trip with gasoline, and coat it with engine oil.

Accessories. Order any bags and accessories you need and mount them securely. Think of every possible way they could fall off or be torn off, and mount them accordingly. Test the installation by riding.

Fanny pack. Check everything in your fanny pack and make sure that it works. For example, make sure that the tire pump actually pumps air and that the tube of patch cement is still in its container. Replace any suspicious items.

Spare tubes. Check spare tubes and replace them if they show any signs of cracking or chafing.

Older bikes. On high-mileage bikes disassemble and clean the carb. Check the needle for wear in the area of the clip. Check the timing chain for wear by removing the chain adjuster and noting how much of the adjustment has been used. Check valve clearance and the condition of the spark plug wire, and cap. Look for worn wiring insulation and corroded or dirty connectors. ■

Now, go back and revise your original itinerary based upon what you have learned. Lay out a specific route and note any side trips that look interesting. Calculate mileage between gas and indicate possibilities for accommodations.

Check again with your friends. Lay out the trip for them and see if they are still interested.

Prepare Your Bike

Get your dual sport into excellent condition before starting any tour. A simple mechanical failure could end the trip and force your riding buddies to spend their vacation towing you to some place where you can arrange transportation back to civilization.

The farther you get from metropolitan areas, with their network of dealers and shops, the harder it is to get parts and repairs. Even simple things like inner tubes may be impossible to obtain locally.

Inspect your bike at least a month in advance. Start earlier if you may need an overhaul. Repairs always take longer than promised and parts are frequently on backorder.

My Honda had worn valve guides and burned a lot of oil prior to my Alaska trip. I took the cylinder head to a local shop three weeks before the trip. The mechanic promised he would remove the old guides and install new ones in a week. For one reason or another, he didn't even start until the week of the trip. I went down to the shop in growing alarm and begged every day. He finally gave me the head on the afternoon before our departure. I had to reassemble the engine that night, and leave for a very long ride, without even going for a proper test.

Don't start a long trip with suspicious parts. If there is any doubt at all, take them off and set them aside for future use when you get home. For example, half-worn brake pads should be replaced for the trip, but you can remount them when you get back.

Reservations

There are two schools of thought on reservations. One is to go without them and retain the flexibility to go slower or faster than originally planned. Why push on to the next reservation if you

discover something to explore near your current location?

The other approach is to have a set itinerary. This is almost mandatory when traveling in areas where gas and accommodations are scarce. A place like northern Nevada has a few small towns on major highways; the rest is empty.

If you plan to travel off the major travel routes, research the possible accommodations and then phone or write to make sure they are still in business and actually have gas. The necessity of reaching a specific destination can create very long days if you need to reroute around snow-blocked passes or high water crossings. However, you will always know that gasoline, dinner, and a place to sleep are waiting.

Less is More

Mobility is what separates dual sport from other forms of touring. A backpack and possibly a fender bag for tools and spare tubes may be all you ever need to tour on a lightweight dual sport. Packing light allows you to explore the roughest roads, travel on famous off-road race courses, and explore sand washes.

Every extra thing is a potential problem. Contents of bike-mounted bags get beaten to a pulp, the bags fall off, and zippers break. Anything that *can* happen *will* happen. Riding is the essence of dual sport; leave your stuff at home and enjoy the experience.

Everything for this eight-day, 1500-mile Baja trip was carried in a backpack, fanny pack, and fender bag. The route went from San Ignacio to Cabo San Lucas and back, touching many places on both coasts.

My friend Don could be the poster boy for traveling light. He has 40 Mexican trips under his belt and 25 of them have been dual sport. He travels exclusively with a backpack, fanny pack, and rear fender bag when he is on a lightweight dual sport. The fanny pack sits on the seat and supports the weight of the backpack when he is sitting.

For trips up to two weeks he adds a few items to his regular emergency gear:

- Rear tube (in addition to the front tube in his fender bag)
- Spare headlight and tail light bulbs
- First-aid kit
- Space blanket
- Antibiotics
- Shampoo
- Diarrhea remedies
- Spare goggle lenses
- Extra jersey and riding socks
- A few carefully chosen clothes

Traveling in Groups

Keeping everyone moving and on course is one of the keys to successful trips. No one likes to spend hours riding in circles, trying to find someone who has become separated from the group.

Everyone should try to stay out of dust on long trips. It is better for the bikes, better for the riders, and it's much safer. It also means that the group will be spread out, possibly over several miles. You can use two approaches to keep together.

The alternating leader approach works well for small groups traveling long stretches of road without turns. One person leads for ten miles and then waits for everyone to pass, looking carefully to make sure that their luggage is riding well. The second person becomes the leader and the old leader brings up the rear. After a set number of leader changes the group stops for a break. With this approach, the leader will never go more than ten miles or so without verifying that everyone is still on course.

The leader/follower approach works well on trips with many turns. The best navigator leads and the second-best navigator follows him. These two discuss any confusing turns and decide which way to go. Other riders follow in a set

This rider is using his Chatterbox helmet-mounted radio to tell the trip leader that stragglers are just coming down the hill.

order. Each person waits at turns for the rider behind and makes sure the follower knows which way to go. The last person should be someone who generally knows the route.

The leader and last rider may want to carry two-way radios, which can be quite useful in re-assembling a splintered group. The Family Radio Service (FRS) is an improved walkie-talkie system authorized in the United States since 1996. This service uses frequencies in the ultra high frequency (UHF) band, and so does not suffer the interference effects found on citizens' band (CB). FRS radios are limited to one-half watt of power in the U.S. General Mobile Radio Service (GMRS) radios offer some additional channels and higher power. They require an FCC license, but enforcement against individuals is rare.

GMRS radios offer different ranges of transmission based on power, but both FRS and GMRS are affected by terrain. They can send and receive for many miles with a clear line of sight from the top of a mountain, but much less when blocked by hills.

Sometimes people forget to wait at turns. Followers should not guess which way to go if the person ahead is out of sight. This can lead to several wrong turns and make it very difficult to re-assemble the group. Anyone who does not know which way to go should simply wait. Then it will be easy for the group to fall back and regroup.

Have a clear understanding about what happens in case of personal injury or a broken motorcycle. Will riding partners get you to aid and continue, or will someone stay with you? Agreement in advance can preserve friendships.

SPECIAL CONSIDERATIONS FOR MIDDLEWEIGHT AND HEAVYWEIGHT TOURING

Heavier dual sport bikes have more carrying capacity and trips with these bikes usually involve more pavement. Here are some added considerations for towing with heavier dual sports.

Tires and Chains

As noted in Chapter 6, tire pressures around 18 psi are best for dirt riding while street pressures may be as high as 40 psi.

At high pressure, tires will bounce excessively on rough dirt roads, resulting in an uncomfortable ride, poor control, and possible damage to brackets and luggage. Underinflated tires will overheat, wear quickly, and may blow out on pavement.

The solution is to "air down" (reduce pressure) for dirt and "air up" for pavement. A lightweight electric air compressor will allow you to quickly re-inflate to highway pressure.

Chains and sprockets wear rapidly when operated primarily in dirt. O-ring chains are lubed at the factory and the rings are supposed to keep the dust out and the lube in. However, there is no automatic lubrication between the chain and

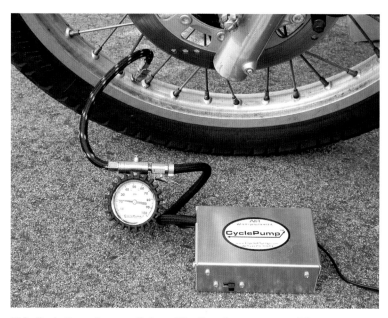

This Cycle Pump is a small, top-of-the line air compressor. It's a snap to change tire pressure from dirt to street levels with one of these.

sprockets. Oil or grease on the outside of the chain has a tendency to attract grit and form a grinding paste. Under these conditions, there is some question about the effectiveness of lubing the chain of a dual sport that is primarily operated in the dirt.

On the highway there is less grit, so regular lubrication will greatly increase the life of the chain and sprockets. Some riders stop after a dirt section and apply enough lubricant to wash away dirt before proceeding on the highway.

Chains operated primarily in dirt seem to last longer when adjusted to the loose side of the factory recommendation. Chains operated primarily on the street seem to last longer when adjusted to the tight side. However, never set a chain significantly tighter or looser than factory recommendations.

How to Pack

Start with a good understanding of your needs. Occasional, casual trips lie at one end of the spectrum while multi-month camping expeditions into remote places lie at the other. There is always one more piece of luggage or gear that can be packed, but should it? Experienced travelers counsel that on a motorcycle trip "less is more."

Short rides in pleasant weather. The same gear that would fit into a backpack is all you really need for a few days if you plan to stay in motels. It will easily fit into a couple of soft tail bags.

Longer trips in all seasons and climates. It takes better gear to stay comfortable on long trips. Traveling in rain and hot or cold weather demands special clothing; see Chapter 4. Areas with wide daily temperature swings expose you to bone chilling mornings and sweltering afternoons. As a minimum you must research likely conditions, decide how to protect yourself from the elements, and equip the bike to carry bulky riding clothes when you are not wearing them.

Camping or motels. Most people who camp settle into a pattern of several nights in the tent followed by a motel or commercial campground to take a good bath and wash clothes. Some travelers cook all of their own meals while others eat a few or all of them in restaurants. Decide which approach you prefer and list the necessary gear. Then plan how you will carry it.

This winter trip to Baja on a V-Strom requires more clothing and more luggage.

Baja, Alaska, or more distant places. Trips like this require careful planning. Research the route—weather, seasons, road conditions, mileage to gas, facilities, etc. Decide whether to camp or stay in motels. List the gear you will need and decide how to pack.

Assemble, weigh, and measure the gear to validate your packing plans. Then get the necessary luggage and other accessories you will need. Install everything and take it on a test ride before starting the real adventure. A test ride may reveal problems securing the luggage, or difficulty getting to it when you stop each night.

DUAL SPORT CAMPING

Camping can add an extra dimension of fun to dual sporting. Your ability to access remote areas can be the ticket to many beautiful and secluded spots. It is best to plan trips in seasons with good weather and a minimum of bugs. Conditions vary locally, but autumn after the first frost is often a good time for camping.

Prepare for the worst if you intend to camp in remote areas. Imagine a dark campsite swarming with mosquitoes and populated with bears. Picture arriving in heavy rain, covered from head to foot with mud. Work out the details of pitching the tent, cooking dinner, safeguarding food, and shedding muddy gear without contaminating the tent or filling it with bugs. Then imagine waking in the rain, fixing breakfast, packing, and continuing the trip.

Chances are, this will never happen to you, but it has happened to many travelers. It's much better to plan for contingencies than to let them catch you unaware.

Camping doesn't require a ton of gear, but you must decide how to carry bulky items such as a

▶ BASIC CAMPING GEAR

These items are in addition to the personal gear you need.

- Sleeping bag
- Sleeping pad
- Tent
- 50 feet of nylon cord (to hang food away from animals)
- Waterproof matches
- Stove and fuel (look for a stove that will burn unleaded pump gas)
- Pot with lid
- Pan (plate is optional)
- Cup
- Knife, fork, spoon
- Dishwashing pad
- Collapsible water bottle
- Food containers (plastic screw bottles)
- Water filter or purification tablets
- Waterproof stuff bags
- Bug repellent; hat with mosquito net (optional)
- Soap
- Towel
- Toilet paper
- Mirror

Many people use freeze-dried backpacking meals, but the supermarket is full of coffee, tea, dried soup, cereal, jerky, raisins, nuts, quick noodles, and energy bars that pack easily and keep well. Check out what is available before spending a lot of money on special backpacker food.

Start with a trial run and go through the process of setting up camp somewhere near home. Stay the night if all is going well. A test like this will tell you a lot about what you need to pack and how to do it. Carrying a lot on the bike restricts your mobility. While loaded with camping gear, it is better to stick to smoother roads. ■

The master chef has created another gourmet entrée using simple, healthful ingredients.

Are you tired of crowded campgrounds? Dual sports can take you to more secluded spots.

Like luggage, less camping gear is preferable. Here is all you really need: tent, sleeping bag, sleeping pad, stove, and cook gear.

tent and sleeping bag and how to keep the bag dry while riding in the rain. Sleeping bags are usually carried across a rear-mounted rack. Backpacking bags, stoves, and tents work well.

COMMERCIAL TOURS

Let's say you're sitting in the middle of Nebraska looking at snow, the bike is a wreck, and your best riding buddy moved to Florida. An organized tour could be the ticket to adventure. It can also be a great experience for riders in less dire circumstances. Either organize your own group for a tour or join strangers.

A quick internet search or scan through *Cycle News* classifieds will reveal several companies offering domestic and foreign tours.

Offerings vary, but generally include:

Outfitters like Baja Off-Road Tours provide the extra security of chase trucks.

- Trips of various lengths and to various destinations
- Freedom to set your own ride schedule
- Route planning that takes you to great places at good times of the year
- Transportation from a designated location to the start of the tour
- Attempt to place you in a small group with riders of similar abilities
- Rental motorcycles
- Experienced guides who speak the local languages
- Full support including sweep riders, 4WD support trucks to carry your luggage, medical equipment, food, drinks, spare parts, and supplies
- Satellite phones in trucks and carried on the trail by the guide
- Complete bike-prep list if you are bringing your own bike

Tours are more expensive than going on your own, but you should get plenty of value in services and security.

FINAL THOUGHTS ON DUAL SPORT TRIPS

Don't fall into the habit of always going on day rides in the same locations. Dual sports can go almost anywhere. Spend at least a few nights each year away from home, either camping or in a motel. Short overnights are always fun and easy to squeeze into your schedule. Longer trips are the ticket to enduring memories. If one day on a dual sport is good, two are better.

INDEX